BIG SPORTS, BIG BUSINESS

BIG SPORTS, BIG BUSINESS

A Century of League Expansions, Mergers, and Reorganizations

Frank P. Jozsa Jr.

Westport, Connecticut
London

Library of Congress Cataloging-in-Publication Data

Jozsa, Frank P., 1941–
  Big sports, big business : a century of league expansions, mergers,
and reorganizations / Frank P. Jozsa Jr.
        p. cm.
  Includes bibliographical references and index.
  ISBN 0–275–99134–2 (alk. paper)
  1. Professional sports—Economic aspects—United States. 2. Sports
franchises—United States. I. Title.
  GV583.J66 2006
  338.4'37960440973—dc22   2006021461

British Library Cataloguing in Publication Data is available.

Library of Congress Catalog Card Number: 2006021461
ISBN: 0–275–99134–2

First published in 2006

Praeger Publishers, 88 Post Road West, Westport, CT 06881
An imprint of Greenwood Publishing Group, Inc.
www.praeger.com

Printed in the United States of America

The paper used in this book complies with the
Permanent Paper Standard issued by the National
Information Standards Organization (Z39.48–1984).

10   9   8   7   6   5   4   3   2   1

To fans of professional sports teams

Contents

A photo essay follows page 80

Preface

In retrospect, this book is a modification and extension of my dissertation, titled "An Economic Analysis of Franchise Relocation and League Expansion in Professional Team Sports, 1950–1975" (Georgia State University, 1977) and *Relocating Teams and Expanding Leagues: How the Major Leagues Respond to Market Conditions.* The latter title, which was published by Quorum Books in 1999, discussed the expansions and relocations in Major League Baseball and in the National Basketball Association and National Football League between 1950 and the mid to late 1990s. Besides the reorganizations within these organizations, *Big Sports, Big Business* also contains the league expansions and mergers, and relocations and transfers of clubs that occurred in the National Hockey League and Major League Soccer, and in various other leagues of these sports between the late 1800s and early 2000s. In other words, this book is a 135-year history of when and how a number of professional leagues had restructured and realigned to compete for fans, market share, and profit in the sports business.

As he did with three of my previous books—that is, *American Sports Empire: How the Leagues Breed Success* (Praeger, 2003); *Baseball, Inc.: The National Pastime as Big Business* (2006); and *Sports Capitalism: The Foreign Business of American Professional Leagues* (2004)—Frank Chance, Pfeiffer University's director of information services at the Charlotte, North Carolina, campus, greatly assisted me with the research of these topics. Besides expertly scanning databases and various journals, magazines, and other literature sources for articles about sports and obtaining several books on interlibrary loan from local and regional public and private libraries, Frank unhesitatingly located different types of raw data and such statistics as teams' attendances per game and season, the populations of U.S. metropolitan areas and world cities, and other details about how clubs had performed in their respective divisions and conferences since the respective professional baseball, basketball, football, ice hockey and soccer leagues were officially established. In accomplishing these tasks, he was reliable, conscientious, and relentless in his efforts, and undoubtedly my most dependable and valuable aide in completing a manuscript. Thus, Frank's contributions are very much appreciated.

I also thank Michael Utsman, who is Pfeiffer's dean of student services at the Charlotte campus. Since the mid-1990s, he has responded to any problems and challenges that were encountered in formatting the aforementioned books' chapters and front and back matters, and in aligning pages, numbering endnotes, and developing indexes. Despite being overworked in his position each semester, Michael never hesitated to apply his knowledge and skills to resolve technological issues with computers and software programs that related to business, economics, and finance, and to the study of professional sports leagues and teams.

My longtime friend and partner Maureen Fogle, a director of nursing services at Mercy Hospital in Charlotte, has supported me for ten years as I have coauthored and authored sports books, wrote articles, and taught classroom and online courses in Pfeiffer's graduate studies programs. Besides being a top-notch administrator in the healthcare industry, Maureen is a doctoral student and part-time university instructor. As such, she understands the commitments and sacrifices that are required to research and produce scholarly work. Because of her experiences and interests, this book and my other titles and documents were successfully published. Finally, our beagle/basset hound Lucy has been a daily companion to me. She enjoys watching her peers on cable television's Animal Planet, playing with her toys in the living room, hallway and office, and harassing me to stop writing in order to take her outside for a stroll in the neighborhood. In short, it has been special and fun to be with Maureen and for us to provide a good home for Lucy and her predecessor, Alice.

Introduction

Since the late 1800s to the early 2000s the professional sports industry has gradually evolved to become a popular and mature institution and a growing segment of America's culture, economy, and society. From different rooms in their homes, millions of people observe sports events on television and the Internet and also listen to the daily broadcast of teams' games on the radio. Meanwhile, other sports fans have an opportunity to attend and enjoy games held on weekdays and weekends in arenas, ballparks, and stadiums that are located in numerous cities, towns, and suburbs of North America. In several of the professional sports, each season there are division and conference playoffs and league championship series that increasingly dominate television broadcasts and frequently crowd out, for example, important news items like political events, ethics violations by corporate executives, military struggles between countries, global business crises, and nations' economic and social catastrophes.

Concurrently, such sports controversies as the illegal use of drugs by prominent professional baseball players, fights between athletes during ice hockey and outdoor soccer games, and interviews with football and basketball coaches and general managers have been published as articles in major magazines and appeared in columns of local, regional, and national newspapers. In a more recent trend, commentators and pundits have passionately discussed an array of sports topics on talk radio shows, prime-time cable channels, and network television stations.

Besides addressing disputes that exist between sports officials and teams' owners and players about league policies, salaries, and other issues, this discourse also focuses on the use of taxpayer funding and communities' public debt to finance the construction of new, multimillion-dollar sports facilities. Even minor and subtle changes in the operation, ownership, and performance of fans' home teams during regular seasons of play may receive top billing in local publications and broadcast on various television programs. It is obvious, therefore, that analysts, journalists, reporters, and scholars each contribute to the hype and popularity of sports, and stimulate the public's seemingly insatiable appetite for news and other information about the behaviors and decisions of athletes and team coaches, general managers and owners, and league commissioners, executives, and other officials.

Mindful of the aforementioned activities, facts, and conditions, *Big Sports, Big Business: A Century of League Expansions, Mergers, and Reorganizations* was written primarily for a general sports audience, and especially for enthusiasts ranging from coaches, owners, and players, to undergraduate and graduate college professors and their students who might major in sports administration, management, or marketing, and to federal and state politicians and municipal government authorities that advocate to further control and regulate organizations in and/or affiliated with the sports industry.

Consequently, this book provides an historical account of two categories of phenomena. The first is reorganizations such as the expansion and merger of specific leagues in professional baseball, basketball, football, ice hockey, and outdoor soccer. The second is the relocation or movement of teams within—and the transfer of clubs between—one or more of the leagues. Although a number of articles, books, case studies and other documents have been published dealing with these topics, there is no single work that focuses exclusively on why, when, where, and to what extent the professional leagues have expanded, merged, and contracted, and the leagues' teams have moved, transferred, and disbanded in seasons from the late 1800s to early 2000s.

In documenting and evaluating these types of decisions and actions, it is argued that the marketplace should primarily determine the emergence, development, and success of various sports and of professional sports organizations. Thus, this book discourages the majority of intrusions from external institutions, and similarly opposes unnecessary government bureaucracy and intervention in, and excessive regulation of, the operation and business of professional sports. Indeed, it is the interactions of suppliers and demanders in local, regional, national, and international markets—which include communities, fans, leagues, franchise owners, coaches, managers, players, private sector organizations, and the media—that provide the most efficient allocation of limited sports resources, measurement of teams' revenues and costs, and assessment of financial returns and risks.

For sure, sports markets and organizations are not purely competitive. Given their economic behavior, conduct, and performance since the late 1800s, the U.S.-based professional leagues are fundamentally cartels that have considerable territorial and pricing powers. That environment exists because a typical league restricts the number of teams and schedules a fixed quantity of games to be played each season at specific sites in metropolitan areas and somewhat distorts how resources are allocated within the sports industry.

Generally, any reforms—such as extensive sharing of revenues or the reallocation of funds from more to less profitable teams, or from high- to low-payroll and large- to small-market clubs—are not preferred as the optimal solutions to a sports league's business problems. Instead of successful franchises subsidizing their respective opponents, the most efficient policies and remedies are for league and team officials to introduce and implement free-market incentives. As such, the leagues' expansions, mergers, and contractions, and the clubs' relocations, transfers, and cancellations are perceived to be natural adjustments to market conditions. In short, there are no individuals or institutions better equipped than each of the league's team owners to either jointly or individually make the expansion, merger, relocation, transfer and other reorganization decisions. After all, from a practical perspective, the owners operate their sports franchises to maximize profit. To perform and accomplish this task, they must anticipate, measure, and respond to changes in market conditions.

In a free, competitive market, a sports team owner's decision to relocate his or her team is an applied short- and/or long-run business strategy. That is, an owner responds to the forces of supply and demand and thus increases the present value of his or her franchise by moving the organization to an available site in an area that has a higher potential to attract fans, generate revenues, and earn maximum profits. An area's potential depends, in part, on the total population base and growth rate of the population; the distribution of households' expenditures, incomes, and wealth; and the demand by residents in local and regional markets to attend sports games and receive broadcasts of them on the Internet, radio, and television. So if an owner fails to maximize profit at a team's current site, the club will be moved to a more lucrative location. Furthermore, the decision model assumes that the other owners in the league will approve relocation if it is in their team's best interests.

Certainly, denying any franchises from relocating to more profitable sites and persuading league officials to consolidate clubs or place expansion teams in particular cities will especially affect the respective communities, sports fans, players, and team owners. Therefore, by applying business, demographic, economic, and financial statistics and sports-related data and information, *Big Sports, Big Business* essentially explores the histories of and reasons for the expansions, mergers, relocations, and transfers that have occurred in five major-league sports.

To that end, the chapters in this book introduce historical trends and any patterns of these actions; incorporates demographic, economic, and financial facts that are related to home sites, local areas, and regional markets; and reveals the strategies of selected leagues and decisions of team owners who seek to manage the number and quality of existing and future franchises. Furthermore, this book's contents evaluate teams and measure their success, in part, based on performances during regular seasons and postseasons, and on such criteria as home-site attendances and estimated market values.

Specifically, *Big Sports, Big Business* primarily examines the expansions and mergers of professional sports leagues and the relocations of teams within—and transfers of clubs between—the American League (AL) and National League (NL) of Major League Baseball (MLB), and within the National Football League (NFL), National Hockey League (NHL), National Basketball Association (NBA), and Major League Soccer (MLS). Also, the text discusses the actions and performances of teams in such alternative and former professional sports organizations as the American Association (AA) and Federal League (FL) in professional baseball, American Football League (AFL) and World Football League (WFL) in professional football, National Hockey Association (NHA) and World Hockey Association (WHA) in ice hockey, American Basketball Association (ABA) and Women's National Basketball Association (WNBA) in professional basketball, and the Atlantic Coast League (ACL) and North American Soccer League (NASL) in soccer. In short, this title represents a response to former kinesiology professor Stephen H. Hardy's call for scholarly studies that regard sport as a unique industry similar to agriculture, steel, and medicine, and for the research that assumes an historical perspective.[1]

In looking ahead to the topics contained in the chapters, much of the demographic data and statistics and the sports facts and other information have been extracted from a wide variety of published materials. For example, between the 1960s and 1990s, several knowledgeable practitioners and well-respected scholars had investigated and analyzed the economic conduct and historical performance of the United States' professional sports teams and leagues and the industry. Their work, in general, discussed the antitrust laws, labor relations, public subsidies, and tax effects with respect to the operations of franchises and stadiums, and the business and structures of leagues.

To illustrate, economists Roger Noll and James Quirk studied the economic and financial reasons for the movements of clubs, and the rationale for the expansions and consolidations of specific leagues. As depicted in their models of the professional sports business, there exist single proprietor- and corporate-owned franchises that are controlled by limited partnerships, syndicates, and investment groups that have agreed to organize and form independent leagues. In turn, each of the franchises has special privileges, including the exclusive right to field a team that plays its home games at a site within a designated geographic area. The franchise's owner operates a team to maximize total profits. Meanwhile, a league behaves like a cartel because it limits competition, sets the operating rules for the franchises, and restricts the supply of teams in the marketplace.

This book acknowledges these models and the contributions of such scholars. In retrospect, the historical studies and research results about the appreciating values of sports franchises and the ever-present competition among cities to build and finance extravagant sports venues with taxpayer money, and about the financial dilemmas of small-market teams to operate and succeed in the long run do, in part, involve and address the basics of league expansions and mergers and team relocations and transfers.

LITERATURE REVIEW

It was during the early 1970s that researchers—who were interested in the reform of sports and restructure of the professional sports industry within North America—had analyzed in detail the business, economic, and financial aspects of team relocations. For example, in 1973 California Institute of Technology professor James Quirk concluded that franchise movements do not provide a viable long-run solution for the tendency of big-city teams to dominate their rivals in a given sport. In other words, the relocations that occurred in organized baseball merely intensified the extent of imbalances in playing strengths among a league's teams instead of mitigating such disparities. Furthermore, he stated that MLB has itself created the problem of franchise instability by implementing and enforcing business rules that, in total, undermine a given club's survival when it is located in any small city. As Quirk put it, only the prudent and equitable application of antitrust legislation will effectively end the abuses stemming from franchise moves and intraleague and interleague imbalances in professional baseball.[2]

After the publication of that research, Quirk later collaborated with Mohamed El Hodiri to produce another work about team movements and league operations in professional sports. Indeed, the significant results reported in their article, in part, echoed those in Quirk's previous study. For one, these two prominent economists discovered that sports franchises located in metropolitan areas with high drawing potential such as Chicago and New York City were more competitive than franchises situated in regions with low drawing potential like Milwaukee and Pittsburgh. For another, they concluded that the higher the proportion of revenues earned by a team from the broadcasting of home games and other local sports events, the greater were the average salaries of players who were listed on its roster. As a result, the chances of the long-run survival for clubs located in such small markets as Cleveland and Kansas City were at best, only mediocre. Moreover, a sports league could better achieve parity of playing strengths among its member teams—as Quirk and Hodiri assert— by assigning franchise rights to equalize drawing potential rather than realigning divisions and conferences and balancing the geographic areas between the clubs. Accordingly, several of the franchise movements and shifts that occurred from the 1940s to 1970s represented the marketing and extension of leagues from being local and regional to national organizations made possible by media exposure, dependable airline transportation, and the growth of population centers in the southeastern United States and in areas on the nation's west coast.[3]

On the heels of Quirk's and Hodiri's seminal work appeared a book of readings titled *Government and the Sports Business* (1974). This analogy, which was edited by Roger G. Noll, discusses the economics of expansion in professional sports relative to home and away game attendances, players' salaries and teams' payrolls, and the taxation of sports enterprises. That is, Noll and the other contributors used economic theories and statistical models to analyze and predict the prospects for sports league expansions that might occur from the 1970s to 1990s. As a result of their research, the authors recommended that sports leagues should pursue open and effective expansion policies as opposed to the restrictive rules that these leagues had voluntarily adopted or that governments had arbitrarily imposed on them before and during the early to mid 1970s. In short, the readings in Noll's book endorsed a larger supply and more efficient allocation of teams, and advocated the elimination of anticompetitive practices of sports enterprises and league organizations. In fact, at least one proposal—the equitable or nearly equal sharing of national broadcasting revenues—was fully adopted by the NFL and to a lesser extent by the NBA, MLB, and NHL.[4]

All published during the mid-1980s, three related articles discuss the relationships among franchise sites, team relocations and the effects of antitrust laws. To illustrate, federal regulatory attorney James Gattuso states that the rules structures governing sports leagues, which act to constrain member teams, have beneficial implications. Because they further the long-run interests and needs of leagues and supposedly sports fans, these rules act to effectively allocate and balance the number of franchises in a region. As a result, this outcome promotes the intensity of interleague competition and thereby enhances the stability of the different leagues. Internal management policies, according to Gattuso, warrant neither meticulous government oversight nor bureaucratic controls. Consequently, regulators should apply the antitrust laws such that franchise owners have the freedom and right to enforce league rules concerning team relocations and transfers, and league expansions, mergers, and contractions.[5]

In contrast to Gattuso's model, political science professor Arthur T. Johnson favors the adoption and implementations of federal legislation and policies that are designed to preserve teams' stability and to maximize the public's access to professional sports events. To remove the scarcity and undersupply of sports franchises in the marketplace, Johnson offers two recommendations. First, he would to require that professional sports leagues reduce their existing barriers to entry for membership and thus permit cities without teams to bid for the rights to secure new franchises. Second, Johnson advocates that the U.S. Congress should protect community interests and ensure team owners have property rights by not overregulating the conduct and operation of professional sports leagues and clubs.[6]

Author David Meggyesy, however, adamantly opposes congressional grants of antitrust immunity to professional sports leagues. In the interests of communities, teams' players, franchise owners, and sports fans, he contends that Congress should instead undertake a comprehensive study of the operation of each professional league. According to Meggyesy, the study should focus on the issue of allowing sports associations to pool and redistribute revenues from the radio and television broadcasts of games and the cash inflows generated from the skyboxes, club seats, and luxury suites within their arenas, ballparks, and stadiums.[7]

In the 1990s, there were three notable books published that dealt with the interplay and enduring relationships among cities, fans, and professional sports franchises. Each book describes or analyzes franchise relocations in the major leagues during various periods of the twentieth century. Authored by Paul Staudohar and James A. Mangan, *The Business of Professional Sports* (1991) explains the dynamics and elements of the sports business and how that business influences, and is affected by, society at large. Indeed, the book stimulates intellectual discourse about the ways to reform and perhaps improve the operation and quality of the sports industry. In addition to examining sport as a product of television, Staudohar and Mangan also provide a concise review of the literature. Interestingly, the review covers various facets of the sports business from player–owner relations to sports as a social science, and to business and public policies relative to amateur and professional sports leagues and clubs.[8]

In *Playing the Field: Why Sports Teams Move and Cities Fight to Keep Them* (1993), Charles C. Euchner discusses the intercity competition that exists to attract and retain professional sports teams. Among other topics, Euchner analyzes the teams' profitability and such previous franchise relocations as the Raiders from Oakland, California, to Los Angeles and the Colts from Baltimore, Maryland to Indianapolis, Indiana. He also examines sports leagues and teams with respect to dependent cities, and franchise mobility from economic, legal, and political perspectives. Euchner declares that professional "sports is not a dominant industry in any city, yet teams receive the kind of attention one might expect to be lavished on major employers and producers located there." According to Euchner's analysis, this attention to teams occurs because "sports franchises have great leverage. Their demands do not directly affect many interest groups, and opponents of stadium projects have difficulty developing coalitions to sports oppose them." As a result, "civic leaders tend to succumb to the blackmail tactics of professional owners rather than develop and support sound economic policies."[9]

As to *The Sports Franchise Game: Cities in Pursuit of Sports Franchises, Events, Stadiums, and Arenas* (1995), industry analyst Kenneth Shropshire refers to quantitative impact studies to evaluate (1) how Philadelphia, Pennsylvania, and Camden, New Jersey, had competed to attract and retain professional sports teams, (2) why franchise shifts had occurred in the San Francisco, California, area, (3) why the Baltimore Colts had moved to Indianapolis during the early 1980s, and (4) what efforts were made by Washington, DC, sports fans to secure a baseball franchise for the nation's capital. In his book, Shropshire provides answers to some intriguing questions. For instance, what value does a sports franchise bring to a city? When should a city battle for a franchise? Why is the competition for a team so vigorous among cities? Should a city build an arena, ballpark, and/or stadium in the hopes of attracting a major sports club? Based on his research, he concludes that a city's decision to pursue a professional sports franchise is largely subjective. As such, local politicians should consider their community's image and civic needs to determine the value of a franchise before financing the construction of a modern sports facility for an existing or new team. Shropshire also advocates the partial public ownership of a franchise if taxpayer funds are invested in a team's facility. Moreover, he states that with public financing of an arena, ballpark, and/or stadium, "it may now be appropriate to expect franchise owners to act more socially responsible in the community." In summary, "a review of economic impact studies of new stadium construction costs and franchise bidding [by cities] warrants the conclusion that there is no clear-cut answer and that there are many issues to consider." Thus in *The Sports Franchise Game*, it is the reader who must ultimately identify, estimate, and evaluate the true economic and social values of professional sports to American cities.[10]

During the past several years, an increasing number of articles have appeared in newspapers across the nation that report on and agonize about the possibility of a team owner deciding to locate or relocate a professional sports franchise. Many of these news items focus on the explicit and implicit threats made by various owners to move their respective clubs if the local taxpayers refuse to fully or partially subsidize the construction and operating cost of a new home-site venue. To illustrate, *Texas Monthly* published an article in 1996 examining Houston's three professional sports teams, the NFL Oilers (now Tennessee Titans), NL Astros, and NBA Rockets. According to a study that was published, the owners of the three Houston-based franchises had extracted large amounts of subsidies from municipal taxpayers to finance new multimillion-dollar facilities that featured amenities like premium seats and luxury suites. Moreover, each franchise owner had demanded a disproportionate share of the venue's revenues that were generated from advertisements, concessions, merchandise sales, and parking fees. Nonetheless, the article concludes that losing one or more of these franchises to other cities should have only a slight and negative economic impact on the Houston area since collectively the teams contribute less than 1 percent of the local economy's output of goods and services.[11]

In his insightful publication "Break Up the Sports League Monopolies," historian Stephen Ross argues that the professional leagues exercise their monopolistic powers by restricting the number of existing franchises in a sport. By holding down and controlling the number of teams in an area, the established franchises realize an increase in revenues because they receive a greater share of the profits from local radio and television rights, and they have the power to induce larger tax subsidies from cities and thus taxpayers. If rival sports leagues had played games in an area, he contends that the established leagues would only earn greater profits if they had expanded and opened other sites. Indeed, the leagues' failure to expand would result in accounting losses or lower profits. Yet, Ross admits that not enough data exists about the competitiveness of expansion practices and policies in professional team sports.[12]

During March 1991, *The Sporting News* printed a series of reports on the expansion plans of some American professional sports leagues. That is, these articles highlight the views of the commissioners of MLB, the NFL, and the NBA. For instance, NBA commissioner David Stern had stated: "Expansion on a precise dollar and cents basis may be less profitable than people think. But if you represent yourself as a national league, and see that there are large regions underrepresented, you have to look carefully at the demand and try to fulfill it." Collectively, the reports underscore the expected and high risks of expansion as espoused by a sample of franchise owners, economists, and sports media analysts. Still, if managed correctly, the reports claim that expansion in the economic environment of 1991 would cause limited financial damage to existing sports teams while helping the leagues to flourish. Finally, the reports conclude that professional sports leagues confront a daunting challenge in the 1990s—that is, reining in costs while finding new and abundant sources of revenue. Six years later, *The Sporting News* offered three proposals for building a successful franchise to the owners of two MLB additions—the NL Arizona Diamondbacks and AL Tampa Bay Devil Rays: select the right star, draft athletes prudently, and have a business plan.[13]

Other scholars have viewed the topics of expansion, merger and relocation from a sociological perspective. In "Blackballing the Inner City," Gary Stix cites Alan P. Sager and Arthur J. Culbert because the two scholars analyzed the exodus of urban baseball teams from inner city neighborhoods like Brooklyn, New York, after the 1957 season. To be sure, the advent of jet travel in the 1950s and the existence of two or more teams in the same sport at the same site partially explain why the Dodgers moved from Brooklyn to Los Angeles. But these academics also conclude that race was a more powerful statistical indicator than the age of the stadium, team standing, or the average annual attendance in a franchise owner's decision to evacuate an inner city site. Thus, Sager and Culbert imply that race proved to be more crucial than personal income, or any other factor, in explaining why fans feared venturing into Brooklyn's poor neighborhoods to attend the Dodgers' home games at Ebbets Field. Even so, critics of the study point out that the majority of teams move because of the greater potential for profits at an alternative site.[14]

Along these lines, former Indiana University professor Mark Rosentraub's *Major League Losers* (1997) explodes the myth that professional sports teams, by virtue of their existence, generate so much economic growth and civic pride that they constitute a public benefit worthy of taxpayer-funded subsidies. When Rosentraub studied the patterns of franchise movements in the major leagues, he revealed that the social and psychological links among sports fans, teams, and cities have frayed as demographic and economic trends redefine the hierarchy of municipalities. Indeed, small and some medium-sized communities that host one or more teams must either subsidize these clubs or lose them to larger or higher-income communities. Rejecting taxpayer subsidies as a solution, Rosentraub endorses a market-based approach that would ultimately and conclusively end the sports welfare game. This approach would stop what he calls "the perverse transfer of public money to wealthy players and wealthier owners."[15]

Some commentators seem to disagree with Rosentraub's compelling thesis. In January 1997, an edition of *SportsTravel* featured an article about the commitments made by cities to build interconnecting infrastructures that link communities, which help them to support their existing, or attract new, professional teams. In such cities as Jacksonville, Florida; Baltimore, Maryland; Hartford, Connecticut; Phoenix, Arizona; Columbus, Ohio; and Toronto, Ontario, Canada, a number of local boosters planned and sought funding for new municipal investments in entertainment and sports complexes. As the promoters of teams see it, the new state-of-the-art hotels and arenas, ballparks and stadiums, and other construction projects promise to spur long-term economic development by creating jobs and marketing the cities' image as sport and entertainment capitals. Furthermore, event sponsors claim that some amateur and collegiate sports games and tournaments will gradually migrate to these cities because of the presence of modern professional sports facilities.[16]

Although some American cities had hoped to attract at least one professional sports franchise, a few regional organizations have become more outspoken about losing teams to other U.S. metropolitan areas and states. In a February 1997 posting on their Web site, the Franchise of Americans Needing Sports (FANS) listed three resolutions relative to the relocation of organized baseball, basketball, and football franchises from various cities in California. The group resolved that the state's senate should sponsor a symposium within three months to discuss the professional sports infrastructure in California and its economic and social impacts on local communities. FANS also requested that the U.S. Congress explore the comprehensive issue of antitrust legislation and its involvement in professional sports, and to investigate the related issues of special tax breaks and incentive programs that induce franchise owners to move their teams to other cities. Last, the group lobbied for Congress to enact specific measures to prevent established teams from being lured away because of the benefits offered by other cities and jurisdictions. Toward that goal, FANS strongly urged Congress to create a federal agency to keep a watchful eye on sports teams that are obligated by contracts and other legal documents to remain in a local municipality for a fixed number of years.[17]

Any astute reader of the United States' business newspapers and magazines realizes the media and press releases that local civic leaders elicit to lure a new or existing sports franchise to an area. Editions of the *Wall Street Journal, Business Week,* and some local publications in the major cities of North Carolina, for example, ran numerous stories in 1997 about the possibility of a major league baseball team immigrating to the 12-county Triad area, which contains the cities of Greensboro, High Point, and Winston-Salem. This region has great demographics—that is, a relatively large total population, above-average economic growth, a high-ranked television market and 12 minor league baseball clubs—and is the home of several investors who were able to finance the $100 million fee for entry into the AL or NL of MLB. Consequently, the Triad area emerged as the leading contender in the race to win a professional baseball franchise since it outdistanced rival sites located in northern Virginia and in such cities as Orlando, Florida; Indianapolis, Indiana; and Charlotte, North Carolina. In a May 1998 referendum, however, the Triad area voters residing in Guilford and Forsyth Counties of North Carolina overwhelmingly rejected a tax proposal to fund and build a $210 million, 45,000-seat baseball stadium for a team. The referendum's outcome suggests, in part, that people in these counties oppose subsidies for a professional baseball facility because county schools, roads, and infrastructure projects each have a higher priority for the use of taxpayer's money.[18]

Meanwhile, in various editions *The Sporting News* recognized several North American cities or areas as the best sports sites in terms of their (1) sports climate and atmosphere, (2) fervent and knowledgeable sports fans, (3) potential venue capacity, and (4) accessible location. Accordingly, having the right combination of these features would make any city or area a strong candidate for an expansion franchise. During the late 1990s, it was Salt Lake City, Utah; Charlotte, North Carolina; and Charleston, South Carolina, that ranked as the three best cities for an MLB club. In contrast, the Los Angeles/Anaheim area and the cities of Toronto and Salt Lake City scored the highest as locations for an NFL franchise, and Pittsburgh, Pennsylvania; St. Louis, Missouri; and the Tampa/St. Petersburg area in Florida seemed to be best suited for an NBA franchise. Nevertheless, these places already have a sample of teams in professional and collegiate sports; a nucleus of hard-core fans who read about, watch, and discuss sports; and an appealing array of indoor and outdoor leisure activities for people to participate in and enjoy. After evaluating these criteria, *The Sporting News* rated Denver, Colorado; the Dallas-Fort Worth area in Texas; and Miami, Florida, as the top three locations for all sports in 1997.[19]

Based on the literature of the sports business, the general procedures to apply for and purchase an expansion franchise or acquire an existing team are formally structured and a straightforward process. In MLB, for example, a prospective owner—individual or group—must have a well-entrenched management system and the know-how of submitting to a league committee a set of financial statements that project the club's operations for at least five years. Furthermore, at the site proposed by the prospective owner, the ballpark must have a capacity of nearly 40,000 seats and its parking facilities must be able to accommodate at least 25 percent of the ballpark's capacity or no less than 10,000 spaces for the spectators' automobiles. Another requisite to becoming a successful owner in baseball is a receptive local government—that is, a group who is enthusiastic and prepared to host a professional sports team. Also, such local demographic statistics as the number of households with television sets must meet a minimum standard that has been established by the league. To be officially selected as a new franchise owner, 75 percent of the current owners in a league—AL or NL—in which the team plays, and 50 percent of the owners in the other league—AL or NL—must approve this transaction.

The prospective owner or ownership group of an NBA expansion franchise must first file an application with the league office in New York City and, second, submit to a committee of current owners a comprehensive business plan that provides specific instructions and other information for how the franchise will operate at a site in its home market. After a thorough check of the application is completed, the NBA's executive committee will conduct an interview of the individual or of the person representing a partnership or syndicate, while other league officials closely audit the business plan. As designated in MLB, at least 75 percent of the existing NBA owners must approve the purchase of a franchise by a prospective buyer.

In the NFL, a potential owner or ownership group initially receives approval from the commissioner's office to acquire a team. Unlike in MLB and the NBA, the NFL requires that one individual must be responsible for a majority interest in the team. If a group seeks ownership of a franchise, one person in the group must own at least 30 percent of the total share. As in MLB, the NFL office wants a managerial structure in place with someone clearly assigned to be responsible for operating the franchise each season. Likewise, it takes 75 percent of the existing owners to approve the sale of any club in the league. In the NHL and MLS, the step-by-step processes to buy and operate a new or relocated team are a modification of those procedures adopted by the other primary sports leagues.

Because of the potential impact on their game schedules, markets, revenues, and profits, the established franchise owners in a league must jointly consent to add a new team or relocate an existing club to another site. In agreeing whether to allow expansion or relocation to be initiated, each franchise owner evaluates the short- and long-run benefits and costs of these proposals. From the standpoint of a current team owner, to approve or deny expansion and relocation might result in more or less national and local broadcasting revenues, an increase or decrease in transportation costs and in home and away attendances at games, and a realignment of competitive rivalries. In short, each existing owner makes two decisions when voting for or against expansion and relocation. That is, whether to approve or not approve either or both of these transactions, and where to geographically locate the new, or move the existing, franchise.

Currently, there are no comprehensive texts or extensive collections of readings dealing with the strategies, tasks, and potential benefits and costs of league expansions, mergers, and consolidations, and team relocations and transfers that occur in professional sports leagues. Therefore, much of the literature on these methods of reorganizations by leagues and teams was derived and applied from articles, reports, and studies, and any data and statistics published since the late 1800s.

BOOK OVERVIEW

After this book's Preface and Introduction, and before the Conclusion and back matter, there are a total of six chapters. In turn, each chapter discusses the different kinds and numbers of reorganizations of professional sports leagues and/or actions of teams that have occurred during a particular range of years. The major types of reorganizations include league expansions and mergers and team relocations and transfers. Furthermore, other types of restructuring consist of a league's cancellation and the termination of one or more franchises.

Relative to Chapter 1, the various sports leagues are listed—given that they had reorganized before 1950—based on the year when they initially expanded. That is, it was the ENL in 1878, NFL in 1923, NHL in 1924, BAA and NBL in 1946 to 1948, and the American Soccer League (ASL) in 1922. Likewise with respect to Chapters 2 through 4, the sports leagues are included and discussed based on whether and when they had reorganized.

Alternatively, the contents in Chapters 5 and 6 involve the various reorganizations of secondary leagues, whose teams are grouped by sport.

Regarding professional baseball, the AA existed in 1882–1891, UA in 1884, and FL in 1914–1915; in professional ice hockey, the WHA performed in 1972–1979; in professional football, the AFL I competed in 1926, AFL II in 1936–1937, AFL III in 1940–1941, All-American Football Conference (AAFC) in 1946–1949, AFL in 1960–1969, WFL in 1974–1975 and U.S. Football League (USFL) in 1983–1985; in professional basketball, the ABA played in the 1967 to 1975 seasons and WNBA since the 1996 season; and in professional soccer, the NASL performed in 1967–1984 and MPSL in 2003–2004.

As stated previously, the first four chapters of *Big Sports, Big Business* identify and explain the different types of reorganizations that took place in North America's dominant leagues and among their respective teams in each of the sports during selected time periods. To be specific, Chapter 1 discusses which of the primary professional sports leagues had expanded, merged, consolidated, and/or contracted their operations for the seasons from 1876 to 1949 inclusive. Accordingly, each of the expansions and/or other reorganizations in the ENL, and then in the NFL, NHL, BAA and NBL, and ASL are highlighted and then briefly analyzed using various demographic, economic, and sports-related statistics, data, and facts. The teams that were added and/or eliminated in each league, and some information about their home sites are presented in tables. As an aside, after the AL and NL reached a consensus in 1902–1903 to become a sports group known as organized baseball, the number of teams in each league remained constant and located at their original sites until 1953 when the AL Browns moved from St. Louis to Baltimore and the NL Braves from Boston to Milwaukee.

Following the concepts and topics disclosed in Chapter 1 are the sports organizations in Chapter 2. Accordingly, the second chapter in this book provides information about the specific professional sports teams that moved from one metropolitan area to another between 1876 and 1950, and discusses why, when, and where these relocations had occurred. Furthermore, the chapter reveals which of the clubs in the various leagues were accepted by and transferred to rival leagues or were forced to cancel their operations. The teams included in this chapter are some baseball franchises that were established before 1901 plus two clubs in the AL, some teams in the NFL after 1922, in the NHL after 1917, in the NBA after 1949 but before the 1950 season, and in soccer after 1920. However, during 1876–1950 there were no MLS teams that moved or transferred since this league did not exist until 1996. For the specific relocations and transfers that happened in the ENL, AL, NFL, NHL, NBA, and the ASL and Eastern Professional Soccer League (EPSL), the performances of the teams before and after they had moved or transferred, and any demographic factors that may have influenced the franchise owners' decisions are discussed and if appropriate, reported as data in the tables.

The next two chapters of *Big Sports, Big Business* are extensions, respectively, of Chapters 1 and 2. That is, Chapter 3 describes the various expansion and merger activities and cancellations of selected professional sports leagues for the regular seasons and postseasons that dated from 1950 to the early 2000s. Chapter 4 examines when and where some of the teams from the given leagues had relocated or moved from one metropolitan area to another after the 1949 season, and why some teams had transferred between two or more leagues. As expected, clubs from several of these sports leagues are represented in Chapters 3 and 4.

Besides identifying the teams that were affected by expansion, merger, relocation, and other forms of reorganization and restructuring, Chapters 1–4 also mention why and how each of the sports had changed from a business perspective. In other words, some content in these chapters highlights whether decisions made by leagues officials and franchise owners to reorganize their operations had improved or impeded the extent of a sport's competitiveness, its market share, and prosperity.

Chapters 5 and 6 examine the different types of reorganization and restructuring that have transpired since 1882 for a sample of alternative professional sports leagues and their teams that were or are based in metropolitan areas of North America. Although these organizations existed and struggled during various years (e.g., the AFL in 1960–1969, the WNBA in 1996–2005), the leagues' expansions and mergers, and the relocations and transfers of their teams are interesting events to study and compare relative to those actions in the primary leagues as discussed in Chapters 1–4. In short, the majority of alternative, secondary, and inferior leagues emerged and failed in the sports industry because of demographic and financial reasons, and due to the market power and tradition of the AL and NL in baseball and the NHL in ice hockey, NFL in football, and NBA in basketball, but not the MLS in soccer since it was formed in the mid-1990s.

The book concludes by highlighting in Chapter 7 the major findings of the research and then speculating with respect to the future development and growth of the U.S.-based professional sports leagues and their teams. For at least the next decade, the demand for quality sports entertainment will continue to grow from avid fans, from American households and other groups, and from sports enthusiasts who live in foreign nations of the world. As such, the direction, trend, and pattern of league expansions and mergers and team relocations and transfers certainly interests current and prospective fans, franchise owners, investors, media companies, communities, and, of course, sports teams' general managers, coaches, and players. Consequently, although *Big Sports, Big Business* documents and reports what has taken place during years from the late 1800s to the early 2000s, the Conclusion consolidates the research results and establishes a foundation for predicting what might occur in the professional sports industry in the future.

1

Expansions and Mergers of Leagues, 1876–1950

Eleven years after the sport's first game—using rules previously devised by Alexander Cartwright—took place in 1846 between the Knickerbockers Baseball Club of New York and the "New York Nine," the National Association of Baseball Players (NABP) was organized with 24 affiliated teams. In effect, the officials of this so-called quasi-amateur league had seized control of baseball from the Knickerbockers, who claimed to have invented the sport and thus insisted that games must be played by the Club's rules. Nevertheless, despite a military conflict between two regions of the United States, throughout the late 1850s and early to mid 1860s baseball games were enthusiastically played on sandlots in urban and rural areas across the north and south. Meanwhile, the NABP existed and continued to perform until the late 1860s when a majority of fans lost interest in baseball because of "sell-outs," illegal betting on games, and other corrupt practices conducted by some of the league's administrators, team owners, and players. Ultimately these events led to the formation of the first authentic professional sports league based in the United States.

That is, in 1871 the National Association of Professional Baseball Players (NAPBP) began to operate because of the constant bickering and power struggles between groups of amateur and professional athletes who had represented and/or played on teams in the 15-year-old NABP. Indeed, these groups argued extensively about such matters as having separate and unequal memberships and rights in the league, whether to charge spectators a fee for admission to games and how to stop illegal payments to players, and about the bribing of players by gamblers and other undesirable elements. As a result of these controversies and infractions, and a successful

U.S. tour initiated by the Cincinnati Red Stockings, who had used salaried players and charged prices to fans for tickets to games, the sport of amateur baseball gradually declined in America, and the NABP collapsed and dissipated after the conclusion of its 1870 convention.

To meet the public's growing demand for organized baseball, the NAPBP opened its first regular season in the spring of 1871 with 10 teams that had home sites and played games in such cities as Boston, Massachusetts; Chicago, Illinois; and Cleveland, Ohio. This league, however, experienced instability during 1872 to 1875 when a total of 28 baseball teams joined to play but, for various demographic, economic and sport-specific reasons, had failed to survive. These sport enterprises included the Fort Wayne Kekiongas and Rockford Forest Cities in 1872, the Troy Haymakers and Brooklyn Eckfords in 1873, the Elizabeth Resolutes and Washington Nationals in 1874, and the Baltimore Lord Baltimores and Philadelphia Pearls in 1875. Also, after one or a few seasons, some of the NAPBP's expansion clubs confronted financial difficulties and had to cancel their operations. This group was composed of the Baltimore Marylands, Keokuk Westerns, Middletown Mansfields, New Haven Elm Cities, Philadelphia Centennials, and St. Louis Red Stockings. Finally, another of the league's problems occurred when some of the teams' owners refused to spend a $10 fee to sponsor and enter their clubs in championship races and play to win games. Invariably, this meant that teams frequently moved into and out of the NAPBP, inferior clubs in small towns competed against those located in major cities, and one city often had two or more teams entered into the postseason playoffs. As a result, the league lacked discipline and cohesiveness, and experienced a high turnover rate of franchises.[1]

In the end, the Boston Red Stockings, New York Mutuals and Philadelphia Athletics were the only NAPBP teams that had survived throughout each of the league's five seasons. Thus, the NAPBP was forced to fold in 1875 because the majority of its clubs performed below the expectations of baseball fans, had small attendances at their games, and incurred increasing amounts of operating losses and debts. Even so, despite the NAPBP's short tenure of operating as a unit during the early 1870s, other prominent professional leagues of various sports gradually emerged before 1950 with teams located in numerous metropolitan areas of the United States.

Based on their formation, development, and success or failure, this chapter identifies and discusses two different types of reorganizations that occurred within and between some of the elite professional leagues in the same sport as of the mid-1870s to late 1940s. The sports groups primarily affected by these changes were baseball's pre-National League (NL) and American League (AL) in Major League Baseball (MLB), and the National

Football League (NFL), National Hockey League (NHL), and National Basketball Association (NBA). Besides these six major organizations, during this time period there were other less-renowned sports leagues in the United States that had consolidated and/or expanded to incorporate new teams to begin play in various seasons. This list included, for example, the Federal League (1914–1915) in professional baseball; and the American Football League I (1926), II (1936–1937), and III (1940–1941); and the All American Football Conference (1946–1949) in professional football. Their reorganizations, franchises, and team performances are, in part, described in other chapters of *Big Sports, Big Business.*

This chapter, therefore, focuses on the restructuring activities and management reforms of a few sports leagues with teams that performed for sports fans and that had operated as competitive businesses prior to 1950. To highlight and discuss these organizations from a historical perspective, the most important leagues will appear in sequence based on the seasons when they each began to expand their membership or had merged with a rival and accepted new clubs. As such, expansion began in the pre-NL in 1878 and MLB in 1901, and then in the NFL in 1923, NHL in 1924, and NBA in 1949. Because it was the first and premier professional soccer league established in the United States, the American Soccer League (ASL) and a number of its new teams are described in this chapter after the NBA.

EARLY NATIONAL LEAGUE

While playing its regular seasons during 1871–1875, the NAPBP experienced a number of conflicts in coordinating and scheduling games and adversities involving dishonesty and corruption of some teams' players, violations of rules, and organizational bureaucracies. These types of problems motivated entrepreneur William A. Hulbert, attorney Campbell Orrick Bishop, and businessman Charles Fowle—who owned the NABPB's St. Louis team—to jointly create a governmental structure and develop a constitution for establishing a new baseball organization in which a set of rules ensured that playing baseball was a respected and honored activity, clarified that the mutual interests of clubs and players were be protected and promoted, and implemented a schedule for playing a baseball championship series each season. In other words, the pre-NL—titled here as the Early National League (ENL)—was organized by Hulbert, Bishop, and Fowle to operate on an ethical basis and as a business system to be dominated by the clubs' owners, who had committed to enforcing league rules that, in part, ended corruption by restricting the rights, freedoms, and salaries of teams' players.

Given these goals, when the NAPBP ceased to operate after the 1875 season, six of its member teams—the Boston Red Stockings, New York Mutuals, Philadelphia Athletics, Chicago White Stockings, Hartford Dark Blues, and St. Louis Brown Stockings—and other professional baseball clubs from Cincinnati, Ohio, and Louisville, Kentucky, agreed to unite and play competitively as the ENL, which proceeded to open its first season in 1876. Late that year, this original major baseball league decided to expel the Mutuals and Athletics for refusing to pay travel expenses and play their away games against teams at ballparks located in Midwestern cities of the United States. As a result of expelling these two franchises, the ENL consisted of only six teams in the 1877 and 1878 seasons. However, a series of changes occurred that expanded the league to an average of eight clubs in the 1879–1891 seasons and then to 12 in the 1892–1899 seasons. To establish their existence and discuss a portion of their histories, the performances of the ENL's 14 expansion teams are depicted in columns four to six of Table 1.1.[2]

As denoted in the table, a total of seven new teams—which excludes any clubs that transferred from the American Association (AA) and Union Association (UA)—had joined the ENL in 1878–1879 and another seven from 1880 то 1887. Due to depressed local business and economic conditions and the teams' inferior performances, the small- to midsized-market Blues, Cream Citys, Stars, and Cowboys each played for only one season in the ENL, whereas the large-market Gothams/Giants and Phillies each competed and existed for 18 seasons. The two latter clubs and the Grays from Providence, Rhode Island, achieved the most success of the group because they won a majority of their games and a total of four league pennants. In contrast, from 1876 to 1900 it was the nonexpansion teams located in the cities of Baltimore, Boston, Brooklyn, Chicago, and St. Louis that were the dominant competitors since each of them won at least three pennants while being members of the ENL.

Because of inferior performances as ENL teams that played in small urban areas, the unsuccessful baseball franchises listed in Table 1.1 had to cancel their operations after a few seasons. To illustrate, in 1880 the cities of Troy, New York; Worcester, Massachusetts; and Indianapolis, Indiana ranked, respectively, 29th, 28th, and 27th in total population. As a result, the Troy Trojans, Worcester Ruby Legs, and Indianapolis Hoosiers were unable to effectively compete with the other clubs, maintain an adequate fan base in their markets, and generate sufficient revenues and profits to exist as ENL teams beyond three or four years. Meanwhile, the underperforming Bisons and Blues, which were located in the midsized areas of Buffalo, New York, and Cleveland, Ohio, respectively, each prevailed for

Table 1.1
Performances of Early NL Expansion Teams, Selected Seasons

| Team | Season | | | Performance | |
	From	To	AW%	AFIN	PENS
Indianapolis Blues	1878	1878	.400	fifth	0
Milwaukee Cream Citys	1878	1878	.250	sixth	0
Providence Grays	1878	1885	.609	second/third	2
Buffalo Bisons	1879	1885	.487	fourth/fifth	0
Cleveland Blues	1879	1884	.451	fifth/sixth	0
Syracuse Stars	1879	1879	.314	seventh	0
Troy Trojans	1879	1882	.408	sixth	0
Worchester Ruby Legs	1880	1882	.362	eighth	0
Detroit Wolverines	1881	1888	.432	fouth/fifth	1
New York Gothams/Giants	1883	1900	.551	fifth/sixth	2
Philadelphia Phillies	1883	1900	.512	fifth	0
Kansas City Cowboys	1886	1886	.248	seventh	0
Washington Senators	1886	1889	.324	seventh/eighth	0
Indianapolis Hoosiers	1887	1889	.368	seventh/eighth	0

Note: Team and Season are self-explanatory. For Performance, the columns AW%, AFIN, and PENS are, respectively, each team's average winning percentage, average finish position while in the league, and the number of pennants won while playing in the ENL. The Gothams team in New York was renamed the Giants in 1885.

Sources: James Quirk and Rodney D. Fort, *Pay Dirt: The Business of Professional Team Sports* (Princeton, NJ: Princeton University Press, 1992), 378–83; *Official Major League Baseball Fact Book 2005 Edition* (St. Louis, MO: Sporting News, 2005), 170–80; "National League Year in Review," at http://www.baseball-almanac.com, accessed 21 August 2005.

at least six consecutive regular seasons. In short, except for the Senators located in Washington, DC, and the Wolverines in Detroit, Michigan, the ENL baseball teams that were located in large sports markets generally outperformed those clubs that played home games at their ballparks in small to midsized urban areas.

To summarize, the three columns of Performance in Table 1.1, on average the 14 expansion teams in the ENL played about six regular seasons, won 41 percent of their games and finished in fifth or sixth place during their existence. Meanwhile, three, or approximately 21 percent of these franchises, won at least one league pennant. With respect to each of the expansion club's lifespan of seasons, only the ENL's large-market New York Giants and Philadelphia Phillies continued to play as NL teams in 1900. Furthermore, the table reveals that the cities of Buffalo, Indianapolis, Kansas City, Milwaukee, Syracuse, Troy, Washington, and Worchester were not profitable sites to host an expansion team in the ENL. Nevertheless, in

1901 Milwaukee and Washington, along with Cleveland and Detroit, had joined Baltimore, Boston, Chicago, and Philadelphia to become the eight cities that hosted an AL baseball team.

In retrospect, there were some important events and circumstances that had influenced the ENL's structure, development, and business strategy. First, after the 1877 season, Louisville resigned as a franchise because it could not assemble and field a competitive team, while the league dropped clubs that were located in Hartford and St. Louis. Second, three years later, the league's team owners unanimously agreed to adopt a 50-cent admission charge for people to attend games played at their ballparks, and also approved the banning of Sunday games and prohibiting the sale of liquor on each of the clubs' premises. In turn, after the 1880 season, these policies led to the expulsion of the Cincinnati team for objecting to and violating the new rules. Third, in 1882 a number of brewers realized that the ENL clubs existed in only seven large U.S. cities. This opportunity led these owners to form the American Association (AA), which began to play its inaugural season with six teams, including one each in Cincinnati, Louisville, and St. Louis. Furthermore, the AA decided to ignore the ENL's rules and charge spectators 25 cents each for admission, schedule games on Sundays, sell liquor at the teams' games, and not honor the reserve clause in player's contracts.

Fourth, after the 1889 regular seasons of the ENL and AA, the Brotherhood of Professional Base Ball Players organized a new league. This was the Players League (PL), which consisted of six teams that equally shared its league's profits. Despite being first in total attendance among baseball's leagues, the PL dissolved in late 1890 because of a compromise that was negotiated with the ENL and AA regarding the addition of a reserve clause in the standard contracts of players and, in part, due to the mergers of teams and the defections of the PL's New York and Pittsburgh franchises to the ENL.

Fifth, some disputes about the officiating, players' contracts, and the free movements of teams between leagues led to the collapse of the AA in 1891. Because of these five facts and other matters, in the 1892 regular season, the ENL included 12 teams, featured a 154-game split schedule, recognized first- and second-half champions, and adopted a six-game postseason playoff. Therefore, from 1892 to 1899, the ENL contained exactly one dozen clubs each season. Then in 1900 the ENL officially became the NL, which existed for 53 years with eight franchises.

One year after Ban Johnson renamed his Western League to be known as the American Baseball League, he assembled eight teams into a group to challenge the monopolistic NL. This new league played its first season in 1901 despite being rejected by the rival NL as a 'major' baseball entity. However, two years later the AL and NL finally settled their differences in policies about teams' locations and began to perform as MLB. Also, the AL and NL agreed to honor the reserve clauses in players' contracts and arranged for their first-place teams to play each other annually in a World Series. As such, the cities that hosted AL and NL professional baseball teams in 1903 remained the same until the early 1950s.

In the end, the efforts to offer and market professional baseball to sports fans in the United States by such rivals as the AA and PL failed to thrive in the short run because they were untested, undisciplined, and under-financed organizations. Furthermore, they had to compete against the creditability, market power, and success of the ENL, and the popularity of this league's teams in various markets of U.S. east and Midwest cities.

NATIONAL FOOTBALL LEAGUE

Before the mid-1890s, football in the United States was primarily a sport played between college teams and among clubs in amateur and semiprofessional leagues. Then, between the late 1890s and very early 1900s, such newly organized professional football teams as the Allegheny Athletic Association and Morgan Athletic Club, and a series of clubs in towns of western Pennsylvania and eastern Ohio had played games for leisure, fun, and competition, and actively participated against each other in local and regional tournaments. Indeed in Ohio, the Canton AC—renamed Canton Bulldogs—and Massillon Tigers became bitter rivals and relatively popular teams.

Even so, America's college and university coaches adamantly resisted and condemned the growth of semiprofessional and professional football, especially because their athletes—who had finished school and graduated with degrees—increasingly accepted money to play on nonamateur teams. Thus temporarily, most adult sports fans refused to attend professional football games, meaning that the sport did not expand beyond its base. Furthermore, by the mid to late 1910s, the few but primitive and unstable leagues existing in professional football were in a state of confusion. This occurred, in part, due to criticism by the media of nonamateur teams that employed current and postgraduate college athletes, and because veteran players continually moved to and competed for the football franchises that offered the highest salaries. It appeared, therefore, that the sport of organized football needed a central and reputable organization whereby all professional teams were subject to and followed the same types of regulations, rules, and standards.

At an organizational meeting that occurred in Canton, Ohio during August 1920, the American Professional Football Conference (APFC) was established as a nationwide league by the representatives of four teams. One month later, the APFC's name was changed to the American Professional Football Association (APFA). For the 1920 regular season, this football league maintained no official standing and several of its 14 franchises—which had each paid an entry fee up to $100—had played some games against non-APFA opponents. Moreover, few people attended home-site games. (Many college coaches rejoiced in the professional league's problems.) Then in 1921, the APFA consisted of 21 teams, and the number of games they played that season varied from 12 each by the Akron Pros and Buffalo All-Americans to 1 by the Tonawanda Kardex. Nonetheless, to effectively introduce, market, and promote itself and the game of professional football to sports fans across America, in June 1922 the APFA adopted its current title. That is, it became the National Football League (NFL). Since the 18-team APFA was officially renamed the NFL and all of its franchises had fielded teams, 1922 is the base year with respect to identifying the expansions, mergers, relocations, transfers, and other types of reorganizations discussed with respect to the league's seasons in this and the following chapters.[3]

As explained previously, the APFA grew from a total of 14 teams in 1920 to 21 in 1921; and then as the NFL it shrank to 18 to begin the 1922 season. During this three-season period (1920–22), the Chicago Tigers and seven rival teams folded, while the competitive Decatur Staleys changed its name to the Chicago Staleys in 1921 and, one year later, to the Chicago Bears. Furthermore, between 1920 and 1922 a total of 12 new clubs were admitted into and joined the APFA, such as the Louisville Brecks, Minneapolis Marines, and Cincinnati Celts in 1921 and the Columbus Panhandlers, Oorang Indians, and Toledo Maroons in 1922. For this chapter, however, the first NFL expansions discussed are those that occurred after the 1922 season had concluded. Therefore, with respect to the 1923 to 1949 regular seasons, the new NFL teams that were added and their performances are each listed in the various columns of Table 1.2.

Before describing this group of 25 football expansion clubs, it is important to remember that the NFL restructured and changed in size from 8 teams in the 1932 season to 10 in 1933. Before the latter season started, however, the league had divided itself into two separate units—that is, a five-team Eastern Division (ED) and five-team Western Division (WD). Based on this two-part geographical distribution of clubs, at the conclusion of a season, the winners of each division had to compete in one game for the NFL championship. In

Table 1.2
Performances of NFL Expansion Teams, Selected Seasons

Team	Season From	To	Season Performance 1	2	3	4	5
Cleveland Indians/Bulldogs	1923	1925	.750	.875	.385	C	–
Duluth Kelleys/Eskimos	1923	1927	.571	.833	.000	.545	.111
St. Louis All-Stars	1923	1923	.200	C	–	–	–
Frankford Yellow Jackets	1924	1931	.846	.650	.933	.400	.786
Kansas City Blues/Cowboys	1924	1926	.222	.286	.727	C	–
Detroit Panthers	1925	1926	.800	.400	C	–	–
New York Giants	1925	1949	.667	.667	.917	.364	.929
Pottsville Maroons	1925	1928	.833	.833	.385	.200	R
Providence Steam Roller	1925	1931	.545	.417	.651	.889	.400
Brooklyn Lions	1926	1926	.273	C	–	–	–
Hartford Blues	1926	1926	.300	C	–	–	–
Los Angles Buccaneers	1926	1926	.667	C	–	–	–
Louisville Colonels	1926	1926	.000	C	–	–	–
Cleveland Bulldogs	1927	1927	.667	C	–	–	–
New York Yankees	1927	1928	.467	.333	C	–	–
Detroit Wolverines	1928	1928	.778	C	–	–	–
Minneapolis Red Jackets	1929	1930	.100	.125	C	–	–
Staten Island Stapletons	1929	1932	.429	.500	.400	.222	C
Portsmouth Spartans	1930	1933	.455	.786	.750	.545	R
Cleveland Indians	1931	1931	.200	C	–	–	–
Boston Braves	1932	1936	.500	.500	.500	.200	.583
Cincinnati Reds	1933	1934	.333	.000	C	–	–
Pittsburgh Pirates	1933	1940	.333	.167	.333	.500	.364
Cleveland Rams	1937	1942	.091	.364	.500	.400	.182
Boston Yanks	1944	1948	.200	.333	.200	.364	.250

Note: Team is self-explanatory. The columns labeled From and To are, respectively, the expansion and final year at the specific site. Season Performance is the winning percentages of the expansion teams during their first, second, third, fourth and fifth season. The C means that the team canceled its operations before or during that season. An R indicates that a team relocated to another city; that is, the Pottsville Maroons moved to Boston in 1929 and was renamed the Boston Bulldogs, and the Portsmouth Spartans relocated to Detroit in 1934 and became the Detroit Lions. The Frankford Yellow Jackets was renamed the Philadelphia Eagles in 1933, Pittsburgh Pirates became the Pittsburgh Steelers in 1941, and the Boston Redskins moved to Washington, DC, in 1937 and was renamed the Washington Redskins. The Boston Yanks relocated to New York in 1949 to play as the New York Bulldogs, and the Cleveland Rams moved to Los Angeles after the 1945 season to compete as the Los Angeles Rams. The original Cleveland Indians became the Bulldogs in 1924, Duluth Kelleys the Eskimos in 1926, and Kansas City Blues the Cowboys in 1925.

Sources: James Quirk and Rodney D. Fort, *Pay Dirt*, 409–34; *Official 2001 National Football League Record & Fact Book* (New York: National Football League, 2001), 300–301; "NFL Franchise Chronology," http://www.hickoksports.com, accessed 27 August 2005.

fact, after the league had established this type of divisional structure, it continued to exist for the 1933 through 1949 regular seasons and with respect to any playoff games. Interestingly, to further serve its needs and embrace a preferred style of play, in 1932–33 the NFL adopted some noncollege rules for the first time, including inbound lines or hash marks and goalposts on the goal lines. As such, the NFL was being transformed into an exclusive, commercial, and independent organization.

During the early to mid 1920s, the U.S. economy boomed, and the nation's stock markets skyrocketed. As a result, a number of business entrepreneurs and investors tended to ignore the financial risks and invest in sports clubs and in public firms of other growth industries. Since professional baseball had become increasingly popular and prosperous in the United States, and because ice hockey was considered a Canadian sport and outdoor soccer primarily a European activity, the ownership of a monopoly such as an NFL franchise offered a once-in-a-lifetime opportunity for individuals to become well-known celebrities, to diversify their portfolio of assets, and to accumulate even more wealth and economic power. Thus, during the 1920s, 1930s, and 1940s some rich and prosperous persons, families, and friends became the owners of new professional football teams. Table 1.2 indicates how well these NFL expansion clubs had performed during their regular seasons of play.

As reflected in the table, 18 of the expansion teams were admitted to the NFL in the 1920s, six in the 1930s and one in the 1940s. Since the majority of these teams had played their home games in stadiums that were located in small to midsized markets, only the New York Giants survived as an expansion franchise of the league beyond the 1948 season. Because of economic uncertainties and social inequalities that were caused by investor speculation, overvalued securities, high inflation and rising interest rates, and problems resulting from the Great Depression and World War II, most of the NFL expansion teams played for a few seasons but eventually failed as sports businesses. If the large-market New York Giants are deleted from the table, on average the remaining 24 teams survived for approximately three NFL seasons. The range in seasons varied from eight for the successful Frankford Yellow Jackets and inferior Pittsburgh Pirates to one for eight of the teams, including the pathetic Brooklyn Lions, Louisville Colonels, and St. Louis All-Stars, and the excellent Cleveland Bulldogs, Detroit Wolverines, and Los Angeles Buccaneers.

Some meaningful and specific relationships, and interesting statistics and other facts about the 25 NFL expansion teams reveal, in part, how the clubs had operated and performed as a group and as individual competitors. First, for each of the seasons listed—or from one through five—the average win-loss percentages of the existing teams were, respectively, equal to .464, .513, .551, .472, and .450. This uneven trend in winning percentages indicates that these teams' performances continuously improved during the first three seasons to a peak, and then declined in seasons four and five. Invariably, a combination of such factors as a change in team ownership; cancellation of a franchise; one or more consecutive losing or winning seasons; home and away game attendances; players' injuries, trades, and retirements; and the replacement of coaches and general managers likely contributed to the fluctuation in teams' performances throughout the five seasons.

Second, based on the gross population of their urban areas in the expansion year, eight, or approximately 32 percent, of the franchises listed in the table were each located in large and small markets, whereas nine, or about 36 percent of the total, existed in midsized markets. Their average win-loss percentages and number of seasons played were, accordingly, equal to .517 and 3.1 for the eight teams located in large markets, .383 and 3.1 for the eight clubs in small markets, and .402 and 2.6 for the nine franchises in midsized markets. Thus, the teams playing at their home stadiums in such urban areas as Detroit, Frankford—which was incorporated into Philadelphia in 1845—and Los Angeles had relatively good performances, whereas those clubs based in Cincinnati, Hartford, and Louisville played poorly. Occasionally, the teams in relatively midsized markets like Cleveland and Minneapolis existed for fewer seasons than some of the clubs that were located in large and small urban areas. In short, these results suggest that, on average, NFL team performances were not always positively correlated with market size, and that the average number of seasons played varied by less than one year between clubs in the three groups of markets.

Third, the number of expansion small-market teams that had performed in their first season exceeded the quantity of new large-market clubs that competed in their initial season. For example, in Table 1.2's group of 25 franchises, such sparsely populated cities as Duluth, Minnesota, and Kansas City, Missouri, outnumbered the densely populated places like Boston and Detroit. Since the NFL Bears and Cardinals jointly shared and played for years in the Chicago area, as did the Eagles and Yellow Jackets in the Philadelphia area and football's Dodgers and Giants in the New York area, the owners and prospective owners of other NFL teams were denied entry into those populated markets and thus forced to select other sites in cities of the Midwest with smaller populations such as Louisville, Kentucky; Pittsburgh, Pennsylvania; and Portsmouth, Ohio.

Fourth, across the five seasons, there were excessively large differences in performances between the superior and inferior NFL expansion teams. To illustrate, the Frankford Yellow Jackets and New York Giants won more than

70 percent of their total games and finished first in the NFL, respectively, in 1926 and 1927. Meanwhile, the win-loss percentages for the Boston Yanks equaled .269 during the 1944–1948 seasons and .307 for the Cleveland Rams in the 1937–1941 seasons. With respect to each of these teams' five seasons, the Yanks never finished higher than third place in the ED and the Rams never exceeded a fourth place finish in the WD. Furthermore, the Philadelphia Eagles, New York Giants, and Washington Redskins dominated in the ED, as did the Chicago Bears, Detroit Lions, and Green Bay Packers in the WD. As a result, in 1949 owner Ted Collins moved the Yanks from Boston to New York and renamed his team the New York Bulldogs, and in 1946 owner Dan Reeves relocated the Rams from Cleveland to Los Angeles and changed the club's title to Los Angeles Rams.

Fifth, eight, or 32 percent, of the NFL expansion teams existed for five seasons, and the same number and proportion played for merely one season. Interestingly, the franchises playing in each group of seasons tended to be located in either large or midsized markets. If these 16 teams are grouped together and identified, the exceptions to that fact were the small-market and successful Providence Steam Roller and the unsuccessful Hartford Blues and Louisville Colonels. As to the other nine expansion teams and their performances, the relatively successful—yet small-market—Pottsville Maroons and Portsmouth Spartans decided to relocate to other cities after completing four seasons. After finishing second, third, and then eighth twice in consecutive seasons, the Maroons moved from Pottsville to Boston, Massachusetts in 1929 and became the Boston Bulldogs. Similarly, after placing second or third during the 1931–1933 NFL seasons, the Spartans went broke in 1933, which, in turn, motivated owner George Richardson to move the team from Portsmouth to Detroit and rename the club Detroit Lions.

Sixth, for various business reasons 15, or 60 percent, of the NFL expansion teams had to suspend operations and cancel their franchises in five or fewer years. The New York Yankees, for example, went broke after the 1928 season; the Minneapolis Red Jackets had combined with and then reassigned its players to the Frankford Yellow Jackets to finish the 1930 season; and the Cincinnati Reds' team folded after it incurred severe financial losses in the 1933 and 1934 seasons.

Seventh, several NFL players abandoned their teams and joined a number of American Football League (AFL) clubs that existed during the 1926, 1936–1937, and 1940–1941 seasons. A sample of these AFL franchises by season included the Los Angeles Wildcats and Philadelphia Quakers in 1926, Pittsburgh Americans and Syracuse Braves in 1936, Boston Shamrocks and Rochester Tigers in 1937, Columbus Bullies and Milwaukee Chiefs in 1940, and the Buffalo Indians and Cincinnati Bengals in 1941.

In summary, between 1923 and 1948, the NFL had decided to add 25 expansion franchises. Eight of these new teams each had located in large and small urban areas, whereas nine competed at home in midsized markets. On average, the 25 clubs played at least three seasons in the league and won approximately 43 percent of their games, and except for the New York Giants, had failed to exist at the original sites after the 1948 season. The three most successful teams for five seasons were the large-market Frankford Yellow Jackets and New York Giants and small-market Providence Steam Roller and Duluth Kelleys/Eskimos, and the least successful clubs for five seasons included the large-market Boston Yanks and Boston Braves, and the small to midsized market Cleveland Rams and Pittsburgh Pirates.

NATIONAL HOCKEY LEAGUE

Since the early 1800s, the people of Canada were interested in watching English field hockey games because they enjoyed the sport's rough body contact, skillful footwork, and expert stick handling as performed by players in Her Majesty's Royal Canadian Rifles and other army units. These historical facts suggest that the evolution of ice hockey, in part, had originated in Canada's eastern provinces and was promoted by a series of amateur and professional activities during the 1850s and 1860s, by the creation of rules to govern ice hockey games when played by students attending Montreal's McGill University in the 1870s, and by an assortment of ice hockey associations and teams that were geographically dispersed within and surrounding the cities of Ontario and Quebec in the 1880s. Accordingly, from those conditions, environments and events emerged several loosely organized Canadian ice hockey leagues and eventually the NHL.

Evolving from a combination of activities and rules, and associations of teams, a number of official ice hockey leagues had formed in Canada during the mid to late 1880s to early 1900s and then, for various reasons, folded within this period. For example, while composed of three teams from Montreal and one each from Ottawa and Quebec, the Amateur Hockey Association (AHA) played its first season in 1888. As a result of financing and scheduling problems and lacking a feasible business plan, the AHA folded in 1898. As such, it was replaced by the seven-team Canadian Amateur Hockey League (CAHL), which existed for seven seasons. Unfortunately, this organization also experienced similar managerial dilemmas and monetary hardships as the AHA. So in 1905, the CAHL failed and was replaced by the six-team Eastern Canada Amateur Hockey League (ECAHL). As clubs had competed in games during the ECAHL's initial season, some of the prominent players decided to quit

their teams while other players moved to clubs that existed in rival associations. Consequently, the ECAHL also folded, allowing the multi-team
Eastern Canada Amateur Hockey Association (ECAHA) to form in 1906.
Because the ECAHA was underfinanced and mismanaged, it succumbed
after three seasons. In turn, this led to the birth of the five-team Canadian
Hockey Association (CHA). However, after being denied higher salaries by
their teams' owners, many of the league's better players constantly shifted
from one club to another, causing some of these hockey enterprises to
bankrupt. Thus, the CHA did not exist beyond fall 1909.[4]

As a result of these failures of former amateur leagues, hockey officials
in Canada decided that the sport needed reforms and the establishment
of a professional league. Thus, they organized the professional National
Hockey Association (NHA), which began to operate in 1909 with clubs
located in such Canadian cities as Cobalt, Haileybury, Montreal, Ottawa,
and Renfrew. In later years, a few teams from hockey associations in Quebec
and Toronto had joined this new league.

Throughout its nine-year history of seasons, the NHA experienced a
number of unique and stressful internal conflicts. The most significant
controversy involved the Toronto Blueshirts' owner Edward Livingstone,
who allegedly had violated the league's regulations in order to gain a
competitive advantage for his team. For instance, he supposedly offered
monetary contracts to other teams' top athletes so that these players would
not participate in hockey games, and also he threatened the NHA concerning his interest in organizing a rival ice hockey league to be based in
the United States. Consequently, Livingstone was officially ejected from the
NHA in early 1917, which thereby prompted the resignation of the league's
president, Frank Robinson. When the remaining NHA franchise owners
met in Montreal's Windsor Hotel in November 1917 and discovered that
Livingstone was covertly negotiating a deal with hockey officials to regain
control of the Blueshirts, these owners became angry and thus formed the
NHL. This new hockey league's founding members included the Montreal
Canadiens, Montreal Wanderers, Ottawa Senators, Quebec Bulldogs, and
the newly renamed Toronto Arenas. During the 1917 season, the Bulldogs
had to temporarily discontinue operations in Quebec, and the Wanderers folded that season because a fire had destroyed Montreal's Westmount
Arena, which contained the team's home ice rink. Therefore, the NHL
existed with three clubs competing in 1917 and three in 1918. One year
later, the Quebec Bulldogs returned to the league and the Toronto Arenas
became the Toronto St. Patricks.[5]

From 1919 to the early 1920s, the NHL team owners increased their
players' salaries to a level that could not be matched by any clubs in the

other Canadian-based ice hockey leagues. As a result of the players' inflated salaries and greater franchise costs, all NHL teams were forced to seek additional revenues from fans who attended games and from other hockey customers, including local businesses and governments. To generate more cash inflows and the required amounts of funding to continue operations, during the 1920s the NHL franchise owners approved the entry of six new teams that would be placed in cities of Canada and/or the United States. As denoted in Table 1.3, two franchises entered the league in 1924, one in 1925 and three in 1926. Each of these clubs' performances and other historical facts about them for various hockey seasons are briefly discussed next in this chapter.

Boston Bruins

In 1923–1924, grocery store magnate Charles Adams persuaded the group of NHL franchise owners to place a new team in Boston. Adams realized this vibrant city of nearly one million people had thousands of sports fans who would enthusiastically support a professional ice hockey club. For an expansion fee of $15,000, Adams acquired the right to place a franchise in Boston and name it the Boston Bruins. As a member of the NHL's Eastern Conference (EC) since 1924, the Bruins have achieved great success: The club won Stanley Cups in 1929, 1939 and 1941, and finished as runner-up for a Stanley Cup in a total of four postseasons playing against such competitors as the Toronto Maple Leafs and other NHL champions. Some of the Bruins' greatest players have established league records while

Table 1.3
NHL Expansion Teams and Stanley Cup, Selected Seasons

Team	Season		Stanley Cup	
	From	To	Champion	Opponent
Boston Bruins	1924	1950	3	4
Montreal Maroons	1924	1938	2	1
Pittsburgh Pirates	1925	1929	0	0
Chicago Blackhawks	1926	1950	2	2
Detroit Cougars/Falcons/Red Wings	1926	1950	4	6
New York Rangers	1926	1950	3	4

Note: Team and Season are self-explanatory. Champion and Opponent are, respectively, the number of seasons that the club won the Stanley Cup and had finished as a runner-up in the Stanley Cup finals to 1950. The Detroit Cougars was renamed the Falcons in 1930 and then the Red Wings in 1933. The Montreal Maroons folded after the 1938 season, and the Pittsburgh Pirates relocated to Philadelphia in 1930.

Sources: James Quirk and Rodney D. Fort, *Pay Dirt*, 463–74, and *The World Almanac and Book of Facts* (New York: World Almanac Books, 2004), 940.

skating in games, including Eddie Shore, who won the Hart Memorial Trophy in 1933, 1935, 1936, and 1938; and Bobby Bauer, who was the league's most gentlemanly player in 1940, 1941, and 1947. Other outstanding Bruins players include Lionel Hitchman and Tiny Thompson in the 1920s, and Dit Clapper and Bill Cowley in the 1930s and 1940s.[6]

Montreal Maroons

In 1924 some sports investors and businessmen Thomas Strachan and Donat Raymond joined together and paid a total fee of $15,000 to a group of NHL team owners as a payment to enter a new hockey franchise into the league. Strachan and Raymond also owned the Montreal Forum, which had opened in 1924 for the Maroons—a nickname assigned by the Montreal media because of the team's almost solid maroon uniforms. With respect to the Maroons' local market, the club drew its hockey fans from the Anglophile neighborhoods of Montreal, whereas its rival, the Montreal Canadiens, appealed primarily to fans of French descent. As a result, there were significantly more friendly French people in Montreal that supported the Canadiens than a passionate English population who rooted for the Maroons. The differences in fan bases, in turn, contributed to the Maroons' deplorable financial position each year and to the termination of the franchise in 1938.

During 15 seasons in the NHL, the Maroons were very competitive. The team won a Stanley Cup in 1926 by defeating the Victoria Cougars and again in 1935 by outplaying the Toronto Maple Leafs, and in 1928 finished runner-up to the champion New York Rangers. Besides competing in these championship series, the Maroons also won NHL division titles in 1930 and 1936, and qualified for playoff appearances in 1926–1928 and 1930–1937. Furthermore, in 1936 a Maroons club played vigorously for approximately three hours but lost to the Detroit Red Wings 1–0 in the longest playoff game in NHL history. Interestingly, the Maroons' least and most productive seasons were, respectively, in 1924 when the team scored 20 points and finished with a win-loss-tie record of 9–19–2, and in 1927 when the club scored 54 points and ended its schedule at 24–14–6.

The Maroons' all-time best athletes were the league's 1926 and 1930 Most Valuable Player Nels Stewart, 1934 Rookie of the Year Russ Blinco, and Hall of Fame players Babe Siebert, Clint Benedict, George Boucher, Hooley Smith, Lionel Conacher, Punch Broadbent, Reg Noble, Toe Blake, and captains Dunc Munro and Stew Evans. Despite the performances of these outstanding players, it was the Great Depression in North America, poor attendances at NHL ice hockey games in the 1935–1937 regular seasons,

Maroons coach King Clancy's failure to discipline his players, and the team's last place finish at 12–30–6 in the 1937 season that created revenue deficiencies and thereby forced the team to officially fold its operations on May 13, 1939. Because of the Maroons' bitter rivalry with the Canadiens, many ice hockey followers living in Montreal eventually became fans of and supported the Toronto Maple Leafs.

In short, for 15 NHL seasons the Maroons were a remarkably competitive but unprofitable expansion franchise. In any event, its teams provided fun and entertainment for ice hockey fans in Canada's largest city and an alternative to watching the Montreal Canadiens score goals for victories and win NHL division and conference titles and Stanley Cups.

Pittsburgh Pirates

After playing as the Pittsburgh Yellowjackets in the U.S. Amateur Hockey Association since 1915 and winning two of the Association's championships, this franchise joined the NHL in 1925 when attorney and owner James Callahan paid the league a fee of $12,000, and spent an additional $25,000 to acquire some skilled ice hockey players from clubs in the Western Canada Hockey League (WCHL). Since the colors of the NHL Pirates' uniforms in 1925 were similar to those of the popular MLB club that was located in Pittsburgh—that is, canary yellow with black horizontal stripes—Callahan chose the Pittsburgh Pirates to be the new name of his ice hockey club. With respect to the club's initial season, the NHL had granted Callahan's Pirates a provisional status of "semi-expansion."

During five years as a franchise in the league, the Pirates won more than 50 percent of its regular season games twice, but failed to play in a Stanley Cup final or to win a divisional championship. Nonetheless, the team competed in the 1926 NHL playoffs and lost to the eventual Stanley Cup champion Montreal Maroons. Also, the Pirates appeared in the 1928 playoffs but was defeated by that season's NHL champion, the New York Rangers. The Pirates' Odie Cleghorne was the first NHL coach to reposition his players during games and to use three set forward lines, which was a significant change from the standard way that coaches assigned lines. This new system, however, meant that Cleghorne's best players were fatigued during games because they remained on the ice for as long as possible. Because of their talents and accomplishments, former Pirates hockey players Lionel Conacher, Frank Fredrickson, Mickey MacKay, and Roy Worters were voted into the league's Hall of Fame. Even so, there were no Pirates players who won NHL awards for being the most valuable player and for rookie of the year, most gentlemanly player, leading point scorer, or outstanding goalie.

When the Pirates experienced serious financial difficulties in 1928, Callahan sold the team to an investment group that included a fight promoter and ex-lightweight boxing champion Benny Leonard. After finishing with a pathetic win-loss-tie record of 5–36–3 in the 1929 NHL season, the club filed for bankruptcy in 1930 because of dull performances, declining attendances at the team's home games that were played in Pittsburgh's Duquesne Gardens, and debts that had accumulated to at least $400,000. As a result of a financial crisis, the Pirates' owners moved the franchise from Pittsburgh to southeastern Pennsylvania and renamed the team Philadelphia Quakers. Nevertheless, because of short-run losses that exceeded $100,000 from playing in the 1930 season, the NHL allowed the Quakers' owners to voluntarily suspend the club's operations in future seasons if a request was made to the league before each season had begun. Thus, at the next five consecutive preseason NHL governors meetings, the Quakers announced and were granted a suspension of operations. When the financing for a new arena to be built for the Quakers in the Philadelphia area was not negotiated and approved, the franchise folded in 1936.

Chicago Blackhawks

When his WCHL franchise—which was named the Regina Capitals—experienced financial problems in 1925, owner Frederic McLaughlin moved the team from Regina to play in the Pacific Coast Hockey League (PCHL) in Portland, Oregon, and changed its nickname to Portland Rosebuds. Then one year later, McLaughlin shifted the team from Portland to Chicago, Illinois; paid an expansion franchise fee of $12,000 to the NHL; and titled his club Chicago Black Hawks. After three regular seasons, the team began playing its home games in the $7 million Chicago Stadium when that facility opened in 1929. Although known as the Black Hawks for 58 seasons, the team's nickname was revised to be the Blackhawks in 1986.

Between 1926 and 1950, the Black Hawks—now Blackhawks—won two Stanley Cups and competed as a final opponent in two other NHL championship series. Because of their contributions during various regular seasons and in the playoffs, this franchise's memorable players throughout its early history included most valuable player and leading point scorer Max Bentley, rookies of the year Mike Karakas and Cully Dahlstrom, and outstanding goalies Charlie Gardner and Lorne Chabot. Indeed, Bentley and Gardiner are in the league's Hall of Fame.

Based on the Black Hawks' prior seasons of wins, losses, and ties, and its previous playoff and championship appearances and the performances of its players, this 80-year-old franchise has achieved average to above average success in the league. As one of six NHL expansion teams of the 1920s, the Blackhawks' performances certainly rank ahead of the former Pittsburgh Pirates and about equal to the former Montreal Maroons, but inferior to the traditions and results of the Boston Bruins, New York Rangers, and Detroit Cougars/Falcons/Red Wings.

Detroit Cougars/Falcons/Red Wings

After spending $25,000 to purchase the Victoria Cougars of the PCHL, a syndicate led by Charles Hughes moved the team from Victoria in 1926 to play in Detroit. Renamed the Detroit Cougars by its owners, the club joined the NHL after paying an expansion fee of $12,000. Since there were no adequate arenas for professional ice hockey teams in Detroit during the early 1920s, the Cougars played the 1926 season on a rink located in Windsor, Ontario. Then, the new $2.2 million Detroit Olympia Stadium opened in 1927, and that facility became the home arena of the Cougars. As a marketing strategy, the team's nickname was changed to the Detroit Falcons in 1930, and three years later to the Detroit Red Wings.

In performances, this ice hockey enterprise has been the most consistent and successful expansion franchise in the league. Specifically, a collection of Red Wings clubs won two Stanley Cups in the 1930s and one in the 1940s. Besides winning these three championships, various Red Wings teams finished runner-up in four Stanley Cup competitions prior to the 1950 season. To accomplish these feats since 1926, the franchise had achieved its victories by relying on the playmaking of Eddie Goodfellow, Sid Abel, and Gordie Howe. According to many experts who have studied this sport, Howe is considered the second or third greatest hockey athlete of all time. To illustrate, during his career on the ice, he scored 1,850 points and in six seasons won the Hart Memorial Trophy for being the league's most valuable player and also the Art Ross Trophy for being the NHL's leading point scorer. Because of the club's 22 total appearances in the Stanley Cup Finals since 1926, it is expected that the Red Wings will remain competitive in the NHL's Central Division during the majority of future seasons.

New York Rangers

Prior to the 1950 season, the sixth expansion team that entered into the NHL was the New York Rangers. The team's owner, Madison Square Garden Corporation, obtained the franchise rights in 1926 when the company paid the league a fee of $12,000 and spent $25,000 to obtain some players from the WCHL. Within weeks following the Corporation's acquisition, Tex Richard hired Toronto Maple Leafs coach Conn Smythe to organize and train the Rangers' team. After Smythe was fired because of his disagreements with the franchise's administration, coach Lester Patrick was appointed to replace him before the start of the 1926 season. As a result, that season the Rangers scored 56 points and finished at 25–13–6, and won the NHL's American Division but lost a series of games in the playoffs to the Boston Bruins. Besides the Maple Leafs and Bruins, the Rangers most competitive rivals have been the Montreal Canadiens, New Jersey Devils, New York Islanders, and Philadelphia Flyers.

Between 1926 and 1950 inclusive, the Rangers had performed well enough to win Stanley Cups in 1928, 1933, and 1940, and to finish runner-up to the NHL champions in 1929, 1932, 1937, and 1950. During the club's early history, its athletes received many honors, including most valuable players Buddy O'Connor and Chuck Rayne, rookies of the year Kilby Macdonald, Grant Warwick, Edgar Laprade, and Pentti Lund, most gentlemanly players Frank Boucher and Clint Smith, outstanding defenseman Doug Harvey, leading points scorer Bryan Hextall, and outstanding goalie Dave Kerr. Because of their athleticism and achievements, some of these players were elected to the NHL's Hall of Fame.

In the next section of this chapter, the contents focus on the expansions, mergers, and other events of a few prominent U.S.-based professional basketball leagues and their teams during the 1930s and 1940s.

NATIONAL BASKETBALL ASSOCIATION

The sport of professional basketball, as played in the United States, began in 1896 at a Young Men's Christian Association (YMCA) event in Trenton, New Jersey. When a dispute occurred between some players on Trenton's YMCA basketball team and the organization's officials, these athletes reacted by forming a local professional team and accepting money from sponsors to play games. Subsequently, in 1898 a group of sports editors from a few New Jersey newspapers met and established the National Basketball League (NBL I), which initially consisted of six franchises that were located in various midsized to large cities in eastern states. With respect to this league's 1898 to 1903 seasons, the championship teams in consecutive years were the Trenton Nationals (twice), and then the New York Wanderers, Bristol Pile Drivers, and Camden Electrics (twice). Unfortunately, in January 1904 the NBL I folded because the Camden Electrics and Trenton Potters—formerly nicknamed the Trenton Nationals—had ceased to operate their clubs as members of the league.[7]

Twenty-one years after the NBL I had failed, the American Basketball League (ABL) was organized and located its headquarters in the New York area. This professional basketball league's culture and image were considered to be ethnic and big city by American sports fans and officials. Nevertheless, the ABL included a variety of Midwest and east coast teams that were frequently owned and managed by local sports promoters who lacked sufficient financial capital to invest in and promote professional basketball. Even so, the team's players were frequently children of first-generation immigrants who had traveled to the United States to escape the repression that existed in European countries.[8]

More specifically, the ABL had consisted of a group of teams from 1925 to 1931 and 1933 to 1954. However, because of a nationwide depression and debts of franchises, the league had to suspend its operations during the 1931 and 1932 seasons. With respect to each decade of performances, the ABL's dominant teams were the Cleveland Rosenblums and Original Celtics in the 1920s and Philadelphia Sphas in the 1930s and 1940s. Interestingly, the Sphas' roster listed Elmore Morgenthaler, who was professional basketball's first seven-foot player. Besides the teams in Cleveland, New York, and Philadelphia, some other midsized and small- and large-market areas with ABL clubs included Baltimore; Brooklyn; Fort Wayne, Indiana; Rochester, New York; Scranton, New Jersey; and Wilmington, Delaware.

During the ABL era, the Firestone Corporation and the General Electric and Goodyear companies sponsored industrial teams. To establish a U.S. professional organization, these businesses jointly created the National Basketball League II (NBL II) in 1937. That season, the latter league consisted of 13 independent corporate teams that were home-based in a number of towns in the United States' Midwest and that played a short to moderate distance in mileage from one or more of the nation's Great Lakes. In performances, it was the Firestone Non-Skids, Fort Wayne Zollner Pistons, and Oshkosh All-Stars that each won two NBL II championships. Meanwhile, one title was won by the Anderson Packers, Chicago Gears, Goodyear Wingfoots, Minneapolis Lakers, Rochester Royals, and Sheboygan Redskins. During the NBL II's 12 years in existence, 29 clubs had played in various seasons, and many of them were expansion teams such as the Chicago Bruins, Cleveland Chase Brassmen, Hammond Ciesar All-Americans, Syracuse Nationals and Youngstown Bears. Despite these competitors, in 1948 the NBL II experienced financial and operational problems after four of its prominent teams—the Fort Wayne Zollner Pistons, Minneapolis Lakers, Rochester Royals and Indianapolis Kautskys (renamed Jets)—decided to join the Basketball Association of America

Table 1.4

Premerger NBA Teams in BAA and NBL, 1946–1947 to 1948–1949 Seasons

| | Season | | |
Team	1946–1947	1947–1948	1948–1949
Anderson Packers	NBL	NBL	NBL
Baltimore Bullets	–	BAA	BAA
Boston Celtics	BAA	BAA	BAA
Chicago Stags	BAA	BAA	BAA
Denver Nuggets	–	–	NBL
Detroit Gems/Minneapolis Lakers	NBL	NBL	BAA
Fort Wayne Zollner Pistons	NBL	NBL	BAA
Indianapolis Kautskys/Jets	NBL	NBL	BAA
New York Knicks	BAA	BAA	BAA
Philadelphia Warriors	BAA	BAA	BAA
Rochester Royals	NBL	NBL	BAA
Sheboygan Redskins	NBL	NBL	NBL
St. Louis Bombers	BAA	BAA	BAA
Syracuse Nationals	NBL	NBL	NBL
Tri Cities Blackhawks	NBL	NBL	NBL
Washington Capitols	BAA	BAA	BAA
Waterloo Hawks	–	–	NBL

Note: The NBL II is abbreviated as NBL. A – indicates that neither a BAA nor an NBL team had existed at the site during the specified basketball season. The Detroit Gems moved to Minneapolis, Minnesota in 1947 and was renamed the Minneapolis Lakers. The Lakers, Pistons, Jets, and Royals switched from the NBL to the BAA in 1948.

Source: James Quirk and Rodney D. Fort, Pay Dirt, 446–59.

(BAA), as indicated in Table 1.4. Then, in 1949 the six surviving teams of the NBL II left the league to become members of the BAA.[9]

The BAA was founded in 1946 by a group of New York City business executives who enjoyed the game and realized its prospects to be a successful sport. That year, 11 professional basketball franchises were granted charters to play in this new league. During the 1947 and 1948 seasons, five of the original franchises had folded because of internal conflicts: the Cleveland Rebels, Detroit Falcons, Pittsburgh Ironmen, Providence Steamrollers, and Toronto Huskies. Then in 1947, the Baltimore Bullets decided to leave the ABL and enter the BAA as an expansion team. Finally, in 1949 six NBL teams joined the BAA, which formed a three-division league that was renamed the National Basketball Association (NBA). Indeed, it was the Anderson Packers, Denver Nuggets, Sheboygan Redskins, Syracuse Nationals, Tri Cities Blackhawks, and Waterloo Hawks that had abandoned the NBL to play in the BAA and NBA. However, after the 1949 NBA season concluded, the

Packers, Nuggets, Redskins, Hawks, Chicago Stags, and St. Louis Bombers each withdrew as members of the league.

In short, the NBA emerged after the NBL and BAA had consolidated their operations in 1949. Although the rival ABL continued to exist as an independent league until 1955, the NBA gradually became the most stable and powerful professional basketball organization in America. In retrospect, this league had its clubs located in small, midsized, and large cities that extended from New York City to Minneapolis, Minnesota. Even so, in 1950 there were no NBA teams existing in the growing metropolitan areas of the U.S. south, southwest, and west.

AMERICAN SOCCER LEAGUE

According to the literature on sport leagues, numerous Native American athletes participated in a rudimentary form of soccer in Massachusetts during the 1600s and 1700s, and so did some students at U.S. colleges in the 1820s. Toward the end of the nineteenth century, a series of amateur soccer competitions were played in the United States, and in 1894 a few teams cooperated with each other to complete one full season of professional league soccer. However, for the sport to grow, it needed a national organization that would adopt and enforce rules, establish discipline, and punish the players and teams who had violated any rules. So in 1913, the U.S. Football Association was founded. This organization—which was renamed United States Soccer Football Association (USFA) in 1945—gradually assumed control of all amateur and professional activities related to the sport.

While the USFA expanded its membership, soccer continued to grow as a secondary sport in American colleges and several players joined local teams after they had graduated. Thus, in response to the growing number of experienced soccer players living in cities across the United States and the rising popularity of the sport in regions of the east and Midwest, and to market soccer to foreigners living in the United States who preferred it to American baseball, basketball, and football, and to Canadian-based ice hockey, some sports entrepreneurs realized that people were willingly to pay admission prices to watch soccer games played by local clubs.

Given this sports environment and potential market, in 1921 the American Soccer League (ASL) was established as a regional organization by the teams' sponsors, and it became the first official professional soccer league in the United States. For its fan base, the ASL tended to attract newly arrived immigrant populations from European countries. Thus, the league's teams recruited their players from these groups of people. Regarding the location of playing sites, ASL teams decided to exist and play games in cities within regions along the east and northeast coasts, and especially in some of the metropolitan areas of Massachusetts, New Jersey, New York, and Pennsylvania. In fact, eight teams had competed in the ASL's first season in 1921. These clubs included three from cities in Massachusetts, two each from cities in Pennsylvania and New York, and one from a city in New Jersey. For the number of expansion teams and their seasons and performances while competing in the ASL, see Table 1.5.[10]

Table 1.5:
Performances of ASL Expansion Teams, by Season, 1921–1933

Team	Season		Performance	
	From	To	Wins	Points
Brooklyn Wanderers	1922	1933	126	323
Paterson Silk Socks	1922	1922	9	22
Philadelphia Field Club	1922	1926	29	73
New York Giants/Soccer Club	1923	1931	92	257
Newark Skeeters	1923	1928	31	95
Boston Wonder Workers	1924	1928	87	253
Fleisher Yarns	1924	1924	11	28
Indiana Flooring	1924	1926	53	127
New Bedford Whalers	1924	1932	174	411
Providence Clamdiggers/Gold Bugs	1924	1930	126	303
Shawsheen Indians	1925	1925	11	25
Springfield Babes	1926	1926	7	21
Hartford Americans	1927	1927	4	10
New York Nationals/Giants	1927	1932	93	233
Philadelphia Celtics	1927	1927	2	5
Jersey City	1928	1928	2	4
Philadelphia Field Club	1928	1929	11	33
Bridgeport Hungarians	1929	1929	0	3
Brooklyn Hakoah/Hakoah All Stars	1929	1932	48	122
Newark Americans	1930	1932	12	32
New York Americans	1931	1933	9	23
New York Field Club	1932	1932	5	11
Queens Bohemians	1932	1933	2	5

Note: The columns of Team, From, and To are self-explanatory. The Wins and Points columns are the totals for each expansion team during their regular seasons.

Sources: Dave Litterer, "American Soccer League I (1921–1933)," at http://www.sover.net, accessed 20 September 2005, and David Goldblatt, *Soccer Yearbook: The Complete Guide to the World Game* (New York: DK Publishing, Inc., 2004), 504–5.

Based on the five columns of data in Table 1.5 and information extracted from other documents, some interesting observations are worthwhile to cite about one or more of the ASL's 23 expansion teams. First, on average a typical soccer club played three seasons, which ranged from 12 by the Brooklyn Wanderers to one by nine teams, including the Paterson Silk Socks, Fleisher Yarn, and New York Field Club. Second, for various reasons some of the expansion teams simply had to withdraw from the league, such as the Philadelphia Field Club and Shawsheen Indians, while others were forced to resign like the Hartford Americans and Philadelphia Celtic.

Third, as the league expanded by adding new teams the ASL's 1927 season was divided into first and second halves. To avoid a soccer war and compete for players, in 1929 the ASL and Eastern Professional Soccer League II (EPSL II) merged to form the Atlantic Coast League (ACL). As such, the ACL consisted of teams from the ASL such as the Boston Wonder Workers and New York Nationals, and of teams from the EPSL II like the Bethlehem Steel and New York Giants.

Fourth, three ASL expansion teams had changed their nicknames: The Providence Clamdiggers to Providence Gold Bugs in 1928, and in 1930 the New York Giants to New York Soccer Club and New York Nationals to New York Giants. Meanwhile, in 1929 the ASL's Brooklyn Hakoah and EPSL II's New York Hakoah merged to become a new team titled the Hakoah All Stars. Fifth, in performances the most successful of the expansion teams were the New Bedford Whalers and then the Brooklyn Wanderers and Providence Clamdiggers/Gold Bugs. Indeed, these four clubs accumulated a total of 426 wins and 1,037 points. Other ASL clubs, however, also played outstanding soccer in various seasons. For example, the Philadelphia Field Club in 1922, Boston Wonder Workers in 1928, and the New York Giants in 1931 had each won the league's championship. Furthermore, as an original franchise in the league, the Fall River Marksmen won seven ASL championships, and the expansion New Bedford Whalers finished as runner-up in five of the league's seasons.

After the ACL renamed itself American Soccer League in 1930, it folded in spring 1933. As a result, a new sport league named American Soccer League II (ASL II) emerged and established a division of nine teams that were frequently based in areas of the New England region. Between 1933 and 1941, the various teams in this division played soccer games in such cities as Boston, Fall River, Pawtucket, Quincy, and Springfield in Massachusetts; and Providence in Rhode Island; and Hartford in Connecticut. Nonetheless, other than identifying and documenting a portion of the games played in the league and some of the teams' win-loss-tie standings and points scored for a few seasons, there is no other reliable information and data about the ASL II's internal operations and its expansion and merger strategies.[11]

Although the ASL II eventually reorganized itself to play soccer games in the 1951–1953 seasons, the New England division experienced problems earlier and had to disband in the early 1940s. Since the events and other detailed facts about the ASL II's history are inconclusive and incomplete, its reorganization activities and team decisions are unknown and thus not discussed in this chapter.

SUMMARY

Chapter 1 identifies and discusses the types of reorganizations within— and some business aspects of—several prominent U.S.-based professional sports leagues, which were established prior to 1950 and existed to entertain fans during various years. As these organizations appeared in this chapter's contents, the sports leagues of interest were primarily the Early National League (ENL) in baseball, and then the National Football League (NFL), National Hockey League (NHL), National Basketball Association (NBA), and American Soccer League (ASL). To support why and to what extent these five leagues had formed, reorganized, and/or merged, there are five tables containing the names, seasons, and performances of each sport's expansion teams that had played home and away games in the arenas, ballparks, or stadiums of their and competitors' metropolitan areas.

With respect to each of the leagues, Chapter 1 reveals which of their expansion franchises were the most and least successful in performances based on such results as average winning percentages, total points scored, number of division and conference titles won and championships in postseasons, and the clubs' final standings at the conclusion of one or more regular seasons. Furthermore, the teams' market sizes—desig- nated as small, midsized, or large—are related to how successful some of them had performed. For an overview, the relevant pre-1950 results and historical facts about the leagues and their respective expansion teams are summarized in no specific sequence as follows.

Except for the ENL—renamed National League (NL) in 1900—and NBA, before 1950 the other sports leagues expanded, consolidated, and/ or folded their operations during and despite such national events as a banking crisis, surging economy in the 1920s, two World Wars, and the Great Depression. These events and the consequences of competing for fans indicate, in part, how different and effective the strategies of professional sports organizations were with respect to implementing expansions, consolidations and mergers.

Since it officially formed in the very early 1900s, Major League Baseball (MLB) was the most popular and prosperous of the groups during the first half of the twentieth century. Rather than expand or contract the number of baseball franchises that played in the American League (AL) or National League (NL), MLB established a loyal fan base in many communities—and thus continuity—because it consisted of the same 16 clubs from 1903 to 1950. In contrast, 23 new teams had joined the ASL, and the majority of them disbanded within four seasons. Such a high failure rate suggests that ASL clubs had sites in underdeveloped markets and the least dedicated fans relative to the expansion teams in the other professional sports leagues. Indeed, this U.S. professional soccer league had to temporarily cancel some of its seasons during the early 1930s and then decided to fold after struggling financially through the years.

Across all sports leagues, on average most of the expansion teams based in small markets had existed for only one or a few seasons. Yet, during their existence they generally performed about the same in winning percentages as their rivals who were located in midsized markets. In contrast, a few of the leagues' large-market clubs had dominate players, maintained relatively high winning percentages each season, and won titles and championships in their respective sport—such as the NL New York Giants; NHL Boston Bruins, Detroit Red Wings, and New York Rangers; NFL New York Giants; and ASL Brooklyn Wanderers. Thus, differences in the quality of players, total population of cities, and franchises' resources and markets significantly influenced the performances of teams that were located in the largest metropolitan areas. It appears, therefore, that the highly successful and rich clubs playing at home in these areas had more of an incentive to resist and prevent the entry of new clubs into their territories than did the clubs located in midsized markets.

Because of such factors as inept leaders, changes in an areas' population and households' per capita income, and conflicts between a host of team owners and their players, there were opportunities for the primary sports leagues to add new teams and for rival secondary leagues to organize and enter the marketplace. Thus, several expansions occurred in metropolitan areas that experienced moderate to high growth and where the number of sports fans had increased. Furthermore, because of the apathy, ignorance, and/or risk aversion of existing league officials to expand into cities in the United States' south and west, and due to the numerous contractual disputes between teams and their underpaid athletes, the ENL and NFL were each challenged by a number of alternative leagues. However, the organizations that threatened these two major sports leagues failed after one or more years since a majority of the local professional baseball and football markets had not developed enough to sustain more than one club in a sport beyond a few seasons. Consequently, the inferior leagues eventually dissolved or merged with the dominant leagues in the same sport, which allowed surviving teams to become more competitive and the respective franchises to improve their operations from a financial perspective.

In summary, prior to 1950 it was extremely difficult for rival groups to form and assemble teams and then challenge the market power and dominance of clubs in the superior leagues. Also, expansion franchises in each sport had a relatively high failure rate, especially in years one to three, during their existence new teams located in midsized and small-market areas tended to perform about the same in winning percentages, and clubs in the different sports leagues had to compete against other forms of entertainment to establish fan bases in their respective local and regional markets.

2

Team Relocations and Transfers, 1876–1950

As discussed in Chapter 1, prior to the 1950 regular season some of the current and former professional sports leagues had reorganized by adding more teams and/or by merging with their rivals in order to enhance current operations, improve their future development and business environment, and increase potential profit. Specifically these leagues—which consisted administratively of a commissioner, an executive staff and the existing franchise owners—had approved the entry of new teams and/or agreed to merge with their competitors to form a parent organization. The National Hockey League, for example, expanded by adding six franchises during the 1920s, and the Basketball Association of America and National Basketball League united in 1949 to establish the National Basketball Association.[1]

Besides such reforms as expansions and mergers, two other activities occurred with respect to one or more of the professional sports. First, some of the leagues granted their member teams the right to move from a city within an area to another before the forthcoming season, and second, a number of franchise owners received permission to transfer their clubs to other leagues in the same sport. To illustrate, the National Association of Professional Baseball Players (NAPBP) existed as a group of clubs from 1871 through 1875. During its five seasons as an organization, the NAPBP expanded by a total of 14 teams, even though several of the association's franchises had failed to remain solvent throughout these seasons and thus did not continue playing games in the league. Given the precarious financial risks and macroeconomic cycles of the late 1800s, it is likely that the owners of—and investors in—the 14 expansion teams were ambitious individuals and optimistic entrepreneurs who had limited capital assets and funds but decided to try and participate in all of the NAPBP's seasons. However, when internal financial and managerial problems occurred, some teams had to cancel their operations and dissolve for several reasons: the league's lack of integrity and its disorderliness, the inferior quality of competition in professional baseball, low attendances at some of the teams' home ballgames, underdeveloped local and regional sports markets, dilapidated baseball ballparks, and apathy of hometown fans, to name a few. Because the NAPBP was the nation's premier and only true professional baseball organization, none of its teams had the opportunity to transfer to other leagues until the 1875 season was completed; moreover, other franchises did not have the resources and know-how to evaluate, select, and move to a site in another city.

The purpose of Chapter 2 is to identify which sports clubs relocated or transferred during the period 1876–1950, as well as when and why they chose to do so. To conform with the sequencing of the sports as presented in Chapter 1, the specific leagues included in this chapter are baseball's NAPBP, Early National League (ENL), American Association (AA), Union Association (UA), and Major League Baseball's American League (AL) and National League (NL); the National Football League (NFL); National Hockey League (NHL); basketball's Basketball Association of America (BAA), National Basketball League (NBL), and National Basketball Association (NBA); and finally soccer's American Soccer League I (ASL I), Eastern Professional Soccer League II (EPSL II), and Atlantic Coast League (ACL). To represent each of the league's reorganizations, there are a few tables that list the respective teams and the years in which they had relocated and/or transferred, and that provide some meaningful statistics and other relevant information about these teams' sites and performances while playing regular seasons and postseasons in their respective leagues before and after the years they had moved or transferred.

BASEBALL TEAM RELOCATIONS AND TRANSFERS

According to the upper portion of Table 2.1, between 1884 and 1903 five professional baseball clubs had moved from their host cities to sites in other places: the ENL's Cleveland Blues, AA's Washington Statesmen and Cincinnati Kelly's Killers, and the AL's Milwaukee Brewers and Baltimore Orioles. In contrast to the Blues' move from Cleveland to St. Louis in 1885, Brewers from Milwaukee to St. Louis in 1902 and Orioles from Baltimore to New York in 1903, the other two baseball teams changed their nicknames after relocating to cities in less populated urban areas. That is, the Washington Statesmen became the Richmond Virginians in 1884 and the Cincinnati

Table 2.1
Team Relocations, Transfers and Performances in Baseball, Selected Seasons

Year	Team	From	To	Performance Premove	Performance Postmove
Relocations					
1884	Statesmen	Washington	Richmond	.190	.286
1885	Blues	Cleveland	St. Louis	.440	.342
1891	Kelly's Killers	Cincinnati	Milwaukee	.430	.583
1902	Brewers	Milwaukee	St. Louis	.350	.574
1903	Orioles	Baltimore	New York	.436	.570
Transfers					
1876	Boston	NAPBP	ENL	.899	.557
1876	Chicago	NAPBP	ENL	.448	.788
1876	Hartford	NAPBP	ENL	.659	.691
1876	New York	NAPBP	ENL	.441	.375
1876	Philadelphia	NAPBP	ENL	.726	.237
1876	St. Louis	NAPBP	ENL	.574	.703
1885	St. Louis	UA	ENL	.832	.333
1887	Pittsburgh	AA	ENL	.584	.444
1889	Cleveland	AA	ENL	.379	.459
1890	Brooklyn	AA	ENL	.679	.667
1890	Cincinnati	AA	ENL	.547	.583
1892	Baltimore	AA	ENL	.526	.313
1892	Louisville	AA	ENL	.396	.414
1892	St. Louis	AA	ENL	.623	.373
1892	Washington	AA	ENL	.326	.384

Note: The baseball leagues affected by team transfers are the American Association (AA), Early National League (ENL), National Association of Professional Baseball Players (NAPBP), Union Association (UA), and American League (AL). Performance is the average winning percentages of the teams for an equal number of seasons prior to and after their relocations. The winning percentages of four clubs in two relocations—Washington to Richmond and Cincinnati to Milwaukee—occurred within, respectively, the 1884 and 1891 seasons because the Washington Statesmen and Cincinnati Kelley's Killers had to terminate their operations midway during these seasons.

Source: James Quirk and Rodney D. Fort, *Pay Dirt: The Business of Professional Team Sports* (Princeton, NJ: Princeton University Press, 1992), 378–409; *Official Major League Baseball Fact Book 2005 Edition* (St. Louis, MO: Sporting News, 2005), 173–81; "Complete Team Index," at http://www.baseball-reference.com, accessed 15 September 2005.

Kelley's Killers were renamed the Milwaukee Brewers in 1891. Generally, the five baseball clubs had shifted to other cities as a result of such factors as being acquired by new owners, failure to establish a sufficient fan base at their former sites, and/or to play home games in larger markets containing a modern ballpark located in an attractive neighborhood.[2]

After relocating, the five teams' average win-loss percentage at their postmove sites in total improved to .471 from .369 while playing in the previous seasons at their former sites. The Blues, however, performed better and won a higher proportion of games during seasons in midsized Cleveland than it did later when known as the Maroons in large-market St. Louis. Otherwise, the movements to facilities in different and more populated metropolitan areas inspired an increase in performances from the players who had performed for the Virginians in Richmond and Brewers in Milwaukee, and also for the Browns in St. Louis and Highlanders in New York City.

Despite the success from winning more regular season games, some of these teams were forced to eventually disband because of incompetent and undercapitalized owners, lack of support from the media and local sports fans, and a number of demographic, economic, and sport-specific reasons. That is, the Richmond Virginians terminated its operations after the 1984 regular season, the St. Louis Maroons before the 1887 season, and the Milwaukee Brewers after the 1891 season. Furthermore, the Highlanders changed its nickname to become the New York Yankees in 1913 and 40 years later, the Browns relocated from St. Louis to Baltimore and was renamed the Baltimore Orioles. In short, the movements of the baseball teams within the AA and AL resulted in improvements of their performances, whereas in the ENL, the Maroons based in St. Louis experienced a 22 percent decline in its average winning percentage during regular seasons. Nevertheless, except for the two AL teams that relocated, the other three clubs had to cancel their operations after one or more seasons. In contrast, the Orioles and Yankees franchises have remained competitive and prosperous while playing, respectively, since 1953 in Baltimore and 1913 in New York City.

With respect to the 15 teams that appear in the lower portion of Table 2.1, after the NAPBP folded in 1875, the league's Boston Red Stockings, Chicago White Stockings, Hartford Dark Blues, New York Mutuals, Philadelphia Athletics, and St. Louis Brown Stockings survived by joining with the Cincinnati Red Stockings and Louisville Grays to form the ENL, which played its first regular season in 1876. That season, the six teams that had transferred from the NAPBP earned victories in approximately 56 percent of their total games, which was a decline from 62 percent in 1875 when they were members of the NAPBP. Regarding the performances of specific teams, Boston placed fourth in the ENL with a winning percentage of .557 in 1876 after winning four consecutive NAPBP pennants in the 1872–1875 seasons, and Philadelphia finished seventh in the ENL at .237 in 1876 after ending each of its five seasons in the NAPBP by placing first, second, fourth, third, and second. Also, the teams in Chicago, Hartford, and St. Louis improved their winning percentages immediately after transferring to the ENL from the NAPBP, and the Red Stockings in Boston won consecutive pennants in the ENL's 1877–1878 seasons.

Between 1885 and 1892, a total of nine clubs had transferred from the UA and AA into the ENL. Because of greater competition, more skilled players, and rivalries between teams in the ENL, these nine clubs' average percentage of games won decreased from 54 percent at their premove sites to 44 percent at the respective postmove sites. Indeed, the Browns and Cardinals in St. Louis, Alleghanys in Pittsburgh, and Orioles in Baltimore each experienced a significant drop in performances in their seasons while based at the postmove sites. Although the Brooklyn Bridegrooms had won an AA title in 1889, that season the club lost a postseason tournament to the NL New York Giants in a nine-game series. When the Bridegrooms dropped out of the AA and entered the ENL in 1890, the team finished in first place with a winning percentage of .667. Nonetheless, in a seven-game playoff against the AA champion Louisville Colonels, the series concluded with each team winning three games and one game finishing in a tie.

Based on the movements of clubs within a league and the transfers of teams between various professional baseball leagues in years from the 1876 to 1903 regular seasons, and given the challenges presented by the formation of the UA in 1884 and Players League in 1890, and despite the turmoil that occurred in the sport of baseball before the merger of the AA and ENL after the 1891 season, MLB's franchises remained intact during the 1903 to 1952 seasons with eight clubs each in the AL and NL, and each of them playing at home in their respective cities. Therefore, for 50 years there were no reorganizations in organized baseball until the NL Braves moved from Boston to Milwaukee before the 1953 season. In short, the longest period of stability of any major American-based professional sports league occurred in the first half of the twentieth century after nearly 25 years of team movements and transfers in baseball's pre-1900 leagues.

FOOTBALL TEAM RELOCATIONS

As described in Chapter 1, the American Professional Football Association (APFA), which had been originally organized in Canton, Ohio, and titled as the American Professional Football Conference (APFC), was officially renamed the NFL in 1922. Two years earlier, the APFA had consisted of 14 franchises. However, after the 1920 season concluded, the 11th-ranked Chicago Tigers withdrew from the league and player-coach George Halas moved the Decatur Staleys—which had finished in second place behind the Akron Pros with 10 wins, 1 loss and 2 ties—from small-market Decatur to northeast Illinois to play as the Chicago Staleys. Following the 1921 season, the Cincinnati Celts, Detroit Heralds, and Washington Senators—with one win each—and the Muncie Flyers, New York Giants, and Tonawanda Kardex—with zero victories each—had terminated their operations, and the APFA champion Staleys were renamed the Chicago Bears.[3]

If the original teams that carried over from 1921 are counted in the total, the 1922 NFL season opened with 18 clubs, including such new teams as the Oorang Indians, Milwaukee Badgers, Racine Legion, and Toledo Maroons. In turn, that season these four clubs finished with number of victories and winning percentages of, respectively, three and .333, two and .333, six and .600, and five and .714. Then, in 1923 the midsized- to large-market Cleveland Indians and St. Louis All-Stars, and small-market Duluth Kelleys joined the NFL as expansion teams, and the winless Evansville Crimson Giants canceled its franchise, leaving 20 teams to compete in the league. With respect to the 1923 season, the two most outstanding NFL teams were the Canton Bulldogs and Chicago Bears. Indeed, in 1922 and 1923 the Bulldogs placed first with a total of 22 wins and the Bears second with 18 victories, followed by either the Chicago Cardinals or Green Bay Packers, which each finished in third place one season, with the Toledo Maroons in 1922 and Milwaukee Badgers in 1923 ended in fourth place.

Table 2.2 indicates that 25 expansion clubs had entered the NFL and played their regular season games in years between 1923 and 1949. Besides that group of clubs, there were also professional football teams competing in the AFL I in 1926, in the AFL II in 1936–1937 and AFL III in 1940–1941, and in the All American Football Conference (AAFC) in 1946–1949. Most likely as a result of evaluating the most profitable potential sites to move their teams, the NFL franchise owners probably considered avoiding the U.S. metropolitan areas where any of the AFL I–III and AAFC clubs were playing their home games. Regardless, to understand the relocation of NFL teams prior to the 1950 season, it is necessary to see and study the entries in Table 2.2.

According to columns one and two of the table, five football clubs moved in the 1920s, another five in the 1930s, and two in the 1940s. Generally, the metropolitan areas surrounding the teams' 12 postmove sites contained larger populations and experienced greater economic growth and more business vitality than did the areas around the respective premove sites. Given the data in the table, the NFL's franchise owners preferred to move their teams from cities in relatively small sports markets to cities in midsized

Table 2.2
Team Relocations and Performances in the NFL, Selected Seasons

Year	Team	Relocation		Performance	
		From	To	Premove Site	Postmove Site
1924	Bulldogs	Canton	Cleveland	1.000	.630
1924	Maroons	Toledo	Kenosha	.500	.000
1928	Bulldogs	Cleveland	Detroit	.667	.778
1929	Eskimos	Duluth	Orange	.111	.375
1929	Maroons	Pottsville	Boston	.200	.500
1930	Triangles	Dayton	Brooklyn	.000	.636
1930	Tornadoes	Orange	Newark	.375	.091
1932	Tornadoes	Newark	Boston	.091	.500
1934	Spartans	Portsmouth	Detroit	.545	.769
1937	Redskins	Boston	Washington	.583	.769
1946	Rams	Cleveland	Los Angeles	.900	.600
1949	Yanks	Boston	New York	.250	.091

Note: The columns labeled Year, Team, and From and To are self-explanatory. Performance is the average winning percentages of the teams during an equal number of consecutive seasons prior to and following their relocations, or otherwise the teams' performances at their premove and postmove sites.

Source: *Official 2001 National Football Record & Fact Book* (New York: National Football League, 2001), 278–301, and James Quirk and Rodney D. Fort, *Pay Dirt*, 409–46.

and large urban areas, usually where professional baseball clubs were based. In short, a market's current size and wealth, its potential for above-average population growth and commercial activity, and the presence of nonfootball professional teams were each specific factors that influenced the decisions of NFL owners to reevaluate the prospective business performances of their franchises and to choose a site in another city within an area to play its home games.

For a number of internal and sport-specific reasons, the dozen teams listed in Table 2.2 tended to play better football and win more games after moving to their postmove sites. In fact, the win-loss percentages of these teams improved marginally: Their average performance rose from .435 at the premove site to .478 at the postmove site. To illustrate, in 1929 the Dayton Triangles ended the season with a win-loss-tie record of 0–6–0 and then 7–4–1 in 1930 as the Brooklyn Dodgers. Alternatively, the Toledo Maroons finished at 3–3–2 in 1923 but one year later achieved a 0–4–1 record as the Kenosha Maroons. Because of deteriorating local, regional, and national economic conditions, and of peoples' and communities' negative attitudes toward the game of professional football and frequent changes in teams' ownership, several NFL franchises experienced financial problems and ceased to exist at their sites. For example, the owners of the Cleveland

Bulldogs and Kenosha Maroons terminated their sports enterprises in the 1920s, as did the owners of the Boston Bulldogs and Newark Tornadoes in the 1930s and Brooklyn Tigers and New York Bulldogs in the 1940s.

Due to personal bankruptcies and business failures prior to 1950, a few of the relocating NFL teams played one or more seasons and then temporarily suspended their operations, which was a relatively frequent strategy implemented by some of the league's franchise owners. First, although finishing 11–0–1 in 1923, the Canton Bulldogs were inactive in the 1924 season after being purchased by millionaire Sam Deutsch for $1,200; second, the Detroit Wolverines earned profits of $7,000 in 1928 after owner Jimmy Conzelman had suspended its operations one year earlier when the club existed as the Detroit Panthers; and third, two years after obtaining a franchise for $125,000, owner Dan Reeves did not enter the Cleveland Rams into the NFL's 1943 season. Meanwhile, some of the NFL teams that were involved in a relocation or had withdrawn from the league did not play their entire schedules during one season or another because of the need to conserve cash and/or due to the franchises' operating problems: the Louisville Brecks and Rochester Jeffersons in 1923, Columbus Tigers and Hammond Pros in 1926, Buffalo Bisons and Duluth Eskimos in 1927, and the Cleveland Indians and Frankford Yellow Jackets in 1931.

With respect to the entries in Table 2.2, some of the teams eventually became well-known and highly valued football enterprises and thus developed into marketable sports brands after they had relocated to another city. For example, four years after the Boston Braves had experienced a net loss of $46,000, owner George Marshall moved the club from Boston to the Washington, DC, area and renamed it to perform as the Washington Redskins. Between 1937 and 1945, the Redskins won five Eastern Division (ED) titles and two NFL championships, and also finished runner-up to the league champions in the 1940, 1943, and 1945 seasons. Interestingly, during the club's first nine years in Washington, DC, the Redskins' worst performance occurred in 1941, when the team finished third in the ED at 6–5–0 and therefore failed to win enough games that season to challenge the Brooklyn Dodgers for second place in the league's standings.

Meanwhile, a few of the NFL teams that had moved continued a tradition of winning games at their postmove sites. For example, during the 1931–1933 seasons, the Portsmouth Spartans were 23–10 in total wins-losses. After the Spartans went broke in late 1933, entrepreneur George Richardson purchased the franchise for $15,000—paying $6,500 to remove its outstanding debts in the process—and then moved the team from Portsmouth to Michigan and renamed it to play as the Detroit Lions. For three consecutive years in the 1934–1936 seasons while in the Western

Division (WD), the Lions won 25 games and lost 10. Led by its scoring leader Earl (Dutch) Clark, the club won an NFL championship in 1936 by defeating the New York Giants 26–7.

Another team listed in Table 2.2 is the Rams, which played regular seasons in Cleveland and then later in Los Angeles. After becoming an NFL franchise in 1937 when a syndicate of investors paid an expansion fee of $10,000, the Cleveland Rams suspended its operations in 1943 and then two years later beat the Washington Redskins 15–14 to win an NFL championship. With a total loss of $82,000 for playing in the league during 1941–1942 and 1944–1945, owner Dan Reeves moved the club from Cleveland to southern California in 1946 and changed its name to the Los Angeles Rams. Although the franchise continued to incur financial losses while operating in Los Angeles, the Rams eventually won one WD and then two consecutive National Conference titles in the 1949–1950 seasons, and won an NFL championship in 1951 after finishing runner-up to the Philadelphia Eagles in the 1949 season and to the Cleveland Browns in the 1950 season.

In short, the 12 NFL teams that had moved between 1924 and 1949 did so because of inferior or below average performances at their premove sites and accumulation of an excessive amount of debts; failure to establish a local or regional fan base; playing their home games in stadiums that were located in small cities, metropolitan areas, and sports markets; and such external and destabilizing events as price inflation in the 1920s, the Great Depression in the 1930s, and World War II and its aftermath in the early to mid 1940s. Nevertheless, an NFL club listed in column four of Table 2.2 that did not survive after the 1949 season was the New York Bulldogs, which owner Ted Collins had relinquished to the league in 1950. That year the AAFC merged with the NFL, which in turn reduced by one the total number of professional football leagues for sports fans in the United States to read about and support. Indeed, this type of monopolistic market structure and competition existed in football until the American Football League was established in 1960, followed by the World Football League in 1974, and 10 years later the U.S. Football League.

ICE HOCKEY TEAM RELOCATIONS

Table 1.3 in Chapter 1 denotes that during the 1920s six new teams began to play as competitors in the NHL's regular seasons: the Boston Bruins and Montreal Maroons in 1924; Pittsburgh Pirates in 1925; and in 1926, the Chicago Black Hawks (renamed Chicago Blackhawks in 1986); the Detroit Cougars (renamed Detroit Falcons in 1930 and then Detroit Red Wings in

1933); and the New York Rangers. Besides adding these expansion clubs, the league also initiated a realignment of its structure twice prior to the 1950 season. That is, because of the league's small size and longstanding tradition, the NHL contained no divisions or conferences in the 1917 through 1925 seasons. Then in 1926, five of its ice hockey teams were each assigned to the Canadian and American Divisions, a 44-game schedule was adopted for all teams, and the Stanley Cup became the exclusive property of the league. This new structure prevailed until 1938, when the NHL eliminated its two divisions and existed as one entity up to the late 1960s.[4]

In short, although the NHL had expanded by six teams before 1950, a few of the league's other franchises did not prosper during the 1920s and 1930s because of game- and facility-related problems. These included low attendances at home, inferior and dull performances during games, and inadequate amounts of revenues and profits generated at their local arenas and from other sources. Four of these troubled teams are listed in column two of Table 2.3, and some facts and history about these clubs and their reasons for relocating are discussed in the following sections.[5]

Quebec Bulldogs

After two years of controlling a franchise that had been authorized to enter the NHL but did not perform as a team in the league, owner Michael Quinn allowed his Quebec Bulldogs to play its first regular season schedule of games in 1919. When the Bulldogs finished the season in fourth place with a total of 4 wins and 20 losses, garnering only eight points, Quinn sold

Table 2.3
Team Relocations and Performances in Ice Hockey, Selected Seasons

| Year | Team | Relocation | | Performance | |
		From	To	Premove Site	Postmove Site
1920	Bulldogs	Quebec	Hamilton	4–20/fourth	6–18/fourth
1925	Tigers	Hamilton	New York	19–10–1/first	12–20–4/ fifth
1930	Pirates	Pittsburgh	Philadel- phia	5–26–3/fifth	4–36–4/ fifth
1934	Senators	Ottawa	St. Louis	13–29–6/fifth	11–31–6/ fifth

Note: The columns labeled Year, Team, and From and To are self-explanatory. Listed in the two columns under Performance is the win-loss and divisional finishes of the NHL's Quebec Bulldogs in the 1919 season and the Hamilton Tigers in the 1920 season. For the other three relocations, Performance is the win-loss-tie and divisional finishes of the teams, respectively, at the premove sites in the 1924, 1929, and 1933 seasons, and at the postmove sites in the 1925, 1930, and 1934 seasons.

Source: "History," at http://www.nhl.com, accessed 24 August 2005.

the club for $5,000 to businessman Percy Thompson. To avoid a substantial financial loss by operating the franchise as the Bulldogs in the 1920 season, Thompson moved his team from Quebec to Ontario, Canada, and renamed it Hamilton Tigers. For the 1920 through 1923 NHL seasons, the Tigers' cumulative win-loss-tie totals were 28–68–0. But in the 1924 season, the Tigers had the best record in the league's final standings when it finished at 19–10–1, with 39 points. Nevertheless, in the NHL playoffs the Tigers were defeated for the regular season title by the Montreal Canadiens.

Despite his club's recent success in the final standings, Thompson sold the Tigers in 1925 for $75,000 to Bill Dwyer, who moved the team from Hamilton to New York and assigned it a new nickname. That is, the club became the New York Americans. Because the Americans were not as popular an ice hockey team in New York as the NHL Rangers, the franchise went broke in 1938 after several seasons of below-average performances while competing in the Canadian Division. Nevertheless, the NHL invested in and subsidized the operations of the Americans for a few years. However, despite a change in names so that it could play as the Brooklyn Americans in the 1941 season, the team finished in seventh place at 16–29–3 with 35 points and was terminated before the 1942 NHL season had begun. Interestingly, the Bulldogs in Quebec, Tigers in Hamilton, and Americans in New York and Brooklyn never competed for a Stanley Cup, although one or more of these clubs had great athletes and such Hall of Fame players as defensemen-forward Billy Burch, left winger Dave Shriner, defensemen Red Dutton, and goalie Roy Worters.

Pittsburgh Pirates

In 1925 the long-time Montreal Canadiens' forward-goalie Odie Cleghorn was appointed to the NHL Board of Governors, and he chose to represent hockey's newest expansion team, the Pittsburgh Pirates, as a coach-player. The league had received an expansion fee of $12,000 from investors who had acquired the Pirates franchise, plus $25,000 was spent by the Pirates' new owners to obtain some ice hockey players from the Western Canada League and U.S. Amateur League. Remarkably, during the 1925–1929 seasons, the team occasionally performed up to Pittsburgh fans' expectations because of Cleghorn's rapid line changes, which meant that fresh players usually appeared for many minutes per game at their positions on the ice. However, despite the coach's strategy, the Pirates never finished above third place in the American Division, and that outcome resulted in relatively small attendances at the club's rink in Pittsburgh.

As such, in 1930 the Pirates' new owner, Benny Leonard, moved the team from Pittsburgh to southeastern Pennsylvania and renamed it to perform as the Philadelphia Quakers. In the 1930 season, the Quakers competed at their postmove site but established three embarrassing NHL records: The team scored the fewest total points (12), claimed the fewest victories (four), and had the league's longest consecutive losing streak (15 games). After placing fifth in the American Division and incurring an operating loss of $100,000, the Quakers suspended operations in 1931. As a result of depleting its cash balances and experiencing a substantial increase in operating debts, the franchise did not enter a team in the 1931–1935 NHL seasons. Consequently, the Quakers dissolved in 1936.

In contrast to the modest success of the Bulldogs in Quebec, the Pirates in Pittsburgh and Quakers in Philadelphia did not effectively compete against their primary rivals in the league. Indeed, in six seasons the Pirates and Quakers teams in total failed to win an American Division title or qualify for a playoff game.

Ottawa Senators

Despite recurring financial problems and ownership issues, and playing its home games in a small city and sports market, the Ottawa Senators competed in the NHL during the 1917 to 1930 seasons, suspended operations in 1931, and then resumed to play in the 1932 and 1933 seasons. Even with its long history of needing money to buy resources, the franchise was previously successful at winning the Stanley Cup—when named the Ottawa Silver Seven—in the 1902–1904 seasons, and as the Senators in the 1908, 1910, 1919, 1920, 1922, and 1926 seasons. To achieve their championships, the Senators clubs' relied on such great players as goalie Clint Benedict, defensemen George Boucher, and forward Harry Broadbent, and coaches Bruce Stuart, Pete Green, and Dave Gill.

However the Senators deteriorated in quality, became uncompetitive, and finished the 1930, 1932, and 1933 seasons in fifth place of the Canadian Division. In 1934, the franchise's owner moved the club from Ottawa to St. Louis, Missouri and renamed it St. Louis Eagles. After ending the 1934 season at 11–31–6 and scoring 28 points in the Canadian Division, the team went broke. As a result, the NHL bought out the club's owner for an unknown price and then redistributed the Eagles' players among other teams in the league. Boston received forward Bill Cowley, who then developed into a star player for the Bruins.

In summary, between 1920 and 1934, four NHL clubs had decided to relocate from their home sites to cities in other urban areas. Except for the

Bulldogs' movement from Quebec to Hamilton, the three other postmove sites contained larger populations and more ice hockey fans than what existed at the respective premove sites. Generally, the teams that moved were unsuccessful: For example, the Philadelphia Quakers and St. Louis Eagles folded after one season, and although the Tigers played 5 seasons in Hamilton, Ontario, and the Americans competed for 16 years in New York, during their existence these clubs failed to win a division title.

Although not classified here as simply a relocation but rather as an example of a franchise transferring a portion of its players to a team located at another site, an ice hockey club nicknamed the Rosebuds was once based in Portland, Oregon, and from 1914 to 1918, it played its games while being a member of the Pacific Coast Hockey Association (PCHA). In fact, the club was the PCHA champion in the 1915 season and became the first U.S.-based team to play for a Stanley Cup, an event that occurred in 1916. Nine years later, the Regina Capitals of the Western Canada Hockey League (WCHL) moved to Portland to play the 1925 season as a member of the newly named Western Hockey League (WHL).

To attract attention and receive more publicity from the local media, and also to establish a large fan base in that northwest city on the coast, the Capitals decided to change names and become known as the Portland Rosebuds. When the 1925 season concluded and the WHL folded, the Chicago Black Hawks' owner, Major Frederic McLaughlin, purchased the contracts of the Rosebuds' players for approximately $15,000. Then McLaughlin transferred these players—whose market values in total amounted to the net worth of the Rosebuds franchise—from Portland to Chicago to play for the Black Hawks in the NHL's American Division.

BASKETBALL TEAM RELOCATIONS AND TRANSFERS

As indicated in Chapter 1, a group of officials from the four-year-old Basketball Association of America (BAA) and 13-year-old National Basketball League (NBL) decided to consolidate their organizations and create the National Basketball Association (NBA) in 1949. As a result, the NBA immediately became the premier professional basketball league in North America, and many years later, one of the most prosperous sports groups in the world. However, before identifying the different teams that participated for seasons in the BAA and NBL and then transferred into the NBA, it is important to note that these two former basketball leagues had an identical organizational structure. In other words, the BAA and NBL were each composed of teams that played in either an Eastern Division (ED) or a Western Division (WD). This distribution of divisions, in turn, had generated rivalries between some of the clubs within these leagues, and benefited the sport of basketball, given the sites of the teams and their geographical dispersion at sites in cities within various areas of the United States.[6]

After the BAA and NBL merged, it was necessary for the NBA to organize its hierarchy such that each team was placed in one of three divisions. Therefore, to balance out the 17 franchises on a regional basis and from a competitive perspective, for the 1949 season the NBA placed five clubs in the ED and six each in the WD and Central Division (CD). Table 2.4 examines and compares some sports-related data and other historical information about these teams, how they performed, and whether they succeeded in their respective divisions. The first section of the table provides the seasons, names, and performances of the NBA clubs that had previously played games while in the BAA, and the table's second section lists the seasons, names, and performances of teams that had transferred from the NBL into the NBA.

BAA Teams into the NBA

According to the final two columns in the top portion of Table 2.4, there were six basketball teams that had shifted to the NBA from the BAA's ED and five from its WD. These two groups of divisions included a few clubs from large and populated markets such as the New York Knicks, Chicago Stags, and Philadelphia Warriors, and some teams from less populated urban areas like the small-market Fort Wayne Pistons, Indianapolis Olympians, and Rochester Royals. Although the BAA was established in 1946, three seasons prior to it becoming the NBA, in 1948 the Indianapolis Jets, Minneapolis Lakers, Fort Wayne Pistons, and Rochester Royals had switched from the NBL to the BAA, as indicated in Chapter 1's Table 1.4. Besides these simple facts about the relationships between some of the teams that had transferred from the BAA to the NBA, other specific observations and matters are interesting to reveal relative to each of the clubs' experiences as enterprises while operating in professional basketball.

First, the 11 BAA teams' average winning percentage remained unchanged at .547 after they had switched into the NBA. Relative to their performances on the court when they transferred from the BAA in 1948 into the NBA in 1949, four clubs had improved their winning percentages at their postmove sites, and six of them won fewer games. Although the Rochester Royals' teams won three-fourths of their games played during the 1948 and 1949 regular seasons and finished in first place of the BAA's ED and NBA's CD, they failed to win a league championship. Regarding the

Table 2.4
Team Transfers and Performances in BAA, NBL, and NBA, Selected Seasons

Seasons			Performance	
BAA+ NBL	NBA	Team	Pre-Transfer Site	Post-Transfer Site
BAA into NBA				
2	6	Baltimore Bullets	.483/third/ED	.368/fifth/ED
3	57	Boston Celtics	.417/fifth/ED	.324/sixth/ED
3	1	Chicago Stags	.633/third/WD	.588/third/CD
8	8	Fort Wayne Pistons	.367/fifth/WD	.588/third/CD
2	5	Indianapolis Jets/ Olympians	.300/sixth/WD	.609/first/WD
2	11	Minneapolis Lakers	.733/second/WD	.750/first/CD
3	57	New York Knicks	.533/second/ED	.588/second/ED
3	13	Philadelphia Warriors	.467/fourth/ED	.382/fourth/ED
4	8	Rochester Royals	.750/first/ED	.750/first/CD
3	1	St. Louis Bombers	.483/fourth/WD	.382/fifth/CD
3	1	Washington Capitols	.633/first/ED	.471/third/ED
NBL into NBA				
3	1	Anderson Duffey Packers	.766/first/ED	.578/second/ WD
1	1	Denver Nuggets	.290/fifth/WD	.177/sixth/WD
11	1	Sheboygan Redskins	.547/third/WD	.355/fourth/ WD
3	14	Syracuse Nationals	.656/second/ED	.797/first/ED
3	2	Tri-Cities Blackhawks	.563/second/WD	.453/third/WD
1	1	Waterloo Hawks	.484/fourth/WD	.306/fifth/WD

Note: The heading labeled Seasons includes a column of the total number of regular seasons of each team while they were members of the BAA and NBL, and a column of the total regular seasons while they played in the NBA at their respective sites through 2005. For example, the Baltimore Bullets existed for two seasons in the BAA (1947 and 1948) and six seasons (1949 to 1954) in the NBA. The heading labeled Performance is the teams' winning percentages and finish positions in their respective divisions at their pre- and post-transfer sites. Specifically, the column designated as Pre-Transfer Site denotes the final winning percentages and league positions of the BAA and NBL teams for the 1948 regular season, and the column titled Post-Transfer Site is these NBA teams' final winning percentages and league positions in the 1949 regular season. ED is the Eastern Division, CD the Central Division, and WD the Western Division.

Source: "Basketball Association of America," at http://www.nbahoopsonline.com, accessed 24 August 2005; "National Basketball League," at http://www.nbl.com, accessed 24 August 2005; "National Basketball Association," at http://www.nba.com, accessed 24 August 2005; James Quirk and Rodney D. Fort, *Pay Dirt*, 378–409, 446–59.

other teams' performances, the Indianapolis Olympians and Fort Wayne Pistons achieved the most significant increases in win-loss percentages after they had joined the NBA. The Olympians—who were formerly the

Indianapolis Jets—performed better, in part, because of competing in the new league's WD, which included five of the mediocre clubs from the NBL. Likewise, while playing at its post-transfer site in Fort Wayne, the Pistons tied with the Chicago Stags for third place in the CD in the 1949 season. In contrast, the Baltimore Bullets, Boston Celtics, Philadelphia Warriors, and Washington Capitols played much worse as NBA teams, as indicated by the large decreases in their winning percentages and final positions in the ED for the 1949 season.

Second, because of the small crowds that attended their home games and struggling to finance operations, the NBA Chicago Stags and St. Louis Bombers had to cancel their franchises and withdraw from the league before the 1950 season. Furthermore, due to inferior performances during the 1949 season and the lack of support from basketball fans and local businesses in the nation's capital, it was necessary in early 1951 for the Washington Capitols to discontinue playing games in midseason when it had 10 wins and 25 losses. As a result of its problems, the club's owners were forced to cancel the franchise. Third, the former BAA Minneapolis Lakers continued its outstanding performances as a member of the NBA's CD. Led by All-Pro center George Mikan and coached by John Kundla, the Lakers won a league championship in the 1949 season and again in the 1950 and 1952–1954 seasons.

NBL Teams into NBA

Except for the Nuggets in Denver—which ranked 24th in population among U.S. cities in 1950—the other NBL teams tended to be located in Midwestern cities with relatively small metropolitan areas and tiny sports markets. That is, the local populations that supported the Duffey Packers in Anderson, Indiana, the Redskins in Sheboygan, Wisconsin, the Blackhawks in the Tri-Cities—which included Moline and Rock Island, Illinois, and Davenport, Iowa—and the Hawks in Waterloo, Iowa each numbered less than 100,000 people. Meanwhile, the Nationals in Syracuse, New York, played in an area that had a population of about 200,000 in 1950. Therefore, to maintain competitiveness between the teams in each division of the league, the NBA's WD was organized in 1949 to include the four very small-market clubs from the Midwest plus the Nuggets and Olympians. As such, there are three specific characteristics about the former NBL teams that are interesting to highlight.

First, the average winning percentages of these six clubs fell from .551 in the NBL's 1948 season to .444 in the NBA's 1949 season. Nevertheless, as indicated in column five of Table 2.4, Syracuse was a superior team in both seasons: The Nationals finished second in the NBL's ED, and one year later first in the NBA's ED by winning approximately 80 percent of its regular season games, and played hard but placed runner-up to the Lakers in the NBA final series. In contrast, in the 1949 season, five of the WD clubs won fewer games and ranked relatively lower in the league than they did at the conclusion of the 1948 season after competing in the NBL.

Second, with respect to the entire group of six WD teams—including the former BAA Jets (now Olympians)—it was the Packers, Nuggets, Redskins, and Hawks that failed early and dropped out of the NBA before the 1950 regular season had begun. Indeed, because of weak attendances at their home-site games and generating insufficient amounts of cash inflows and revenues to sustain their operations, the four clubs could not continue to exist in future seasons as competitive and viable business enterprises in the NBA.

Third, during the 1937 to 1948 seasons several different franchises had existed as teams within the NBL. Besides the league's six clubs listed in Table 2.4 that had transferred in 1949 into the NBA, there were other prominent teams that played and won NBL titles. These champions included the Goodyear Wingfoots, Firestone Non-Skids, Oshkosh All-Stars, Chicago Gears, Fort Wayne Pistons, Rochester Royals, and Minneapolis Lakers. As discussed previously, the Pistons, Royals, and Lakers had transferred into the BAA from the NBL before 1949. However, because of indecisive and unenthusiastic owners, low attendances at games, small fan bases, and coaching problems, officials refused to admit the NBL Dayton Rens and Hammond Calumet Buccaneers into the NBA even though they had performed moderately well as clubs in the 1948 season.

Prior to 1950, the majority of reorganizations involving teams in the U.S.-based professional basketball leagues happened during the mid to late 1940s—after the relocations that had occurred among clubs in MLB and the NHL and about the same time period as those in the NFL. That is, when the BAA and NBL merger concluded then concurrently, the NBA was officially named and organized to begin its first season in 1949. As discussed previously, most of the basketball teams that transferred from the former BAA and NBL—which officially ceased to exist after the transition—had to eventually cancel their operations as members of the NBA or were motivated to relocate to a site in a city of another area within years after the 1950 season. Simply put, in 1949–1950 the business of marketing and promoting an elite professional basketball organization and its member teams to American and international sports audiences had been formally established.

SOCCER TEAM REORGANIZATIONS

The American Soccer League I (ASL I), which initially consisted of eight professional teams that were located in various U.S. cities within the northeast region, had played its first season in 1921. During this organization's existence, 19 new teams were permitted to join the league and compete in the 1920s and another four entered the ASL I in the early 1930s. The expansion years, the names, and performances of these clubs appear in Table 1.5 of Chapter 1.[7]

Besides the league's 23 expansion franchises, a number of teams withdrew from the ASL I because of poor performances and low attendances at their home games and the lack of financial support from the clubs' owners and sponsors. Based on total points scored in their final seasons, the three best and worst performing ASL I clubs that had to cancel operations were, respectively, the highly competitive Todd Shipyards in 1921, New York Field Club in 1923, and Philadelphia Field Club in 1926, and the average to below-average performing Jersey City Celtics in 1921, Philadelphia Celtics in 1927, and Newark Skeeters in 1928. In fact, between 1921 and 1928, a total of 17 ASL I club owners determined that it was necessary to terminate their franchises. Subsequently, in 1933 the league finally dissolved because of operating problems and teams' debts, and after it became involved in a power struggle with the U.S. Soccer Football Association (USFA) and Federation Internationale de Football Association (FIFA) to control the sport.

Two years before the ASL I had ceased to operate in 1929, some officials of the league vehemently opposed the New York Giants, Bethlehem Steel, and Newark Skeeters entering and participating in a U.S. Open Cup tournament. As a result of this dispute, these three major clubs withdrew from the ASL I and joined the Eastern Professional Soccer League II (EPSL II), which the USFA had organized. To launch its 1928 season, the EPSL II included the Giants, Steel, and Skeeters plus five soccer teams from the Southern New York State Association. Fortunately, for business reasons, after the 1928 and fall 1929 seasons, the ASL I, USFA, and FIFA settled their differences about national and international soccer policies, teams' territorial and ownership rights, and other matters of mutual interest.

In 1929, to consolidate operations and establish revenue streams, and to increase professional soccer's market share among the nation's sports fans and improve the quality of soccer teams and games, some franchises from the ASL I and EPSL II formed and then shifted into the Atlantic Coast League (ACL). During its first season, the ACL included 11 soccer teams that had transferred from one or the other league. For some pertinent facts about the history and performance of each club, the ACL's teams are listed and ranked in Table 2.5 from first to eleventh based on their final standings in the 1929 regular season. An overview of these clubs is discussed in the next few paragraphs.

While it performed as one of the original ASL I franchises, the Fall River Marksmen won league championships in the 1923–1925 and 1928 seasons, and in the fall 1929 season. In 1930, the Marksmen again became a champion by leading the ACL with 43 points and a win-loss-draw record of 18–1–7. The New Bedford Whalers, which had entered the ASL I in 1924 as an expansion team, was a runner-up to the Marksmen in the 1925 season and two years later, won the league's playoff by outscoring Bethlehem Steel 2–0. After the Whalers joined the ACL in late 1928, it finished the 1929 season with 35 points and tied for second place with the Hakoah All Stars. Recall from Chapter 1 that the All Stars consisted of players from a merger between two Hakoah teams—that is, Brooklyn of the ASL I and New York of the EPSL II. As a result, the club was a very strong performer during its existence in the league.

Table 2.5
Team Transfers into ACL, Ranked by Performances, 1929 Season

| Team | Former League | | Season Performance | | |
	ASL I	EPSL II	Games Played	Points	Percent
Fall River Marksmen	1921–1929	NA	26	43	.814
New Bedford Whalers	1924–1927	1928–1929	33	35	.530
Hakoah All Stars	1928–1929	1928–1929	33	35	.530
Providence Gold Bugs	1924–1929	NA	25	28	.519
New York Nationals	1927–1929	NA	33	33	.500
Pawtucket Rangers	1921–1929	NA	28	27	.483
Bethlehem Steel	1922–1927	1928–1929	27	26	.481
New York Giants	1923–1927	1928–1929	30	28	.467
Brooklyn Wanders	1922–1929	NA	32	28	.438
Newark Skeeters	1923–1927	1928–1929	15	3	.100
Boston Bears	1924–1929	NA	4	2	.250

Note: The ASL I's Brooklyn Hakoah and EPSL II's New York Hakoah teams merged in 1929 to form the Hakoah All Stars. In 1928, the New Bedford Whalers, Bethlehem Steel, New York Giants, and Newark Skeeters withdrew from the ASL I to form the EPSL II. Formerly named the Boston Wonder Workers, the Boston Bears withdrew from the ACL after the club played four games and had scored two points in 1929. NA means not applicable.

Source: Dave Litterer, "American Soccer League I (1921–1933)," at http://www.sover.net, accessed 20 September 2005.

Four years after entering the ASL I as the Providence Clamdiggers, the team was renamed Providence Gold Bugs in order to play in the 1928 and 1929 seasons. During these campaigns, the Gold Bugs' teams had played competitive soccer against major rivals and thus finished in a tie for second place behind the Marksmen, which became the league's champion. Meanwhile, in 1927 the New York Nationals joined the ASL I as an expansion team and in the second half of the 1928 season, the J&P Coats franchise was renamed the Pawtucket Rangers. In 1923, J&P Coats was the ASL I champion. The Nationals' clubs generally scored about average in points and winning percentages each season as a member of that league.

Before the club withdrew from the ASL I in the early portion of the 1928 season and joined the EPSL II, Bethlehem Steel had finished runner-up to the Marksmen in 1924–1925 and then two years later won a league championship. With respect to its performances, the Steel's average winning percentage in the 1924–1927 seasons exceeded 65 percent, and while playing in the EPSL II, it was 88 percent. Similar to Bethlehem Steel's success, the New York Giants also performed relatively better in the seasons when the club played in the EPSL II than in the ASL I. That is, in the EPSL II the Giants finished with 24 points and in second place in the fall 1928 season, with 13 points and fifth place in the spring 1929 season, and with 18 points and third place in the fall 1929 season.

During its 13-year tenure as the most prominent soccer league in America, the ASL I admitted such expansion teams as the Brooklyn Wanderers in 1922, Newark Skeeters in 1923, and in 1924 the Boston Wonder Workers—which was renamed the Boston Bears in fall 1929. With regard to these teams' individual performances while playing in the ASL I, the Wanderers finished at .677 and in second place to the Marksmen in the first half of the 1928 season, but at .353 and seventh place in the fall 1929 season. Meanwhile, the Skeeters played above .300 in one season and at or near the bottom of the league in its other seasons, and the Wonder Workers was runner-up to the ASL I champion Bethlehem Steel in the 1926 season and one year later defeated the New Bedford Whalers to win the club's first and only ASL I championship. With one victory, three losses and only two points scored in the 1929 season, the Boston Bears was an inferior team and thus withdrew from the ACL after playing only four of its games. Furthermore, because of inadequate funding from their sponsors and lack of support from local fans, in 1930 the New York Nationals and Bethlehem Steel also decided to drop out of the league.

To schedule a season of soccer games and play as a league in fall 1930, the ACL reverted to its original title, which was ASL I. As such, several of the league's teams decided to modify their organizations' operations in various ways. To illustrate, in 1930 the Newark club reentered the ASL I as the New Jersey Americans, the New York Giants became the New York Soccer Club, and the New York Nationals renamed its team New York Giants. Then in the first half season, or spring 1931, the Soccer Club and Marksmen merged to play as the New York Yankees, and the Gold Bugs moved from Providence to Fall River and became the Fall River Football Club, which proceeded to absorb the New Bedford Whalers.

In the second half season, or fall 1931, the New York Americans entered the ASL I as an expansion team. Meanwhile, the Yankees was absorbed by the Fall River Football Club, which then relocated to New Bedford to play as the New Bedford Whalers. Unfortunately, the teams' standings for the season in spring 1932 were incomplete. Even so, in the first half season, or fall 1932, the ASL I added the Brooklyn Wanderers, New York Field Club, and Queens Bohemians as expansion teams. Finally, in the second half season, or spring 1933, the information available about this soccer league reveals that the five remaining teams in the ASL I were the Wanderers, the Bohemians, the New York Americans, the Prague Americans, and the New York Brookhatten, and that the Brookhatten won the league's title. Ultimately the ASL I folded as a league after the spring 1933 season because of mismanagement and internal disorganization, inadequate publicity and exposure in the media, and worsening economic conditions in the United States.

SUMMARY

The primary purpose and goal of Chapter 2 are to identify and analyze two specific types of reorganizations that involved the dominant professional leagues prior to the sports' 1950 regular seasons. That is, the chapter highlights the changes in performances that occurred when clubs had moved from one city to another as members of a league and when teams transferred between one or more leagues in the same sport.

According to the information contained in Tables 2.1–2.5, there were 64 affiliated sports teams that relocated or transferred between 1876 and 1950. With respect to the professional baseball leagues, these actions included six in the NAPBP, three in the ENL, one in the UA, eight in the AA and two in the AL. As to the other sports leagues, the numbers of teams affected were, respectively, 12 in the NFL, 4 in the NHL, 17 in the NBA and 11 in the ACL. When listed by the numbers of teams—from most to least—that had relocated and transferred during eight 10-season intervals, there were as follows:

- Nineteen sports clubs affected in 1940–1949
- Eighteen in 1920–1929
- Seven each in 1890–1899 and 1930–1939
- Six in 1870–1879—which actually transpired in 1876–1879 since no activity had occurred from 1870 to 1875
- Five in 1880–1889, two in 1900–1909 and
- Zero in 1910–1919.

Thus, for different reasons the professional leagues discussed in this chapter tended to expand and/or contract in size, and various teams had moved from their home sites and markets to facilities in other cities of metropolitan areas, or had transferred to other leagues as distributed in these eight decades of seasons.

Some key themes are incorporated in Chapter 2. Generally clubs were moved to sites in other cities because they had performed below expectations at home against their rivals, could not sustain their operating losses from playing games before small crowds, and/or were sold and purchased by a new group of owners. After moving to different areas, some of the teams' average winning percentages tended to increase, and more fans attended their home games, at least for a few seasons, while they competed to qualify for the league's playoffs and perhaps win a number of division and conference titles. On average, the postmove areas of relocated clubs had larger populations and experienced higher growth rates, and contained renovated or new arenas, ballparks, or stadiums.

Beyond one or more regular seasons, however, most of the franchises that had moved operated at a loss and eventually dissolved, merged with other teams, or transferred to rival leagues. In other words, these teams could not survive and succeed at either their pre- or postmove sites. Also, some clubs had to relocate to different places because there were other and more popular professional teams and sports in their local and/or regional markets.

Due to the sport's expanding nationwide audience and popularity, the baseball clubs that relocated prior to 1950 normally existed at their postmove sites for more seasons than their counterparts in football, ice hockey, and soccer. Meanwhile, since the NBA was officially named and began operating in 1949, several of this league's clubs did not relocate until after the 1950 season, a topic discussed in Chapter 4.

In summary, between the late 1800s and 1940s, sports in the United States experienced an increase in demand, especially from fans and also the general public. Even so, because of local, regional, and national demographic and economic events, some teams in the professional leagues were unprofitable at their original sites and thus compelled to move to different metropolitan areas in order to survive. In contrast, other teams continued to operate as sports enterprises by transferring to rival leagues. Consequently, as the various leagues developed and their teams matured in this 75-year period, the leaders of these organizations gradually learned how to be more effective at marketing, managing, and financing their businesses within a dynamic, competitive, and expanding sports industry.

To continue and extend the history and business of professional sports from 1950 to the early 2000s, Chapter 3 examines expansions and mergers involving the prominent U.S. sports leagues. Chapter 4 focuses on the relocations and transfers of teams within and between these and other leagues. After Chapters 3 and 4, the core contents of this book conclude with presenting similar topics and actions of some alternative leagues in Chapter 5 and these organization's franchises in Chapter 6. Finally, there is a Conclusion, which highlights the contents in Chapters 1–6.

3

Expansions and Mergers of Leagues since 1950

According to political affairs professor Michael N. Danielson, "The push of demographic and economic change has been reinforced by the ability of [professsional sports] leagues to sell expansion franchises for ever-higher prices, attract offers from places that want big-league teams, political pressures to make professional sports more accessible, and fears that rival leagues will set up business in bypassed markets." In conjunction with professor Danielson's viewpoint, this chapter essentially focuses on why, when, and where some U.S.-based professional baseball, football, basketball, ice hockey, and soccer leagues had added a number of teams between 1950 and 2005 and, furthermore, had merged their operations with rival leagues in the same sport.[1]

Based on an array of articles, research studies, and other documents, the professional sports leagues' decisions to expand and/or merge after 1950 were implemented for several reasons. First, the total U.S. population had increased from approximately 160 million in 1953 to 179 million in 1960, which is nearly a 12 percent growth rate. As a result, several cities that were existed within metropolitan areas of the nation's southeast, southwest, and west became larger population centers that could support one or more professional teams in a variety of sports. Second, after the 1940s, the infrastructure of the United States continued to improve because new airports, railroads, regional and national interstate highways, city streets, and rural roads were constructed or redesigned and then periodically upgraded. In turn, these types of expenditures and public investments across the nation lowered travel times for consumers and reduced the transportation costs for businesses, thus encouraging the penetration of small, midsized, and large sports markets and dispersion of commercial activities.

Third, after the post–World War II era the disposable income, tangible wealth, and standard of living of U.S. households measurably increased, and this phenomenon caused numerous entrepreneurs to emerge as prospective and enthusiastic owners of—and investors in—existing and future professional sports franchises. Indeed, a number of these rich individuals and families—and their friends and colleagues—were ambitious and successful business people and private groups that who had previously assumed known and unknown financial risks to generate their companies' revenues and profits in various industries such that they accumulated personal fortunes. Fourth, it became apparent to some observers that officials in the major U.S. sports leagues, including those in professional baseball, football, basketball, ice hockey and soccer would evaluate the potential risks, costs, and returns, and eventually encourage and approve the placement of new teams in different metropolitan areas of the nation, and also for officials to merge their organizations with rival leagues in the same type of sport.

In short, these four reasons and other demographic, economic, financial, and social factors had provided the incentives and opportunities for expansion teams to locate and play their home games at new sites in cities of North America. A portion of teams were members of the American League (AL) and National League (NL) in Major League Baseball (MLB) and of the National Football League (NFL) and National Basketball Association (NBA) during the early 1960s, of the National Hockey League (NHL) during the late 1960s, and of Major League Soccer (MLS) during the late 1990s and early 2000s. Furthermore, to prosper in the long run, it seemed likely that some of the rival professional sports leagues would have to merge and streamline their operations. Consequently, in this chapter each of these sports leagues' expansions and mergers is addressed, discussed, and evaluated as superior, neutral, or inferior business strategies.

MAJOR LEAGUE BASEBALL

To highlight baseball's pre-1950 history, between 1878 and 1887 the Early National League (ENL) had agreed to admit 14 new teams. However, excluding the New York Giants and Philadelphia Phillies, the other dozen ENL clubs were unable to exist at their initial sites and within nine seasons had either moved to another city or folded. Evidently, it was such factors as the lackluster and inferior performances of the clubs as observed by spectators at their ballparks, poor attendances at home and away games, inability to establish a local or regional fan base, managerial mistakes and financial problems of the franchises' owners, and being located in a small or midsized metropolitan area and sports market that caused each of these

12 teams to fail at their expansion or relocation sites. In contrast, while performing at home in large markets, the Giants and Phillies each won more than 50 percent of their games and a total of two ENL pennants, and had played competitive and exciting baseball at their ballparks before capacity crowds, respectively, in New York City and Philadelphia.[2]

Organized baseball's AL and NL had each consisted of eight teams in 1901. Two years later, they settled their differences and agreed to honor the reserve clause in player contracts and to establish an annual World Series. During the next 10 years, professional baseball became increasingly exposed and more popular in the United States such that not only did the original 16 MLB teams remain solvent, but also a portion of them were profitable. In turn, that prosperity provided business opportunities for investors to collaborate and provide more baseball games to fans in various market areas. So in 1913, a rival alternative league titled the Federal League (FL) was formed as a national baseball organization. After promoting itself as a "major" sports league, this group opened its first season in 1914 with clubs located in such non-MLB cities as Baltimore, Buffalo, Indianapolis, and Kansas City; in Brooklyn and Pittsburgh—which had hosted NL clubs; and in Chicago and St. Louis, where rival AL and NL teams were playing their games. Nonetheless, after filing a lawsuit challenging organized baseball to be an illegal trust and advocating that it be dissolved, the FL arranged a peace agreement with the AL and NL and then disbanded in 1915, meaning its teams had to discontinue their operations.

Despite scandals involving some professional baseball teams, coaches, and players; destruction of two World Wars; and economic damages from the Great Depression, the eight franchises in the AL and the NL coexisted with each other as sports enterprises and performed at their respective home and away sites until the early to mid 1950s, when a few owners requested and received approval from league officials to move their teams to other metropolitan areas. Then during the early 1960s, MLB decided to enlarge its membership beyond the longstanding total of 16 franchises. Consequently, baseball's commissioner and the respective franchise owners jointly implemented a management process to consider proposals and evaluate the bids from various individuals and groups, screen and interview each of the candidates, unanimously select the most qualified individual and/or syndicate to be the new teams' owners, and agree to the location of sites.

Table 3.1 identifies and discusses the 14 expansions that have occurred in MLB since 1950. Beside the expansion year in column one, it contains—for each U.S.-based AL and NL franchise—the metropolitan area population and population rank during the team's first year at its home site in columns three

Table 3.1
MLB Expansion Teams and Performances, by League, Selected Seasons

Year	Team	SMSA		Performance	
		Population	Rank	Pennant	World Series
AL					
1961	Los Angeles Angels	6.7	2nd	1	1
1961	Washington Senators	2.0	10th	0	0
1969	Seattle Pilots	1.4	17th	0	0
1969	Kansas City Royals	1.2	26th	2	1
1977	Toronto Blue Jays	2.8	NA	2	2
1977	Seattle Mariners	1.6	23rd	0	0
1998	Tampa Bay Devil Rays	2.2	21st	0	0
NL					
1962	Houston Colts	1.2	16th	1	0
1962	New York Mets	10.6	1st	3	2
1969	Montreal Expos	2.6	NA	0	0
1969	San Diego Padres	1.3	23rd	2	0
1993	Colorado Rockies	2.2	20th	0	0
1993	Florida Marlins	3.4	11th	2	2
1998	Arizona Diamondbacks	2.9	14th	1	1

Note: The column Year is each club's initial season or the expansion year. The Standard Metropolitan Statistical Area (SMSA) Population and Rank is reported for each U.S.-based club as of the expansion year, and the city populations of Toronto and Montreal are included in column three. (NA indicates that the SMSA population ranks are not available for Toronto and Montreal.) Performance includes the number of AL or NL pennants and the total World Series that each team has won from its expansion year through the 2005 season.

Source: *Official Major League Baseball Fact Book 2005 Edition* (St. Louis, MO: Sporting News, 2005), 210–57; "Major League Baseball," at http://www.mlb.com, accessed 8 August 2005; *The World Almanac and Book of Facts* (New York: World Almanac Books, 1961–2004).

and four, respectively, and in columns five and six the clubs' performances based on the total number of pennants and World Series won since their expansion year. Also, the table includes the city populations of Toronto and Montreal as of the expansion year, and the number of pennants and World Series won by the Toronto Blue Jays and Montreal Expos.

To revise and modernize their internal structures as single leagues and the scheduling of games during regular seasons and in the playoffs, MLB restructured in 1969 when the AL and NL were each subdivided into an East and West Division (ED and WD), and again in 1994 when the composition of each league consisted of three divisions—ED, WD, and

Central Division (CD). Furthermore, in 1995 MLB established a wild card system, whereby each AL and NL team that had not won a division title but finished with the highest winning percentage at the conclusion of the regular season could further compete and qualify for a postseason. As a result of this incentive, some wild cards have advanced during the postseason and eventually won a World Series, such as the Florida Marlins in 1997 and 2003, and the Anaheim—formerly Los Angeles and California—Angels in 2002.

American League

In 1961 two syndicates each paid an expansion fee of $2.1 million to MLB. These payments permitted the large-market Los Angeles Angels and midsized-market Washington Senators to join and play in the AL. Each city contained ballparks and enough households with disposable incomes to support an MLB team. Moreover, the NL Dodgers played in the huge and growing Los Angeles area, and previous Senator's clubs had existed for several seasons in the Washington, DC, area. In fact, there was pressure on MLB from members of Congress and an implicit agreement to replace the Senators team that had moved from Washington to Minneapolis, Minnesota, in 1961.

With respect to the MLB seasons prior to the Angels winning a pennant and World Series in 2002, the club had never appeared in the league's playoffs. Meanwhile, the expansion Senators experienced a series of ownership changes during the 1960s; then, because of attendance problems and disappointing seasons at 43,500-seat DC Stadium in the nation's capital, owner Bob Short moved his team from Washington to Texas in 1971 to play in the 35,200-seat Arlington Stadium as the Texas Rangers. Since 1971, the Rangers have won four WD titles but no AL pennants and World Series.

After the expansions of the Angels and Senators in 1961, five new AL teams made their debut in the AL and played their home games in new or renovated stadiums built with taxpayer money. These included the Seattle Pilots, which failed and went bankrupt after the 1969 season, when the club won about 40 percent of its scheduled games, finished in sixth place in the WD, and drew only 678,000 fans to 25,400-seat Sick's Stadium that was located in the small market of Seattle, Washington. Besides the Pilots, in 1969 businessman Ewing Kaufman paid a $5.5 million expansion fee to MLB so that he could own and place the Royals in 35,500-seat Municipal Stadium within the very small market of Kansas City, Missouri. Despite the club's depressed and inferior performances during most regular seasons, the Royals won a WD title and the AL pennant in 1980; five years later, it won another division title, league pennant, and then a World Series.

Eight years following the expansion of the Royals in Kansas City, a new AL team settled in a city located in southeastern Canada to play at home in 38,000-seat Exhibition Stadium, and another team based itself in a city on the U.S. west coast to compete at home in the 59,100-seat Kingdome. These two ballparks were publicly owned, and the teams' new owners realized the economic benefits of playing games in these facilities. That is, after paying MLB expansion fees that cost $7 million and $6.25 million, respectively, individual syndicates became the principal owners of the Blue Jays in mid-sized Toronto, Ontario, and the Mariners in the small market of Seattle. Regarding these teams' lifetime performances since 1977, the Blue Jays won consecutive World Series championships in the 1992–1993 seasons; the Mariners, however, have yet to compete for an AL pennant, in part, because of such competitive rivals in the WD as the recently named Los Angeles Angels of Anaheim, the Oakland Athletics, and Texas Rangers.

Finally in 1998, an investment group led by Vince Namoli purchased the right to place a team nicknamed the Devil Rays in Tampa Bay, Florida and to play its home games in 45,200-seat Tropicana Field, which was built by the community in 1990 to lure the White Sox from Chicago. As a member of the ED, the Devil Rays has generally finished each season in fourth or fifth place and was recently sold to and acquired by a new ownership group headed by Stuart Sternberg. Unless Sternberg and his associates are willing to significantly increase the club's payroll, and somehow arrange for a new taxpayer-funded ballpark to replace the 16-year-old Tropicana Field, the Devil Rays will continue to lose a majority of home and away games to such teams in the division as the highly competitive Boston Red Sox and New York Yankees.

National League

The seven NL expansion teams have collectively won nine pennants and five World Series as of the 2005 MLB season, outperforming their counterparts in the AL. Specifically, in 1960–1961 the Houston Sports Association (HSA) paid the NL a fee of $1.8 million for the right to own and operate a team named the Houston Colts. Then in 1963, HSA member Roy Hofheinz became the sole owner of the franchise; one year later, he renamed it the Houston Astros. Regarding the Astros' performances since the 1962 season while performing in the 42,200-seat Harris County Domed Stadium and later in the 62,400-seat Astrodome, the team won WD titles in 1980 and 1986, CD titles in 1997–1999 and 2001, and finished in second place behind the St. Louis Cardinals in the final standings of the

2004–2005 seasons. During fall 2005, the club defeated the Cardinals for the NL pennant and appeared in its first World Series against the Chicago White Sox. Despite three outstanding pitchers and veteran sluggers, the Astros was beaten in four consecutive games by the mighty White Sox, which had not won a World Series since 1917.

After paying an expansion fee of $1.8 million to MLB, a syndicate headed by Joan Payson became the owner of the New York Mets during 1960, three years after the Dodgers left Brooklyn for Los Angeles and the Giants vacated New York City for San Francisco. Since the 1962 season, the Mets have won NL pennants in 1969, 1973, and 1986, and finished as World Series champions in 1969 and 1986. However, from the mid to late 1980s to the early 2000s, the club has been an inconsistent performer in the ED, despite the relatively high average cost of its annual payroll for players and the team's home site at 55,600-seat Shea Stadium, which exists in baseball's most populated and wealthiest market. Although the franchise has not won a pennant in 20 years, the Mets' market value has greatly appreciated because of its location in a city that is celebrated as the "Big Apple."

For an expansion fee that amounted to $12.5 million, in 1968 a syndicate led by John McHale and Charles Bronfman purchased the right to place their Expos team in midsized Montreal and perform as a member of the ED. This city was selected as a site because of its history of supporting such sports teams as the Montreal Alouettes and Montreal Canadiens, and because of McHale and Bronfman's commitment to the local community. Since the 1969 season, this franchise has won one title—in 1981 after defeating the Philadelphia Phillies in a divisional playoff. During the 1990s and early 2000s the Expos had failed to establish a loyal fan base, generate sufficient revenues from its local broadcasting agreements, and draw spectators to the team's games played in 46,500-seat Olympic Stadium. As a result, the team relocated to the Washington, DC, area in early 2005 and was renamed Washington Nationals.

Since 1969—or one year after it became an expansion team for a fee of $12.5 million—the WD San Diego Padres won NL pennants in 1984 and 1998. Nevertheless, in these seasons the Padres lost in the World Series to, respectively, the AL Detroit Tigers in five games and New York Yankees in four games. In 2004 the Padres moved from 56,133-seat Qualcomm Stadium into a modern ballpark that is named Petco Park. As a result of higher ticket prices and the cash inflows generated from concessions, club seats, luxury suites, and larger attendances at the 42,445-seat Petco Park, the club's revenues and payrolls of its players have increased. Consequently, in 2005 the Padres won a WD title but was defeated in the playoffs by the CD St. Louis Cardinals. In short, from playing at Petco Park in the high-growth area of

San Diego, the Padres' teams should remain moderately competitive each season and profitable for the owners of the franchise.

With respect to the performances of three other NL expansion teams that are listed in Table 3.1, while located in Miami's small-market area and playing at home in 42,500-seat Pro Player Stadium, the Marlins won a pennant and World Series in 1997 and again in 2003. However, the club's owner, Jeffrey Loria, has threatened to leave the city of Miami if a modern ballpark is not constructed for his team, in part, with taxpayer funds. In fact, Marlins president David Samson has visited Portland, Oregon; San Antonio, Texas; and Oklahoma City, Oklahoma, to meet with baseball officials and search for a new site. Apparently, the sports fans in southern Florida prefer to read about, support, and attend the games played by Miami's NFL Dolphins and NBA Heat, and NHL Florida Panthers.

In contrast to the Marlins, since 1993 the expansion Colorado Rockies in the midsized market of Denver has yet to win a WD title, whereas the Arizona Diamondbacks has played its home games in midsized Phoenix and won an NL pennant and World Series in 2001 by defeating the New York Yankees in seven games. Interestingly, the Rockies' attendances in Denver's 50,400-seat Coors Field have steadily declined since the mid to late 1990s. Meanwhile, the Diamondbacks—while playing at home in 49,000-seat Bank One Ballpark (renamed Chase Field in 2005)—has gradually lost some local market share to Phoenix's NBA Suns, NFL Cardinals, and NHL Coyotes. In short, MLB's post-1950 expansion teams with the best performances through the 2005 season have been the AL Royals and Blue Jays, and the NL Mets and Marlins. In contrast, the most disappointing expansion teams in MLB include the AL Pilots and Senators, and the NL Rockies and former Expos.

NATIONAL FOOTBALL LEAGUE

Prior to 1950 there were 25 new professional football teams that had entered the NFL. With respect to that particular group of clubs, the New York Giants is the only expansion franchise that has continued to operate in the same metropolitan area through the league's 2005 season. The names, seasons, and performances of the other 24 clubs appear in Table 1.2 of Chapter 1. As denoted in the table, the last pre-1950 expansion team to vacate its original location was the Boston Yanks; that is, the club moved from Boston to New York City in 1949 after finishing fourth, fourth, fifth, third, and fifth in the NFL's ED during the 1944–1948 seasons. As a result, it was 11 years later when the league's owners decided to compromise and authorize the entry of more expansion teams as a strategy to penetrate a

Table 3.2
NFL Expansion Teams and Performances, Selected Seasons

Year	Team	SMSA		Performance	
		Population	Rank	Conference	Super Bowl
1960	Dallas Cowboys	1.0	20th	9	5
1961	Minnesota Vikings	1.4	14th	4	0
1966	Atlanta Falcons	1.3	20th	1	0
1967	New Orleans Saints	1.1	31st	0	0
1976	Seattle Seahawks	1.6	23rd	0	0
1976	Tampa Bay Buccaneers	1.5	24th	1	1
1995	Carolina Panthers	1.3	33rd	1	0
1995	Jacksonville Jaguars	1.0	46th	0	0
2002	Houston Texans	4.6	10th	0	0

Note: See the Note below Table 3.1 for the columns labeled as Year, Team, Population, and Rank. Performance includes the number of American and National Football Conference titles and Super Bowls that each team has won from the expansion year to the 2004 season.

Source: NFL 2001 Record & Fact Book (New York: National Football League, 2001), 290–99; "National Football League," at http://www.nfl.com, accessed 8 August 2005; The World Almanac and Book of Facts, 1960–2004.

number of promising sports markets surrounding some of America's growing urban areas.[3]

Table 3.2 identifies when and which new teams were approved as members of the league after 1950, and how they have performed. Note that the table excludes the 10 clubs that had joined the NFL in the 1970 season as a result of the league's merger with the American Football League (AFL). Because of that merger, such teams as the Cincinnati Bengals, Miami Dolphins, and New York Jets had transferred into the NFL from the AFL. As such, a discussion of their home sites and performances is included in Chapter 4.

Businessmen Clint Murchison and Bedford Wynne jointly paid the NFL a $600,000 expansion fee for the right to own and operate the Dallas Cowboys in the league's Western Football Conference (WFC) beginning in the 1960 season. The league supported these owners, who placed their franchise in Dallas because of the area's population growth, large fan base and demand for football, and the availability of the 68,200-seat Cotton Bowl as a stadium for the team. In 1988 a syndicate headed by multimillionaire Jerry Jones acquired the club for $95 million from owner H. R. Bright, who had purchased the franchise from Murchison and Wynne in 1984 for $60 million plus a payment of $26 million for the operating lease to Texas Stadium and for other real estate. While located in the midsized

Dallas area, the Cowboys have won a total of nine Eastern Football Conference (EFC) and National Football Conference (NFC) titles and also Super Bowls in the 1971, 1977, 1992–1993, and 1995 seasons. Because of former coaches Tom Landry and Jimmy Johnson and such players on the team's offense as quarterbacks Roger Staubach and Troy Aikman, receivers Drew Pearson and Michael Irvin, running backs Emmitt Smith and Tony Dorsett, and field goal kickers Rafael Septien and Richie Cunningham, for years the Cowboys have been ranked as one of the most competitive and highest valued franchises in professional sports. Indeed, the team's value will especially appreciate if a new football stadium is built soon for Jones' club with local and state taxpayer funds to replace 35-year-old, 65,675-seat Texas Stadium, which is located in the city of Irving.

In addition to the Cowboys, the Minnesota Vikings, Atlanta Falcons, and New Orleans Saints also entered the league during the 1960s. Although the franchise owners had placed their expansion teams in small-to-midsized sports markets, the NFL invaded these three areas to discourage AFL teams from expanding into the cities. To be specific, after a syndicate spent $600,000 as an expansion fee to own and control the Vikings in the Minneapolis-St. Paul area in the NFL's 1961 season, the fee increased in the mid-1960s to $8.5 million for Rankin Smith to operate the Falcons in Atlanta and $8.5 million for John Mecom Jr. to own the Saints in New Orleans.

In total, these three franchises have not been very successful during most NFL seasons at winning their respective divisions and NFC championships. Although the Vikings previously won four of its conference titles, the club was then decisively defeated in Super Bowls by the Kansas City Chiefs 23–7 in 1970, the Miami Dolphins 24–7 in 1974, the Pittsburgh Steelers 16–6 in 1975, and the Oakland Raiders 32–14 in 1977. Since the late 1970s, the Vikings have experienced a number of disputes among its owners, and in 2005 an embarrassing scandal occurred involving some of the team's players who had leased a charter boat and hired strip dancers and prostitutes for entertainment. Despite the negative publicity from this event and other distractions, the Vikings recovered to win a series of games but performed below expectations, which was a Super Bowl victory in the 2005 NFL season.

Meanwhile, the Falcons won an NFC title in the 1998 season, and in 1999 lost to the American Football Conference (AFC) champion Denver Broncos 34–19 in a Super Bowl that was played in Miami's Pro Player Stadium. (The Falcons' current owner, Arthur Blank, is the cofounder of Home Depot, Inc.) In 2003, Blank's general manager drafted All-American quarterback Michael Vick, who had performed as a superstar football player at Virginia Tech University. Because of Vick's speed when he runs with the football and his improved skills in passing to receivers, the Falcons are more competitive and a threat to the other teams in the NFC's South Division (SD). In fact, some observers of the sport predict that within a few seasons, Vick will lead his club to win another NFC title and perhaps a victory in a Super Bowl.

In contrast, in fall 2005, the Saints franchise was demoralized after Hurricane Katrina destroyed levees that caused the flooding of New Orleans and damaged the Louisiana Superdome. As a result, Los Angeles and San Antonio, Texas were each mentioned as a future home for the team after the conclusion of the 2005 or 2006 season. Therefore, it is likely that Saints owner Tom Benson prefers to find another site for his club because of the decline in the values of New Orleans' infrastructure and real estate, the pessimism about the city's current and future business environment, and the disengagement of the club's fan base in the southern Louisiana region.

During the mid-1970s, two U.S. cities contained stadiums and population bases that had the potential to support NFL teams. To play in the 1976 season, the Seattle Seahawks and Tampa Bay Buccaneers each became new members of the league. Despite the Seattle and Tampa Bay areas being relatively small markets in the mid to late 1970s with respect to hosting professional football teams, the Seahawks' Lloyd Nordstrom and Buccaneers' Hugh Culverhouse each paid a $16 million expansion fee to the NFL for the right to enter a team in the league. Although the Seahawks have failed to win an AFC or NFC championship from its inception to 2004, the club won the AFC's WD in the 1988 and 1999 seasons, and in 2006 overwhelmed and defeated the Carolina Panthers in the NFC championship game.

Relative to the average to below-average long-run record of the Seahawks, the Buccaneers has performed moderately well in some seasons against its opponents in the NFC's Central Division (CD) and then in the SD. Specifically, the Buccaneers won or tied for CD titles in the 1979, 1981, and 1999 seasons, and in the 2002 season won the SD and NFC, and then Super Bowl XXXVII by defeating the Oakland Raiders 48–21 at Qualcomm Stadium in San Diego, California. Similar to the Falcons and perhaps Seahawks, for a number of years the Buccaneers' teams are expected to be leading contenders to compete for the NFC's SD title.

Because of the above-average economic growth and sustained increases in the per-capita incomes of households, and the growing profits of businesses in several metropolitan areas of the southern United States during the late 1980s and early 1990s, NFL team owners agreed in 1993 to admit the 29th and 30th franchises into the league. A syndicate that was headed by former Baltimore Colts player Jerry Richardson convinced the clubs' owners to approve his bid for a team—named the Carolina Panthers—to be located in Charlotte, North Carolina, and so did businessman Wayne Weaver for his club—which is named the Jacksonville Jaguars—to be located in northeast Florida,. In performances, the Panthers won the NFC's WD title with a record of 12–4 in the 1996 season but was later defeated by the Green Bay Packers 30–13 in the conference's championship game. Then in 2004, the Panthers won the SD and NFC titles, and, in a hard fought game, lost to the New England Patriots 32–29 in Super Bowl XXXIX played in Houston's Reliant Stadium. Meanwhile the Jaguars—a member of the AFC's CD—was beaten in conference championship games in the 1996 and 1999 postseasons.

In 1970, the Houston Oilers transferred from the AFL into the NFL and played in the league's CD of the AFC. Although the Oilers had won or tied for CD titles in the 1980, 1991, and 1993 seasons, the club failed to win a conference title. So after the 1996 season, the NFL agreed to allow the Oilers' owner Bud Adams to move his team from southeastern Texas to Memphis, Tennessee to temporarily play in the 62,400-seat Liberty Bowl, and then permanently to Nashville, Tennessee to perform in the 67,000-seat Coliseum. While located in Nashville, the former Oilers—renamed Tennessee Titans—won division titles in the 2000 and 2002 seasons but lost to the NFC champion St. Louis Rams 23–16 in Super Bowl XXXIV.

For nearly two years, NFL officials had debated with each other about the economic benefits and costs of placing an expansion team in the Los Angeles and/or Houston areas. Then by a unanimous vote of 29–0, in 1999 the league approved businessman Robert McNair's bid of $700 million to locating a new NFL team in Houston, which in 2000 had a metropolitan area population of nearly five million residents. A component of McNair's bid was a plan to construct and finance a new 69,500-seat retractable-roof football stadium for the team within or near the city of Houston.

After naming his expansion club the Houston Texans, McNair hired the Jacksonville Jaguars' defensive coordinator Don Capers to be the Texans' first head coach. From 1995 to 1998 Capers had coached the Carolina Panthers, and as previously stated, in the 1996 season his Panthers team won the NFC's WD title and finished runner-up to the Green Bay Packers in the conference championship game. Although the Texans' teams had won only one-third of their games during the NFL's 2002–2004 regular seasons, the club's paid attendance at Reliant Stadium exceeded 70,000 per game in each season. To compete and excel in the AFC's SD, the Texans' primary competitors are the Indianapolis Colts, the Jacksonville Jaguars, and the Tennessee Titans. Based on the team's performances in previous seasons, it may be several years before the Texans are capable of winning a division title.

Clearly, since 1950 the Dallas Cowboys is the NFL's most successful expansion franchise because of the team's performances and division titles in the AFC and then NFC, and the club's five Super Bowl championships. Regarding the league's other expansion teams, the performances of the Minnesota Vikings and New Orleans Saints have been disappointing, whereas in recent seasons the Atlanta Falcons, Seattle Seahawks, Tampa Bay Buccaneers, Carolina Panthers, and Jacksonville Jaguars have been increasingly competitive against opponents in their respective divisions. Whether the Texans will eventually be successful and play above .500 each season in its division and win a conference championship depends on the managerial decisions of owner Robert McNair, game strategies of the team's coach and his staff, and the attitudes, talents, and efforts of the Texans' players.

NATIONAL BASKETBALL ASSOCIATION

Although they are not regarded as expansion franchises in this chapter, 11 clubs from the former Basketball Association of America and six from the National Basketball League jointly organized and formed the NBA to start the 1949 season (see Table 1.4 in Chapter 1). However, after one or more years of competing in the NBA, the majority of these clubs had to either suspend their operations or move to sites in cities within other areas. So in the 1960 regular season, the NBA consisted of eight Eastern Division clubs and eight Western Division clubs. To exploit a business opportunity by introducing the sport of professional basketball into other U.S. metropolitan areas and consumer markets in North America, and to remain entertaining as an elite sports organization in competition for fans with MLB, the NFL, and the NHL, the NBA officials decided to begin adding new teams to the league during and after the early 1960s.[4]

Table 3.3 lists 18 NBA expansions and the total population of the teams' metropolitan areas, or of Canadian cities, in the expansion year. Except for Vancouver and Toronto, the table also provides the Standard Metropolitan Statistical Area population ranks of 16 clubs in column four and the performances of all teams at their original sites in columns five and six. For more insight, the following four sections of this chapter highlight some interesting aspects of these expansion teams' seasons and business histories.

1960s

According to the table, the NBA's membership increased by six teams in the 1960s, four in the 1970s, five in the 1980s, two in the 1990s, and thus

Table 3.3
NBA Expansion Teams and Performances, Selected Seasons

Year	Team	SMSA		Performance	
		Population	Rank	Champion	Runner-up
1961	Chicago Packers	6.2	3rd	0	0
1966	Chicago Bulls	7.0	2nd	6	0
1967	San Diego Rockets	1.2	23rd	0	0
1967	Seattle Supersonics	1.4	17th	1	2
1968	Milwaukee Bucks	1.4	19th	1	1
1968	Phoenix Suns	.9	34th	0	2
1970	Buffalo Braves	1.3	24th	0	0
1970	Cleveland Cavaliers	2.0	12th	0	0
1970	Portland Trail Blazers	1.0	33rd	0	1
1974	New Orleans Jazz	1.1	31st	0	0
1980	Dallas Mavericks	3.9	8th	0	0
1988	Charlotte Hornets	1.1	35th	0	0
1988	Miami Heat	8.0	11th	0	0
1989	Orlando Magic	1.1	37th	0	1
1989	Minnesota Timberwolves	2.5	16th	0	0
1995	Vancouver Grizzlies	1.8	NA	0	0
1995	Toronto Raptors	4.3	NA	0	0
2004	Charlotte Bobcats	1.5	34th	0	0

Note: See the Note below Table 3.1 to interpret the columns labeled Year, Team, Population, and Rank. The NA indicates that the population ranks of Vancouver and Toronto, or of their respective provinces, are indeterminate since these cities' metropolitan areas are not measured as SMSAs. Performance includes the number of seasons that each team has won an NBA championship and finished as a runner-up to the champion from the expansion year to the 2004 season.

Source: "National Basketball Association," at http://www.nba.com, accessed 8 August 2005, and *The World Almanac and Book of Facts*, 1961–2004.

far one in the 2000s. After joining the league in 1961 for an unknown fee, during its first two seasons the Chicago Packers—which was renamed the Chicago Zephyrs in 1962—won approximately 22 percent of total games, averaged fifth place in the league's WD, attracted small crowds to its home-site games played in the Chicago Amphitheater in 1961–62 and Chicago Coliseum in 1962–63, and thus failed to establish a sufficient market of fans in the Windy City area. As result, in 1963 the Zephyrs' owner, Dave Trager, moved his team from Chicago to the state of Maryland and renamed it to perform as Baltimore Bullets.

Three years later, a syndicate headed by Dick Klein paid an expansion fee of $1.25 million to locate a new team nicknamed the Chicago Bulls to play its home games at the 17,300-seat Coliseum in Chicago, whose population in 1966 had exceeded six million people. After a series of ownership changes, in 1984 the Bulls drafted Michael Jordan—who was a first-team Division I All-American basketball player at the University of North Carolina, and in 1985 a syndicate featuring Jerry Reinsdorf purchased 56 percent of the club for $9.2 million. Coached by Phil Jackson and led by the NBA's highest scorer and most valuable player Jordan, the Bulls won CD titles and NBA championships in the 1991–1993 and 1996–1998 seasons. Because of Phil Jackson, Michael Jordan, and these former outstanding performances, the club was able to establish a national fan base and become such a business success that it and the league have each developed into popular international sports brands.

During 1967, two small-market West Coast teams were added to the NBA. That is, when syndicates of investors each paid an expansion fee of $1.75 million, the Rockets began playing in the 14,500-seat San Diego Sports Arena in southern California, as did the Supersonics in the 14,000-seat Seattle Center Coliseum in the state of Washington. After concluding four dismal seasons in the league's WC, the Texas Sport Investment group purchased the Rockets for $5.6 million from its owners and then moved the team from San Diego to southeastern Texas to perform as the Houston Rockets. Meanwhile, the Supersonics had played well enough to win four of the NBA's Pacific Division (PD) titles, finishing runner-up to the champion Washington Bullets and Chicago Bulls in, respectively, the 1978 and 1996 seasons, and in the 1979 season won an NBA championship while coached by Len Wilkens. Recently, the Supersonics' owner threatened to move the team from Seattle if the city did not renovate 17,100-seat Key Arena.

In exchange for an expansion fee of $2 million each, the Milwaukee Bucks and Phoenix Suns franchise owners were allowed to enter their teams into the NBA and compete in the 1968 season. Because the two teams have existed in cities in small to midsized sports markets while some of their rivals play at home in midsized to large markets, the Bucks and Suns winning division titles, and especially conference or league championships, were unanticipated events. Yet, since 1968 the Wisconsin-based team had won seven CD and six Midwest Division (MD) titles, and in the 1971 season an NBA championship. The Suns, meanwhile, won the NBA's PD in the 1981, 1993, and 1995 seasons and was runner-up to the league champions in the 1976 and 1993 seasons. In retrospect, the Milwaukee Bucks and Phoenix Suns have each triumphed more often than did the teams of the Chicago

Packers and San Diego Rockets, and performed about the same as the various clubs that represented the Seattle Supersonics.

1970s

The seventh, eighth, and ninth NBA expansion teams in the post-1950 era played their initial seasons in 1970. That year the expansion fee—which was an incentive for NBA owners to admit new teams from marginal cities to enter the league—was $3.7 million each for the owners of the small-market Buffalo Braves, Cleveland Cavaliers, and Portland Trail Blazers.

After eight seasons without winning a division or conference title while playing in Buffalo's 13,000-seat Memorial Auditorium, the Braves became increasingly frustrated with its performances and operating losses. As such, in 1978 owners Irv Levin and Harold Lipton moved the team from Buffalo to San Diego, California. Besides the disappointment of not winning most games during the regular seasons and struggling with financial problems, the Braves relocation also occurred because avid sports fans in the Buffalo area had preferred to support the NFL Buffalo Bills and NHL Buffalo Sabres.

In contrast to the Braves, the Cleveland Cavaliers won the EC's CD in the 1976 season. Moreover, since drafting high school player LeBron James in 2004, the Cavaliers have improved as a team and now challenge their rivals to win division and conference titles. The Portland Trail Blazers, meanwhile, won the PD in 1979 and 1992–1993, and an NBA championship in the 1977 season. Nevertheless, during most years in the league, the Cavaliers and Trail Blazers have been inconsistent. Yet, these franchises seem to generate enough revenues from their operations to remain solvent from playing, respectively, in the 20,500-seat Quicken Loans Arena in Cleveland, Ohio, and the 21,500-seat Rose Garden in Portland, Oregon.

The final club to enter the NBA during the 1970s was the New Orleans Jazz, whose owners paid $6.15 million in expansion fees to join the league. Even though New Orleans is a tourist city that struggles to support its professional sports teams, a syndicate headed by Fred Rosenfield convinced NBA officials of their commitment to promote the team while playing at home in the 72,900-seat Superdome. After six seasons of weak performances and despite the showmanship and charisma of scoring leader and all-star "Pistol" Pete Maravich, principal owner Sam Battistone moved his franchise from New Orleans to small-market Salt Lake City in Utah and then renamed the club Utah Jazz.

1980s

To place the sport at sites in other emerging sports markets in the United States, the NBA admitted the Dallas Mavericks into the league in 1980 for an expansion fee of $12 million, and then at an average cost of $32.5 million per team approved the entry of the Charlotte Hornets and Miami Heat in 1988 and one year later the Orlando Magic and Minnesota Timberwolves. Even without ever winning a conference championship, the Mavericks have been popular as an entertainment option for the sports fans in the Dallas area. Indeed, the team's attendances at its home games in the 19,200-seat American Airlines Center are frequently above the league's average. The Mavericks' Mark Cuban, who became a billionaire after selling his telecommunications company, is a clever, controversial, flamboyant, and outspoken owner who enthusiastically roots for his team and individual players while pacing on the court's sidelines during home games. However, in order to win the WC's Southwest Division, Cuban's club must play more competitively to defeat the champion San Antonio Spurs and the improving Houston Rockets and Memphis Grizzlies.

Since entering the NBA in 1988, the Hornets led the league in attendance per game at the 24,000-seat Charlotte Coliseum until the mid-to-late 1990s. Then, when the voters in the Charlotte area overwhelmingly defeated a referendum to finance the construction of a new downtown basketball facility with taxpayer money, and when the local community failed to adequately support the franchise at home games played in the Coliseum, co-owners George Shinn and Ray Wooldridge moved the club from Charlotte to the City of New Orleans following the 2002 NBA season. After the damages to the 18,500-seat New Orleans Arena as a result of Hurricane Katrina, the Hornets choose to play their 2005 regular season home games at the Ford Center in Oklahoma City, Oklahoma.

The Miami Heat won the Atlantic Division (AD) in the 1997–2000 seasons, and the Southeast Division (SED) title in the 2004 season when center Shaquille O'Neal had joined the franchise after playing several seasons for the Los Angeles Lakers. With O'Neal and backup center and shot blocker Alonzo Mourning, and with high-scoring guard Dwayne Wade and veteran player Gary Payton, the Heat is a team that won the SED, EC, and the NBA championship in the 2005 season and is favored to win the 2006 and/or 2007 seasons. At the 19,600-seat American Airlines Arena in Miami, the Heat play before capacity crowds because of local basketball fans' interest in watching O'Neal, Mourning, Wade, and Payton perform during each home game.

Even with the sport's most versatile player, 6-foot-11 forward Kevin Garnett, the Timberwolves have struggled to win their division's title. Generally, the club plays in front of relatively large crowds at the 19,000-seat Target Center in Minneapolis, and in 2005 played in the WC's Northwest Division (NWD) against four other teams, including the Utah Jazz. If another of the team's athletes performs above expectations, such as swingman Ricky Davis or rookie guard Rashad McCants—who played for the 2005 NCAA champion University of North Carolina—and if Garnett avoids missing games because of serious injuries or illnesses, then the Timberwolves will win the NWD, and in the playoffs likely compete for a WC title against the San Antonio Spurs, Dallas Mavericks, or Phoenix Suns.

1990s–2000s

The NBA granted original franchise rights to the owners of the Vancouver Grizzlies and Toronto Raptors so that each group would provide a team in the league's 1995 season. Because of poor performances and losing most games during regular seasons in Vancouver at the 19,200-seat General Motors Place, and due to the lack of support from fans and businesses in its local market, the Grizzlies were an inferior NBA franchise. Consequently, in 1998 owner Michael Heisley moved his club from Vancouver to the state of Tennessee and changed its nickname to Memphis Grizzlies. Meanwhile, since 1995 the Raptors have not been a successful team at the 19,800-seat Air Canada Centre in Toronto. Unfortunately, the club has failed to win even one AD title in the EC. However, if the Raptors' coach Sam Mitchell can inspire his players, including center Loren Woods, forward Charlie Villanueva, and guard Morris Peterson, then each season the club may challenge such prominent division teams as the New Jersey Nets and Philadelphia 76ers.

During 2003–2004 the league's owners authorized billionaire Robert Johnson, who founded and sold Black Entertainment Television, to assemble a club—the Charlotte Bobcats—and enter the team into the NBA. In its initial season, the expansion Charlotte Bobcats won only 18 games and compiled the league's third-lowest average attendance record at 14,500 per game while playing in the 24,000-seat Charlotte Coliseum. Nonetheless, during early November 2005, the city's new taxpayer-funded but yet to be named 18,000-seat arena opened for the Bobcats in downtown Charlotte. The arena features a giant scoreboard, which models Charlotte's uptown skyline, and contains a number of exclusive inner circle club seats, party suites, and discount merchandise outlets that generate cash inflows for the team in excess of the revenues produced at the former Coliseum. If the

Bobcats gradually improve by winning more games during each season in 2005, 2006, 2007, and 2008, and especially against its opponents in the SED, then the club's operating profit and market value will each increase—but most likely to a lesser extent than the amounts realized by its predecessor, the Charlotte Hornets.[5]

Based on such criteria as team performances, number of titles won, home attendances per season, and appreciation in market values, the NBA's three most successful expansion teams listed in Table 3.3 are the Chicago Bulls, Seattle Supersonics, and Phoenix Suns; the least successful clubs include the Chicago Packers, San Diego Rockets, and Vancouver Grizzlies. Ranked between these two groups of three teams each are the other 12 franchises in column two of the table.

NATIONAL HOCKEY LEAGUE

Prior to 1950, six new teams were admitted into the NHL (see Table 1.3). As a result, the Boston Bruins, Chicago Blackhawks, Detroit Cougars—renamed the Falcons in 1930 and Red Wings in 1933—and the New York Rangers continued to perform at their respective rinks through 2003 and in the 2005 regular season while the Philadelphia Quakers—former Pittsburgh Pirates—folded in 1932, as did the Montreal Maroons in 1939. Thus, between 1939 and 1967 the NHL consisted of four of the pre-1950 expansion teams plus the Montreal Canadiens and Toronto Maple Leafs.[6]

To establish more intense rivalries among some of the league's teams despite the mileage between their home-site locations, the NHL decided to reorganize and subdivide itself after the 1966 season. These realignments in the grouping of teams included, respectively, an Eastern and Western Division (ED and WD) to represent the 1967–1973 seasons, a Prince of Wales Conference (PWC) and Clarence Campbell Conference (CCC) each with various divisions to represent the 1974–1992 seasons, an Eastern and Western Conference (EC and WC) each with two divisions to represent the 1993–1997 seasons, and an EC and WC each with three divisions to represent the 1998–2003 and 2005 seasons. Meanwhile, after the league and National Hockey League Players Association (NHLPA) failed to mutually negotiate a collective bargaining agreement that involved a number of economic issues, the teams' owners locked out the players and then canceled the 2004 NHL season.

After MLB, the NFL, and the NBA had added more teams to their leagues beginning in the early to mid 1960s, NHL officials decided to emulate these decisions by implementing a set of its own short- and long-run strategies. That is, in the mid to late 1960s the league's officials met and agreed to increase the number of professional ice hockey teams, and also to place them at sites in predominately midsized and large areas of the United States but not in such metropolises as Boston, Chicago, Detroit, and New York City. Generally, the areas of new NHL teams were located on the U.S. West Coast and in the northern and Midwestern regions of the nation. Furthermore, there were some teams in the other major professional sports that played their regular season games at ballparks, stadiums, and/or arenas within these areas. Then, to extend its strategy over time, the NHL expanded its markets even further geographically during and after the 1970s by allocating teams to areas in the southern United States and also to cities in Canada other than Montreal and Toronto.

Between the late 1960s and early 2000s, the NHL had expanded by a total of 21 teams. According to Table 3.4, the distribution of these clubs indicates that 19, or approximately 90 percent of them, were based in U.S. cities, and 2 or 10 percent of them had established their home sites in areas of Canada. If listed by country and decade, it was six NHL expansion clubs placed in the United States and zero in Canada in the 1960s and respectively, five and one in the 1970s, six and one in the 1990s, and two and zero in the early 2000s.

To reveal some unique facts and sports history about each of these teams and their home sites, Table 3.4 includes the various expansion years and teams' nicknames, the population and population rank of each urban area (except for Vancouver and Ottawa in Canada), and the number of seasons that each club had won a Stanley Cup and finished runner-up to the champion from the expansion year through the 2003 NHL season. Based on the columns of information, what does the table expose about the league and the results of its short- and long-run strategies to increase in size during the post-1950 era of seasons?

First, 18, or 85 percent, of the NHL's expansion teams have remained at their original sites to play in the 2005 season, whereas three or 15 percent of them relocated to other areas. Although their nicknames changed after relocating, the Seals—which was named the California Golden Seals in 1970—moved from Oakland to Cleveland; the Scouts from Kansas City to Denver in 1976; and the Flames from Atlanta to Calgary in 1980. Interestingly, the Seals, Scouts, and Flames had never played in an NHL final to compete for a Stanley Cup. Although each of them is discussed more thoroughly in Chapter 4, the three NHL clubs were forced to relocate and play on ice rinks in, respectively, the cities of Cleveland, Denver, and Calgary for several reasons: the inability to win or tie and score points in games against their divisional opponents, failure to attract capacity crowds to their arenas at home-site games, inability to adjust to frequent changes in ownership, and incurring operating deficits each season that had accumulated into relatively large amounts of debt on their financial statements.

Second, based on the numbers in column three of Table 3.4, the 21 teams' areas averaged 3.7 million in population during the expansion year. The Kings, Islanders, and Mighty Ducks each performed at home in large areas,

Table 3.4
NHL Expansion Teams and Stanley Cup Performances, Selected Seasons

| Year | Team | SMSA | | Stanley Cup | |
		Population	Rank	Champion	Runner-up
1967	St. Louis Blues	2.3	10th	0	3
1967	Philadelphia Flyers	4.8	4th	2	5
1967	Los Angeles Kings	7.0	2nd	0	1
1967	Minnesota North Stars	1.8	15th	0	2
1967	Pittsburgh Penguins	2.4	9th	2	0
1967	Oakland Seals	3.1	6th	0	0
1970	Vancouver Canucks	.9	NA	0	2
1970	Buffalo Sabres	1.3	24th	0	2
1972	Atlanta Flames	1.4	20th	0	0
1972	New York Islanders	11.5	1st	4	1
1974	Kansas City Scouts	1.2	26th	0	0
1975	Washington Capitals	3.0	7th	0	1
1991	San Jose Sharks	6.2	5th	0	0
1992	Tampa Bay Lightning	2.0	21st	1	0
1992	Ottawa Senators	.9	NA	0	0
1993	Anaheim Mighty Ducks	15.3	2nd	0	1
1993	Florida Panthers	3.4	12th	0	1
1998	Nashville Predators	1.1	37th	0	0
1999	Atlanta Thrashers	4.1	11th	0	0
2000	Columbus Blue Jackets	1.5	23rd	0	0
2000	Minnesota Wild	2.9	15th	0	0

Note: See the Note below Table 3.1 for the columns titled Year, Year, Population, and Rank. The NA means that SMSA population ranks were not available or measured for Canadian cities or provinces. The total populations of Canadian cities with respect to the expansion year are reported in column three of the table. The two columns for the Stanley Cup include the number of championships won, and the number of runner-up appearances of each team from the expansion year to the 2003 season. The table does not include the NHL's 2004 regular season because it was canceled before the 2005 season had finished.

Source: "National Hockey League," at http://www.nhl.com, accessed 8 August 2005, and *The World Almanac and Book of Facts*, 1967–2001.

whereas the other clubs played at home in midsized or small areas. These latter 18 markets varied in population from 6.2 million in 1991 for the Sharks in the San Jose area to 900,000 in 1970 for the Canucks in the City of Vancouver and in 1992 for the Senators in the City of Ottawa. Besides the Sharks, Canucks, and Senators, it is likely that some of the U.S. teams that played at home in areas containing between one and two million and ranked greater than 25th in total population, had operated each season at a loss during the early 2000s, and also had struggled to win their division and conference titles and thus to compete for a Stanley Cup.

Third, since their expansion years, the 21 teams listed in the table have won a total of nine Stanley Cups and finished runner-up to the league champions in 19 seasons. Specifically, the Flyers became champions in the years 1974–1975, Penguins in 1991–1992, Islanders in 1980–1983, and Lightning in 2004. Furthermore, the Flyers' five runners-up occurred between 1976 and 1997 and the Blues' three in 1968–1970; with two runners-up each were the North Stars in 1981 and 1991, Canucks in 1982 and 1994, and Sabres in 1975 and 1999; and finishing with one runner-up each were the Kings in 1993, Islanders in 1984, Capitals in 1998, Mighty Ducks in 2003, and Panthers in 1996. Based on these numbers of victories in Stanley Cup series, the most successful teams that have joined the NHL as expansions since 1967 have been the New York Islanders and Philadelphia Flyers; the least impressive expansion clubs include three former and five current clubs that had—or have not—competed in a Stanley Cup championship through the 2003 season.

Fourth, because of how the 30 teams were distributed among the six divisions and two conferences during the NHL's 2005 season, it will be a tremendous challenge for some of the low to moderate achieving expansion clubs to compete each year and qualify for the league's playoffs. In the EC, for example, the two primary rivals of the Pittsburgh Penguins are the New York Rangers and New Jersey Devils in the Atlantic Division, of the Buffalo Sabres are the Boston Bruins and Montreal Canadiens in the Northeast Division, and of the Washington Capitals are the Carolina Hurricanes and Tampa Bay Lightning in the Southeast Division. Relative to the WC, the two strongest competitors of the St. Louis Blues are the Detroit Red Wings and Chicago Blackhawks in the Central Division, of the Minnesota Wild are the Edmonton Oilers and Colorado Avalanche in the Northwest Division, and of the San Jose Sharks are the Dallas Stars and Phoenix Coyotes in the Pacific Division.

Fifth, despite the imbalances in exchange rates between the U.S. and Canadian dollars during the 2005 NHL season, as of early 2006 four clubs based in Canada are currently performing at or near the top of their divisions, whereas the other two are struggling to score points and win games. The four former teams are the Ottawa Senators and Toronto Maple Leafs in the Northeast Division and Calgary Flames and Vancouver Canucks in the Northwest Division, and the latter two teams are the Montreal Canadiens in the Northeast Division and Edmonton Oilers in the Northwest Division. In fact, this modest improvement in the overall performances of Canadian-based teams from previous seasons may have resulted from the NHL's new collective bargaining agreement. This document redistributes a larger portion of the league's revenues from the large- to small-market teams, and establishes a salary cap on payrolls whereby club owners have an economic incentive to negotiate in good faith with players' representatives and to restrict the amounts of money paid to ice hockey athletes drafted from colleges and those current players who are superstars and aging veterans qualified as free agents.

Sixth, the 21 teams listed in Table 3.4 exclude the four clubs that entered into the NHL in 1979 from the World Hockey Association. Consequently, the former Winnipeg Jets, Quebec Nordiques, and Hartford Whalers, and the current Edmonton Oilers are not considered to be expansion teams but rather clubs that transferred from a rival league. As a result, their markets and performances, and those of the NHL clubs that had relocated from one area to another after 1950 are each discussed in Chapter 4.

MAJOR LEAGUE SOCCER

Since 1950, a number of men's amateur, semiprofessional, and professional soccer leagues have been based in the United States. These sports organizations, which contained different teams and existed for various years included the American Soccer League II (1934–1983) and American Soccer League III (1988–1989); the United Soccer Association (1967) and National Professional Soccer League (1967), which merged to form the North American Soccer League (1967–1984); and the United Soccer League (1986–1999, 2003–2005), which was formerly known as the United States Interregional Soccer League. In retrospect, the emergence and operation of these leagues and the interactions between each of their teams reflect, in part, the sport's development and progress in the United States for a significant portion of the twentieth century.[7]

Prior to, during, and after a series of thrilling games played against very competitive clubs from other countries in 1993 and then successfully performing at the 1994 World Cup and other tournaments, the U.S. national men's soccer team and its players received extensive coverage in newspapers and on television broadcasts from the mainstream sports media, and more attention and support from local soccer fans in the United States. It became apparent, therefore, that the United States was ready to accept and adopt a new professional outdoor soccer league. Consequently, this environment led to the establishment of a league titled Major League Soccer (MLS), which was initially conceived in 1994–1995.

Before discussing the number and results of expansions, the league's original plans specified that MLS would be organized as a single-entity corporate structure with investors owning and managing teams, which in turn exist as independent business franchises. Furthermore, it was determined that MLS's central office has the responsibility to endorse contracts, to compensate the teams' players, and to control the trading and distributing of players among the franchises.

In 1995–1996 the league signed 10 corporate sponsors, concluded television contracts with four networks, limited each team to 5 foreign and 15 American players, assigned a salary cap of $1.25 million per team, and set a maximum salary of $175,000 to be paid a player. Also, after evaluating the bids from a group of 22 cities, MLS selected 10 teams to compete and perform before fans at home and away sites in the 1996 season. In the EC, the league had placed the Columbus Crew, DC United, MetroStars, New England Revolution, and Tampa Bay Mutiny, and in the WC were the Colorado Rapids, Dallas Burn, Kansas City Wizards, Los Angeles Galaxy, and San Jose Clash.

During 1996–2005, the MLS teams in total averaged 164 games per season and had an annual attendance of approximately 2.48 million spectators in each year. The number of total games played ranged from a high of 192 in each season of 1998–2000 to a low of 140 in 2002, and the league's total attendance varied from a maximum of 2.78 million in 1996 to a minimum of 2.21 million in 2002. Relative to the initial or 1996 season, the league drew more soccer fans than anticipated because the quality of play exceeded expectations, and thus the franchises' financial losses were less than the estimated amounts. However, despite the improvement in teams' performances in 1997, the average attendance at games declined by 16 percent from 1996, and the league's television ratings remained relatively constant.

Nevertheless, in 1998 MLS officials decided to admit one new franchise each from two reputable sports cities where there were currently no professional soccer clubs: One team was based in Chicago and the other in Miami. Accordingly, the populations of these cities contained an abundant number of ethnic fans who were passionate about the sport. Indeed, they would more likely attend a local soccer team's games than those played by professional baseball, basketball, football, and ice hockey clubs. Consequently, during the 1998 to 2004 seasons there were either 10 or 12

Table 3.5
MLS Expansion Teams and Cup Performances, Selected Seasons

Year	Team	SMSA		MLS Cup	
		Population	Rank	Champion	Runner-up
1998	Chicago Fire	9.2	3rd	1	2
1998	Miami Fusion	3.9	12th	0	0
2005	Chivas USA	16.4	2nd	0	0
2005	Real Salt Lake	1.3	35th	0	0

Note: See the Note below Table 3.1 for the columns titled Year, Team, Population, and Rank. The two columns of MLS Cup include the number of seasons that each team has won a championship and also finished as a runner-up to a champion from the expansion year to the 2005 season.

Source: "Major League Soccer," at http://www.mlsnet.com, accessed 8 August 2005, and The World Almanac and Book of Facts, 1998–2005.

teams competing in MLS. Then in 2005 another set of expansions occurred when a club to be based in Los Angeles and one to be located in Salt Lake City each became members of the league. Table 3.5 indicates data from the four expansion teams.

1998

While competing in eight of the MLS seasons, the large-market Chicago Fire averaged 15 victories and 7 losses per season and also accumulated a total of 36 ties. Besides winning Central Division titles in 2000 and 2001, the club defeated DC United 2–0 in 1998 to become the league's champion and then finished runner-up in 2000 after losing in a title game to the Kansas City Wizards by a score of 1–0, and in 2003 with a loss to the champion San Jose Earthquakes in a close game by 4–2. To achieve its wins at home in 63,000-seat Soldier Field, the club's best athletes have been midfielder Peter Nowak, defenders Lubos Kubik and Carlos Bocanegra, and such exciting players as Damani Ralph, Chris Armas, Hristo Stoitchkov, and Mark Chung. These performers improved the club's support from local fans as well. During the 1998–2005 regular seasons, the Fire ranked sixth in the league with an average annual attendance of approximately 15,500. In short, this franchise has contributed to the entertainment value of MLS because of the team's location in a highly populated area and exceptional quality of its players, and how it has performed each season in Chicago and at games in other MLS cities. According to plans, in the 2006 season the Fire is scheduled to play its home games in a new $85 million soccer stadium located in Bridgeview, Illinois.

The Miami Fusion, meanwhile, played in the league for four seasons—1998 to 2001—and competed in games at home in Fort Lauderdale's 20,400-seat Lockhart Stadium. As a member of the EC, the team finished fourth at 15–17 in 1998, fourth at 13–19 in 1999, and then third at 12–15–5 in the EC's Eastern Division (ED) in 2000. However, in 2001 the Fusion won the ED with a record of 16–5–5 but lost in the playoffs. While playing in MLS, the club established a total of four lifetime and single records. During its four-year span of 62 games, the Fusion had the league's lowest total attendance at 579,402 and average attendance at 9,345, and in the 2000 season the club's home attendance was only 7,460. In contrast, from 2000 to 2001 the team's per-game attendance while playing in Miami increased by 49.8 percent, or from 7,460 to 11,177. Despite the popularity of such outstanding players as Alex Pineda, Jay Heaps, and Pablo Mastroeni, and because of poor performances and attendances at its games in 1998–2000 and Miami area sports fans' commitments to the NBA Heat, NFL Dolphins, and MLB Florida Marlins, the Fusion experienced financial problems each year and had to suspend its operations after completing the 2001 season.

2005

Between 1999 and 2005, Toronto and several U.S. cities were mentioned in the literature as potential places to be the hosts of new MLS teams, including (listed alphabetically) Atlanta, Cleveland, Houston, Kansas City, Minneapolis, Oklahoma City, Philadelphia, San Antonio, San Diego, Seattle, and Tulsa. Basically, the league's decision about whether, when, and where to expand depends on such factors as each city's total population and average population growth, the wealth—and commitment to professional soccer—of the prospective investors in the franchises, the availability and condition of a local soccer-only stadium, and the ethnicities and passions of sport's fans in a region. Because of the city's and area's large and growing Hispanic community and the owner's successful experiences with soccer organizations in Mexico, in 2005 MLS choose Los Angeles to be the best place for a team that would play as and be named Chivas USA. For similar and other business reasons, such as the managerial ability and experience of Utah sports entrepreneur Dave Checketts, in 2005 the league also selected Salt Lake City as a site for a new team, which is named Real Salt Lake.[8]

For how well the teams performed in the 2005 season, Chivas USA had a win-loss-tie record of 5–22–5 and thus finished fifth in MLS' WC. Meanwhile, Real Salt Lake ended its first season at 4–22–6 and sixth in the WC. Even so, these teams received large attendances to the home games in their stadiums. Indeed, Chivas USA ranked fourth in the league in attendances by attracting 17,080 people per game to the 27,000-seat Home Depot Center in suburban Los Angeles while Real Salt Lake—who performs at home in 45,000-seat Rice-Eccles Stadium—ranked second in attendance among MLS teams with 18,037 per game. Therefore, it appears that Chivas USA and Real Salt Lake will prosper at their respective sites if they perform and show improvement when playing against rival teams in the WC.

SUMMARY

In total, Chapter 3 identifies the number of new teams that joined the AL and NL in MLB between 1950 and 2005, and those that entered the NFL, NBA, NHL, and MLS during this period. To evaluate these various expansion clubs as business enterprises and sports competitors, in this chapter there are five tables that provide each of the franchise's SMSA population and population ranks—except for the Canadian franchises—as of the expansion year, and the performances of the clubs. Furthermore, some demographic, economic, and sports-specific reasons are given to explain when and where the teams had located to play their home-site games. The chapter's contents also include samples of the regular season titles, post-season playoffs, and the types of championship series that the teams had participated in and won or were defeated.

According to the information gathered and presented in the tables, since 1950 MLB has expanded by 14 teams; the NFL, by nine; the NBA, by 18; the NHL, by 21; and the MLS, by 4. Reasons given for why some team owners decided to suspend operations include the replacement of franchise owners, lack of fans attending home games, teams' financial and managerial problems, and the construction of new venues with taxpayer money for why a portion of the expansion clubs had moved to other cities in small, midsized and large areas, and for why some team owners decided to suspend operations and cease to exist as members of a league. Regarding the teams that have survived, 11, or 78 percent, of baseball's post-1950 expansion teams played in the 2005 MLB season; so did nine, or 100 percent, of the new clubs in the NFL; 11, or 61 percent, in the NBA; 18, or 85 percent, in the NHL; and three, or 75 percent, in MLS.

Four of the leagues' last year to admit an expansion team was, respectively 1998 in MLB, 2002 in the NFL, 2004 in the NBA and 2000 in the NHL. Consequently, a few cities are attractive and feasible sites for expansion teams. These include Monterrey, Mexico, and Portland, Oregon, in baseball; Los Angeles and San Antonio, Texas, in football; Las Vegas, Nevada, and Louisville, Kentucky, in basketball; and Hamilton, Ontario and Quebec City in ice hockey.

Finally, because amateur, semiprofessional, and professional soccer games and events have become increasingly more popular among sports fans and specific age groups in the United States, and since the participation rate of men and women athletes in the sport has significantly accelerated since the mid to late 1990s, there is an emerging shortage in the number of MLS franchises that have home sites in the United States. As such, several cities in metropolitan areas would welcome the opportunity to host a new MLS team. Besides locating a second club in Chicago and Los Angeles, and/or in an area near New York City, five other U.S. cities are potential MLS sites: Kansas City, Kansas; Milwaukee, Wisconsin; Philadelphia, Pennsylvania; Rochester, New York; and St. Louis, Missouri. Meanwhile, in early 2006, MLS chose Houston, Texas, to be the future home of the relocating San Jose Earthquakes' franchise. The soccer team in Texas—which will play its home games in 33,000-seat Robertson Stadium—is nicknamed Houston 1836, since the City of Houston was founded in 1836.

To differentiate themselves from the American Association's Cincinnati Red Stockings, the Early National League's Boston Red Stockings changed their nickname to Boston Beaneaters in 1882. After winning six league pennants between 1883 and 1906, the Beaneaters were renamed the Boston Doves before the 1907 season. [National Baseball Hall of Fame Library, Cooperstown, N.Y.]

The Indianapolis Hoosiers played in the Western League in 1885 and 1894–99. Sam Thompson was the club's only Hall of Fame player, who in 1887 had led the National League in hits, total bases, and runs batted in as a member of the champion Detroit Wolverines. The Hoosiers won the Federal League championship in 1914. One year later, the team moved to Newark, New Jersey and finished the 1915 regular season in fifth place and six games behind the pennant-winner Chicago Whales. [National Baseball Hall of Fame Library, Cooperstown, N.Y.]

In 1890, the Players League was formed with eight teams, including the Buffalo Bison. Despite defeating the Cleveland Infants 23–2 in its first game, the Bison ended eighth at 36–96 and disbanded when the league folded after its initial season. [National Baseball Hall of Fame Library, Cooperstown, N.Y.]

After entering the American Association in 1882, the Baltimore Orioles withdrew from the league in 1889 but rejoined it the next season to replace the Brooklyn club. When the Association folded in 1892, the Orioles joined the National League and won pennants in the 1894–96 seasons and the Temple Cup Series in 1896–97. [National Baseball Hall of Fame Library, Cooperstown, N.Y.]

Detroit Tigers' great player Ty Cobb and Major League Baseball's first commissioner, Kenesaw Mountain Landis, meet in 1920. Cobb's .366 career hitting average is the best in baseball history, while Landis served as commissioner from 1921 to 1944, during which he banned eight Chicago White Sox players from the game for conspiring to fix the 1919 World Series. [Photofest]

As a group, forwards Bill and Bun Cook and Frank Boucher formed a great combination called the "Bread Line" of the New York Rangers in the National Hockey League. Their leadership led the Rangers to win Stanley Cups in the 1927–28 and 1932–33 seasons. [Hockey Hall of Fame]

Edmonton Oilers' Wayne Gretzky celebrates his fourth Stanley Cup championship with teammates in 1988. During 20 regular seasons, Hall of Famer Gretzky established 61 NHL records including all-time leading scorer (2,857 points), most goals in a season (92), and eight consecutive most valuable player awards (1980–87). [Paul Bereswill/Hockey Hall of Fame]

Center Bill Russell and coach Red Auerbach led the National Basketball Association's Boston Celtics to win numerous championships during the 1960s. In fact, Russell was a five-time most valuable player and 12-time all-star while Auerbach was the league's first coach to win 1,000 games and the only one to earn eight consecutive NBA titles. [HBO/Cinemax/Photofest]

During the early-to-mid-1970s, Julius Erving played four seasons with the American Basketball Association's New York Nets. He was voted the league's most valuable player and scoring leader twice, was voted an all-star each season, and he led the Nets to win championships in the 1974 and 1976 seasons. [Photofest]

The San Diego Siege joined the National Women's Basketball League in 2006 as an expansion team. The Colorado Chill defeated the San Diego Siege 78–71 in March 2006 to win the NWBL Championship. [Joseph Wallace/*Imperfeckshun Magazine*]

The Fall River Marksmen won American Soccer League titles in the 1923–25 and 1928–30 seasons; an Atlantic Coast League championship in 1930; and the U.S. Open Cup in both 1924 and 1930. One year later, the Marksmen merged with the New York Soccer Club to form soccer's New York Yankees. [From the archives of the National Soccer Hall of Fame, Oneonta, NY]

Pele gives tips to players at North American Soccer League games in 1979. Being an extraordinary athlete, Pele played on three World Cup championship teams, nine San Paulo championship teams in Brazil, and scored 1,281 goals in his 22-year professional career. [Photofest]

Former Yale University All-American guard William "Pudge" Heffelfinger became the first professional football player in 1892 when he was paid $500 by the Alleghany Athletic Association to play in a game against the Pittsburgh Athletic Club. Alleghany won the game 4–0 after Heffelfinger picked up a Pittsburgh fumble and ran 35 yards for a touchdown. [© Pro Football Hall of Fame/WireImage.com]

During the early 1920s Walter Lingo, who owned dog kennels located in LaRue, Ohio, organized the Oorang Indians. The team, which featured the world's greatest athlete Jim Thorpe (center, back row), played two seasons in the NFL and finished 12th at 3–6–0 in 1922 and 18th at 1–10–0 in 1923. [© Pro Football Hall of Fame/WireImage.com]

Dubbed the "Foolish" Club" by skeptics, these were the original owners of the eight American Football League franchises. Within the group are three owners of current NFL teams: the Tennessee Titans' K.S. "Bud" Adams (sitting left), Buffalo Bills' Ralph Wilson (standing, third from left), and Kansas City Chiefs' Lamar Hunt (standing, fourth from left). [© Pro Football Hall of Fame/WireImage.com]

4

Team Relocations and Transfers since 1950

In review, Chapter 2 focuses on the professional sports teams that—prior to 1950—either moved from a city in a metropolitan area to a site in another area or had transferred into another league from a rival one in the same sport. To be specific about each of the sports leagues affected, the last teams to relocate before the 1950 regular season were as follows: in Major League Baseball (MLB), the Baltimore Orioles to New York City in 1903; in the National Football League (NFL), the Boston Yanks to New York City in 1949; and in the National Hockey League (NHL), the Ottawa Senators to St. Louis in 1934. The final sports teams that had previously transferred included 4 clubs from baseball's American Association (AA) into the Early National League (ENL) in 1892, 11 from the Basketball Association of America (BAA) and 6 from the National Basketball League (NBL) into the National Basketball Association (NBA) in 1949, and a total of 11 clubs from the American Soccer League I (ASL I) and Eastern Professional Soccer League II (EPSL II) into the Atlantic Coast League (ACL) in 1929. Thus, according to the history and statistics about the respective sports leagues and franchises discussed in Chapter 2, before 1950 there were no movements of NBA teams or transfers of MLB, NFL, and NHL clubs. Furthermore, the teams in Major League Soccer (MLS) were not mentioned in that chapter because this U.S.-based league did not exist until 1996.

After considering the expansions and team relocations and transfers that had occurred thus far, each league's members may or may not have changed from the original seasons to 1950. That is, there was a total of 16 teams, or 8 each in MLB's American League (AL) and National League (NL) from the 1901 to 1950 seasons. Meanwhile, 5 clubs performed in the Central Division (CD) and 6 each in the Eastern Division (ED) and Western Division (WD) for a total of 17 in the NBA's initial or 1949 season, and in the NFL 18 teams played in the 1922 season and by 1950 a total of 13—there were 6 in the league's American Football Conference (AFC) and 7 in the National Football Conference (NFC). Finally, in the NHL, 4 teams competed in 1917 and 6 in the 1949 season.[1]

To continue on with the topics depicted in Chapter 2 and thus identify why, when, and which sports teams had relocated and/or transferred after 1950, the following four sections of this chapter are titled according to the primary leagues that had restructured and experienced changes in reorganizing their franchises. The first groups of teams discussed are those that had moved from a site to another area either within or between the AL and NL in MLB, and then those groups of teams that had relocated within and/or transferred into the NBA, NFL, and NHL. Note that between 1996 and 2005 there were no movements of teams within MLS or the transfer of clubs into MLS from any rival soccer leagues.

MAJOR LEAGUE BASEBALL

During the early 1950s there were some MLB teams whose performances and home attendances had significantly declined from previous seasons, and some clubs that played in obsolete ballparks located within small or midsized cities. Also, other baseball franchises existed at sites in areas containing another AL and/or NL team. It was a combination of these factors and new technological innovations in air, automobile, and rail transportation systems that provided an opportunity for a few franchise owners to receive permission from MLB and successfully move their teams to more profitable sites. The following relocations occurred in baseball's AL and NL after 1950.

American League

As denoted in columns three and four of Table 4.1, except for the Athletics' move from Kansas City to Oakland in 1967, the other five AL teams had relocated to less populated metropolitan areas. Even so, three, or 50 percent of the clubs—including the Oakland Athletics—improved performances at their respective postmove sites while the other three that relocated had played worse based on their lower average winning percentages.

Relative to each of the six AL relocations, two years after a syndicate headed by Bill Veeck purchased 78 percent of the Browns and a share of

Table 4.1
MLB Team Relocations and Performances, by League, Selected Seasons

				Performance	
Year	Team	From	To	Premove	Postmove
AL					
1953	Browns	St. Louis	Baltimore	.368	.389
1954	Athletics	Philadelphia	Kansas City	.409	.377
1961	Senators	Washington	Minneapolis	.426	.366
1967	Athletics	Kansas City	Oakland	.404	.532
1970	Pilots	Seattle	Milwaukee	.395	.415
1972	Senators	Washington	Arlington	.453	.409
NL					
1953	Braves	Boston	Milwaukee	.483	.575
1958	Dodgers	Brooklyn	Los Angeles	.596	.519
1958	Giants	New York	San Francisco	.467	.523
1966	Braves	Milwaukee	Atlanta	.531	.500
2005	Expos	Montreal	Washington	.479	.500

Note: Year is when each team moved from the Premove to Postmove site. The columns Team, From, and To are self-explanatory. Based on the number of seasons played at each location, Performance is the one-, two-, or three-year average winning percentages of the teams at their premove and post-move sites, that is, prior to and after relocation. For example, in the AL the Browns won 36.8 percent of its games during the 1951–1953 seasons in St. Louis and the Orioles 38.9 percent of its games in Baltimore during the 1954–1956 seasons. Regarding other types of reorganizations in professional baseball, the Milwaukee Brewers' shift from the AL to NL in 1998 was a transfer within MLB, not the transfer of a team from a rival league into MLB and is thus not included in Table 4.1.

Source: *Official Major League Baseball Fact Book 2005 Edition* (St. Louis, MO: Sporting News, 2005), 206–57, and "Major League Baseball," at http://www.mlb.com, accessed 8 August 2005.

30,000-seat Sportsman's Park in St. Louis, these owners moved the team from that city to 48,000-seat Memorial Stadium in eastern Maryland and renamed the club the Baltimore Orioles. Since 1953, the franchise in Baltimore has won AL pennants in 1966 and 1969–1971, and a total of three World Series. However, despite the opening of 48,876-seat Camden Yards in 1992, the Orioles have struggled to win games against its opponents in the ED such as the Boston Red Sox and New York Yankees. As a result, after the 2005 season the club released power hitters Sammy Sosa and Rafael Palmeiro but also established a plan to rebuild the team for the future with free agents and veterans, and with a number of Orioles players promoted from the organization's excellent minor league system.[2]

Businessman Arnold Johnson paid Connie, Earl, and Roy Mack a total of $6.7 million and acquired the Athletics in 1954. Since local baseball fans had preferred to support the NL Phillies, Johnson decided to move his team that year from 33,000-seat Connie Mack Stadium in Philadelphia to play at home in Kansas City's 30,300-seat Memorial Stadium. In a total of 13 seasons, the various Athletics teams won about 37 percent of their games and finished no higher than sixth place in the AL. As a result, in 1967 the Athletics' owner Charlie Finley—who had acquired the franchise in 1960 from the Johnson estate for approximately $3.8 million—relocated the team from Kansas City to play its home games in the 50,000-seat Oakland/Alameda County Coliseum in California, and then renamed his club Oakland Athletics. Since MLB's 1968 season, the Athletics have won six AL pennants plus World Series victories in 1972–1974 and 1989. In part, it was such pitchers as Dave Stewart and Vida Blue, and strong sluggers like Reggie Jackson and Jose Canseco that propelled the Athletics to win a majority of regular season and postseason games in their championship years and survive as a sports business franchise in the relatively small market of Oakland.

About halfway between the years when the Athletics were moved from Philadelphia to Kansas City and then had relocated to Oakland, Washington Senators owner Calvin Griffith realized that after winning a World Series in 1924 and finishing runner-up in other Series to the Pittsburgh Pirates in 1925 and New York Giants in 1933, his team needed to leave that East Coast city in order to expand its attendances, receive more exposure in the media, and generate additional revenue and perhaps some profit for the franchise. Consequently, in 1961 Griffith moved his club from 32,000-seat Washington Stadium in Washington, DC, to the city of Minneapolis to perform as the Minnesota Twins. Within 10 years after the 48,678-seat Metrodome opened in Minneapolis, the Twins had defeated the St. Louis Cardinals and Atlanta Braves each in seven games to win two World Series. Although the Twins were very competitive while in the AL's CD during the 1990s and early 2000s, Minneapolis' municipal government has refused to demolish the 34-year-old Metrodome and build a new ballpark for the club, in large part, with taxpayer money. Nevertheless, despite this resistance from government, the Twins and Hennepin County officials reached a consensus in April of 2005 to construct a $360 million, 42,000-seat open-air baseball stadium in the Minneapolis-St. Paul area.

In 1968, a group of investors paid $5.3 million for the right to own and operate the Pilots as an AL team within the relatively small city of Seattle, Washington. The franchise, however, went bankrupt because of low attendances at games played in Seattle's 25,400-seat Sick's Stadium, and the team's final standing in the 1969 season of sixth place in the WD. As a result, in 1970 a syndicate headed by the current MLB commissioner Bud Selig purchased the Pilots for $10.8 million from its owners and then moved the club from Seattle to southeastern Wisconsin to compete as the Milwaukee Brewers. Although the Brewers played its home games in 43,400-seat Milwaukee Stadium amid a very small sports market, the club won an ED title in 1981 and then in 1982 defeated the California Angels to win an AL pennant. Despite such athletes as home run hitter Gordon Thomas, Cy Young award winner Pete Vuckovich, and Most Valuable Player Robin Yount, the Brewers lost the 1982 World Series in seven games to the St. Louis Cardinals. Since the early 1980s, the club has not won a division title. Thus, when the Tampa Bay Devil Rays was assigned by MLB to the AL's ED in 1998, the Brewers shifted as a member of the AL to the NL's CD.

After playing 11 MLB seasons in Washington, DC, before limited crowds and finishing with a dismal win-loss record of 63–96 in 1971, the Senators' owner Bob Short perceived the Dallas-Fort Worth, Texas, area as a lucrative baseball market. So he moved his team from the nation's capital to 35,100-seat Arlington Stadium to perform as the Texas Rangers. Although the club has yet to win an AL pennant, the Rangers won WD titles in 1996 and 1998–1999. Because of competition from the Oakland Athletics, Los Angeles Angels of Anaheim, and Seattle Mariners during the early 2000s, the Rangers have struggled to lead the WD in the final standings or qualify as an AL wild card team.

National League

As a group, the average winning percentage of the five NL teams listed in Table 4.1 had increased from .511 in various seasons at their premove sites to .523 in an equivalent number of seasons at their postmove sites. After they had moved, three of the teams improved their performances; the Dodgers in Los Angeles and Braves in Atlanta, however, won fewer games in the seasons following their relocations. Similar to five of the teams that moved in the AL, the NL clubs also tended to relocate from more to less populated areas and from sites within large and midsized cities to smaller sport markets. Indeed, the NL team owners' decisions to relocate and select new sites were based on demographics, financial matters and local ballpark conditions, and their clubs' performances.

Two years after purchasing 100 percent of the Boston Braves—which was valued at $3.5 million in 1951—the club's principal owner Lou Perini and his brothers moved the team from 40,000-seat Braves Field in Boston to Milwaukee in order to avoid sharing a baseball market with the popular Boston Red Sox and to play in 43,400-seat Milwaukee County Stadium, which was built for the club with taxpayer money in 1953. While performing in Milwaukee, the Braves won consecutive NL pennants in 1957–1958 and a World Series in 1957 by defeating the AL New York Yankees in seven games. However, during the early 1960s the Braves played inferior baseball and finished each season in fourth to sixth place of the NL. These below-average performances and a decline in the team's home attendances at County Stadium compelled the franchise's new owners— William Bartholomay and Donald Reynolds—to relocate the team from Milwaukee in 1966 to the 51,500-seat Atlanta-Fulton County Stadium in Georgia and exist there as the Atlanta Braves. Between 1991 and 2005, the Braves excelled by winning 14 consecutive ED titles, five NL pennants and in 1995, a World Series. In fact, since the early 1990s the Atlanta Braves has been the most successful relocated franchise in MLB.

Although the Dodgers had won the 1955 World Series and nine NL pennants since 1915, the club played its home games in Brooklyn's 32,000-seat Ebbets Field, which was an obsolete facility with few commercial amenities and located in an old, ethnic, and declining neighborhood. When some government officials from the Los Angeles area offered the Dodger organization hundreds of acres of prime real estate and the construction of a new 56,000-seat baseball-only stadium as business incentives, in 1958 owner Walter O'Malley moved his club from Brooklyn to the City of Angels and renamed it Los Angeles Dodgers. Likewise, the New York Giants, which had won five World Series and 14 NL pennants between 1905 and 1954 inclusive, was also eager to play in a new stadium rather than in the dilapidated 47-year-old, 55,000-seat Polo Grounds. Thus, in 1958 the Giants' owner Horace Stoneham rejected Joan Payson's bid to keep the team in New York City. So he moved the franchise from New York to northern California and changed its nickname to San Francisco Giants. Since moving to the West Coast, the Dodgers have won five World Series and the Giants three NL pennants. Yet, in recent seasons the Dodgers and Giants have underperformed against their rivals in the WD. Indeed, the two clubs have not been consistent at winning games each season and especially at defeating the small- to midsized-market Arizona Diamondbacks, Colorado Rockies, and San Diego Padres. The Dodgers and Giants are both large-market clubs that should be more competitive in their quest to be NL champions. As such, the Dodgers' new owner Frank McCourt has committed to improving his club's performances and so has the Giants owner Peter Magowan.

While playing in Montreal's 43,739-seat Olympic Stadium, the Expos' best season was in 1994, when the club led the ED. However, because of a league-sponsored lockout, that season was cancelled after the team completed 114 games. Despite the dominance of the Atlanta Braves, the Expos had played competitively during most of its seasons while in the ED. Nevertheless, after a number of successive operating losses and a relatively large amount of debt, MLB purchased the team for $120 million from its owners in 2002 and operated the franchise with subsidies until late 2004 when the league selected Washington, DC, as the club's new home territory. Other proposals to host the Expos were also submitted from groups representing Northern Virginia and from the cities of Portland, Oregon; Las Vegas, Nevada; Norfolk, Virginia; and Monterrey, Mexico. To explain MLB's decision in choosing an optimum site for the team, Commissioner Bud Selig said in two articles, "They [Washington, DC, officials] were very aggressive. They were very tenacious. This was a very impressive bid. It shows their commitment, their dedication."[3]

During the 2005–2007 MLB seasons, the Nationals played home games in Washington's 45,000-seat RFK Stadium while a new $300 million–500 million ballpark was being evaluated and constructed in the Washington, DC, area. With respect to the 2005 season, the club led the ED for two months, and its average attendance at home exceeded 30,000 per game. As a result of this good performance in the division and above-average attendance in the 2005 season, the franchise will likely sell for more than $350 million when MLB selects a group to own and operate the club.

Based on the AL and NL teams' long-run performances, attendances per game and other results and factors at their postmove sites, the two most successful relocations in MLB since 1950 have been the Brooklyn Dodgers to Los Angeles and Milwaukee Braves to Atlanta; the least successful, the Philadelphia Athletics to Kansas City and Washington Senators to Arlington. Furthermore, according to columns five and six in Table 4.1 the five relocating NL teams as a group had higher average winning percentages and thus superior performances at their premove and postmove sites than did the six AL clubs combined.

NATIONAL BASKETBALL ASSOCIATION

Since the BAA and NBL had jointly merged their organizations to form the NBA in 1949, the movements of professional basketball teams playing in the latter league initially occurred in 1951. Then, when the American Basketball Association (ABA) folded in 1976, four of its superior teams applied and were allowed to transfer into the NBA. The years, teams' former and new locations—or rival leagues—and their performances at the premove and postmove sites during various seasons are each listed, respectively, in the six columns of Table 4.2. To explain the table's contents

Table 4.2
NBA Team Relocations, Transfers, and Performances, Selected Seasons

Year	Team	From	To	Performance Premove	Performance Postmove
Relocations					
1951	Blackhawks	Tri-Cities	Milwaukee	.410	.310
1955	Hawks	Milwaukee	St. Louis	.344	.499
1957	Pistons	Fort Wayne	Detroit	.527	.415
1957	Royals	Rochester	Cincinnati	.421	.325
1960	Lakers	Minneapolis	Los Angeles	.351	.598
1962	Warriors	Philadelphia	San Francisco	.615	.398
1963	Nationals	Syracuse	Philadelphia	.531	.539
1963	Zephyrs	Chicago	Baltimore	.269	.441
1968	Hawks	St. Louis	Atlanta	.538	.536
1971	Rockets	San Diego	Houston	.422	.402
1971	Warriors	San Francisco	Oakland	.463	.577
1972	Royals	Cincinnati	Kansas City	.402	.459
1973	Bullets	Baltimore	Washington	.536	.628
1978	Braves	Buffalo	San Diego	.418	.463
1979	Jazz	New Orleans	Salt Lake City	.406	.313
1984	Clippers	San Diego	Los Angeles	.292	.304
1984	Kings	Kansas City	Sacramento	.463	.366
2001	Grizzlies	Vancouver	Memphis	.236	.410
2002	Hornets	Charlotte	New Orleans	.565	.431
Transfers					
1976	Denver Nuggets	ABA	NBA	.642	.589
1976	Indiana Pacers	ABA	NBA	.479	.426
1976	New Jersey Nets	ABA	NBA	.666	.337
1976	San Antonio Spurs	ABA	NBA	.579	.585

Note: Table 4.1 explains the meaning of the Year, Team, From, and To columns, and also the statistics that are entered for the Premove and Postmove Performance. Table 4.2 includes the teams that relocated within the same metropolitan or market areas such as the Warriors from San Francisco to Oakland in 1971 and the Bullets from Baltimore to Washington, DC, in 1973. The movement of the Hornets from the Louisiana Superdome in New Orleans to the Ford Center in Oklahoma City to play its home games in the 2005 season was not a permanent relocation and thus is excluded from Table 4.2. The ABA is the former American Basketball Association.

Source: James Quirk and Rodney D. Fort, *Pay Dirt* (Princeton, NJ: Princeton University Press, 1992), 446–59, and "National Basketball Association," at http://www.nba.com, accessed 8 August 2005.

and expose other details about these clubs in the next two sections of this chapter, the 19 NBA teams that moved are examined as one group and then the four ABA teams that transferred are discussed.

Relocations

Based on the metropolitan areas' populations at the premove and postmove sites, some teams relocated from small and midsized to large areas, whereas others had moved from dense to less populated areas. Except for the Warriors' 1962 move from Philadelphia to San Francisco, the Zephyrs' 1963 move from Chicago to Baltimore, and the Hawks' 1968 move from St. Louis to Atlanta, the other six NBA teams had relocated to larger areas during the 1950s and 1960s. However, in the 1970s and 1980s, 50 percent of the team movements were to smaller areas, whereas in the early 2000s, the city of Vancouver was more populated than Memphis, and Charlotte's population about equaled the number of residents in New Orleans. Interestingly, the Warriors in 1971 and Bullets in 1973 each played at sites in different cities—specifically, Oakland, California, and Washington, DC—that were located within the same Standard Metropolitan Statistical Area (SMSA) as, respectively, their premove sites in San Francisco and Baltimore. In short, prior to 1970, the number of people living in a metropolitan area was a primary factor in the NBA team owners' decisions of where to relocate their clubs, but not as important a factor regarding the movements of teams that occurred from the 1970s through the early 2000s. Indeed, the latter movements depended, in part, on the availability, quality, and size of the basketball arenas at the teams' pre- and postmove sites.

After moving to other areas, 10 of the teams had improved their average winning percentages, whereas the other 9 won fewer games per season. Because of player trades and these athletes' injuries and retirements, and performing in unfamiliar venues at home before a different group of fans, some of the relocating clubs had significant changes in winning percentages at their postmove sites. The table denotes, for example, that the Lakers played much better in games at its arena in Los Angeles and elsewhere than in Minneapolis, as did the Bullets in Washington, DC, versus Baltimore, and the Grizzlies in Memphis relative to Vancouver. In contrast, the Warriors performed below expectations after leaving Philadelphia in 1962, and so did the Jazz after vacating New Orleans in 1979 and the Hornets after moving to New Orleans in 2002. Prior to relocating, the most inferior teams in the group of 19 were the Vancouver Grizzlies, Chicago Zephyrs, and San Diego Clippers, and the worst performers at their postmove sites included the Los Angeles Clippers, Milwaukee Bucks, and, while in Salt Lake City, the Utah Jazz.

From a business perspective, it is interesting to reveal when, why, and where some of the prominent NBA teams had decided to change locations and play their home games at sites in cities of different metropolitan areas. To illustrate, a syndicate headed by Bob Short became the principal owner of the Minneapolis Lakers in 1958 when the league had placed the team on probation for its financial problems. However, prior to 1958, a group of businesses and other investors in the Minneapolis area had contributed $200,000 to a fund that was established to maintain the team's solvency and its commitment to remain in that city. Even so, to succeed in winning five NBA championships between 1949 and 1954, undoubtedly the Lakers had extensive operating expenses, including the salary payments made to professional basketball's best player, George Mikan, who was the league's scoring leader. Since the team could not sustain its high-caliber performances while located in the small to midsized market of Minneapolis without significantly boosting ticket prices to home games and adding more space to the Minneapolis Auditorium, in 1960 Short decided to move his team from Minneapolis to the new 16,012-seat Los Angeles Sports Arena in southern California. As a result of relocating to a larger market, before 1971 the Lakers won five WC titles and finished runner-up in seven postseasons to either the NBA champion Boston Celtics or New York Knicks.

Prior to the club's movement to the West Coast in 1962, the Philadelphia Warriors had won a BAA championship in 1948 and NBA Eastern Conference (EC) titles in 1951 and 1956. The Warriors' Neil Johnston led the league in scoring during the 1952–1954 seasons, as did Philadelphia's center Wilt Chamberlain, when he averaged 37.9 points per game (ppg) in 1960 and 38.4 ppg in 1961, and an NBA record of 50.4 ppg in 1962. Nevertheless, despite the points scored by these two great athletes, the Warriors failed to win a league championship while based in Philadelphia. After a syndicate paid $850,000 to own the franchise, the club decided to increase home game attendances and improve its operating revenue streams by relocating from Philadelphia to northern California and play in the 12,953-seat Cow Palace with the nickname the San Francisco Warriors. Even though Chamberlain led the league again in scoring during the 1962–1964 seasons as a Warriors player in San Francisco, it was in 1967 that all-star forward Rick Berry and his teammates led the club to win an NBA title after defeating the Philadelphia 76ers. Interestingly, the 76ers' squad featured Wilt Chamberlain, who was voted the league's Most Valuable Player in 1966–1968.

The third relocation to be considered in this section involved the Bullets, which moved a distance of 50 miles within its metropolitan area when it relocated from Baltimore, Maryland, to Washington, DC, in 1973. Between 1963 and 1973, the team had won an EC championship and also three consecutive CD titles. However, even with these performances, the Bullets' owner Abe Pollin was disappointed in the club's attendances at home games and upset about the terms of its lease agreement with the city at the 11,100-seat Baltimore Arena. After being renamed the Capital Bullets when it moved in 1973 to Washington, DC, and play in the 18,700-seat Capital Centre, two years later the clubs finished runner-up to the league's champion Golden State Warriors. Then while competing in the Atlantic Division (AD) as the Washington Bullets, the team defeated the Seattle Supersonics in 1978 to earn its only NBA championship. Since 1979, the Bullets—renamed the Washington Wizards in 1997—has not appeared in an NBA final championship series.

The fourth team of special interest here and listed in Table 4.2 is the Grizzlies, a franchise that relocated from Vancouver, British Columbia, to Memphis, Tennessee, in 2001. While playing home games in Vancouver, the team was chastised by the media because of its inept performances on the court in the 19,193-seat General Motors Place. Moreover, a majority of the local businesses in the Vancouver area refused to purchase luxury suites at—and season tickets to—games and thus adequately sponsor and promote the franchise. When a Tennessee county commission agreed to finance and construct a new $250 million arena if the Grizzlies would move there from Vancouver, owner Mike Heisley choose Memphis in southwestern Tennessee as the team's new location rather than such cities as Norfolk, Virginia; New Orleans; or St. Louis, Missouri. After three NBA seasons, the Grizzlies shifted from playing at home in the 13-year-old 20,142-seat Memphis Pyramid to the new 18,165-seat FedExForum. Because of more revenues and profits generated from performing in a modern arena, and by scouting, investing in and hiring better athletes, the team increased the number of its regular season wins and has gradually become more competitive in the WC's Southwest Division.

The final team movement to be highlighted in this section is the Hornets' relocation from Charlotte, North Carolina, to New Orleans, Louisiana in 2002. During the late 1980s and early to mid-1990s, the Hornets' home games were sold out at Charlotte's 24,000-seat Coliseum. However, the community's support of the franchise had diminished after a popular Hornets player was killed in an automobile accident while racing another teammate following a practice session at the Coliseum, and after the club's co-owner George Shinn was involved in a well-publicized sexual encounter with an acquaintance that led to a lawsuit being settled in a local court. These incidents and other issues inspired Mecklenburg County area voters to defeat a bond referendum that was created to finance and build the team a new downtown arena. As a result, Shinn and his partner Ray Woolridge—who was an Atlanta resident—received permission from the NBA to relocate their franchise. After visiting several cities and evaluating the infrastructures and facilities in the metropolitan areas, the Hornets relocated from Charlotte to New Orleans to play the 2002 regular season. Because of injuries to and the trading of its key players, the Hornets' average winning percentage per season has tended to decline since 2002 while the team played at home in the 18,500-seat New Orleans Arena. Because of a damaged basketball court from Hurricane Katrina, the Hornets played their 2005 season's home games in Oklahoma City's Ford Center.[4]

Transfers

After the ABA stopped operating and disbanded in 1976, the owners of the ABA Denver Nuggets, Indiana Pacers, New Jersey Nets, and San Antonio Spurs each paid the NBA a fee of $3.2 million to join the league. Furthermore, these clubs' owners provided $1.6 million in compensation to the other ABA teams that did not enter the NBA, and the Nets furnished the New York Knicks with $4 million for invading that team's territory.

In retrospect, these four ABA teams decided to transfer into the NBA for the following three reasons. First, each of the club's regular season home attendances in their arenas was greater than the ABA teams' average. In fact, during the early 1970s the Pacers played at home before enthusiastic crowds in Indianapolis's 11,000-seat Fairgrounds Coliseum and later in the 17,400-seat Market Square Arena, and the Spurs competed at home in San Antonio's 10,100-seat HemisFair Arena. As a result, each franchise ranked in the top five in attendances among the ABA teams. Meanwhile, the Nuggets and Nets frequently played before 6,000–8,000 spectators per game in, respectively, Denver's 6,900-seat Auditorium Arena and 18,200-seat McNichols Sports Arena, and New Jersey's 8,500-seat Island Garden and New York's 17,800-seat Nassau Coliseum.

Second, while performing in the ABA, the average winning percentages of the Nets, Nuggets, and Pacers each exceeded .550. Moreover, the Pacers won league championships in 1970, 1972, and 1973 and so did the Nets in 1974 and 1976. Thus, the three teams' performances reflected their success in the league and ensured that they—and the Spurs—were valuable franchises to be welcomed by the NBA. Third, the NBA's decision to increase its size by these four clubs in 1976 likely discouraged any rival professional basketball leagues of organizing and placing a team in the metropolitan areas of Denver, Indianapolis, and San Antonio, and another team in the New York City-New Jersey area. Indeed, other existing and potential minor and major professional basketball leagues in the United States would rather locate one or more of their current or expansion teams in such former ABA cities as Anaheim, California; Charlotte, North Carolina; Dallas; Houston; Louisville, Kentucky; Memphis, Tennessee; Miami; Minneapolis; Pittsburgh; Salt Lake City; and St. Louis.

With respect to how the four ABA clubs that transferred into the NBA had performed a few seasons before and after they had shifted from one league to another, their average winning percentage in the seasons decreased from .591 to .484. That is, the Nuggets, Pacers, and Nets each played relatively worse as NBA teams for a few seasons than they did while competing in the ABA. Even so, on average the three teams outperformed some of the NBA clubs that had migrated to new locations in other years, including the Cincinnati Royals, Los Angeles Clippers, Milwaukee Bucks, and Utah Jazz.

Between the 1976 and 2005 seasons, these four teams had mixed performances while playing in the NBA. Based on winning their divisions, the most successful of the clubs has been the Spurs, which earned 14 titles, and then the Nuggets with 4, the Pacers with 3, and Nets with 2. Relative to being league champions from the 1976 to 2004 season, the Spurs won NBA titles in 1999, 2003, and 2005; the other three teams had finished as runner-up in three of the league's final series. Since the early 2000s, the Spurs' best players include first-team All-League and All-Defensive, and Most Valuable Player Tim Duncan; the club's former center David Robinson; current guard Tony Parker; and current small forward Manu Ginobili. If the Nuggets' Marcus Camby and Carmelo Anthony, Pacers' Jamaal Tinsley and Jermaine O'Neal, and the Nets' Jason Kidd and Vince Carter were to considerably excel on the court at their respective positions, then these clubs could perform above expectations during regular seasons in the future and thus qualify for the NBA playoffs.

In short, since 1979 there have been a total of four relocating teams within the league and zero transfers into the NBA. As such, the inertia of basketball teams to move from one city to another suggests that the sites of NBA clubs are increasingly viable and in stable locations. That is, the teams generate enough media exposure and earn sufficient amounts of revenues and profits to maintain their competitiveness while operating as businesses in professional basketball. Nevertheless, for demographic, economic, and sport-specific reasons, a few of the current clubs in the NBA are potential candidates for relocation. In the EC, the teams most likely to move sometime after the 2006 or 2007 season include the Raptors from

Toronto in the Atlantic Division, Hawks from Atlanta in the Southeast Division, and Bucks from Milwaukee in the Central Division. In the WC, the clubs most vulnerable to initiate a change in location are the Hornets from New Orleans in the Southwest Division, Timberwolves from Minneapolis in the Northwest Division, and Supersonics from Seattle in the Pacific Division. Accordingly, there are at least three cities that have publicly expressed an interest in providing an arena and hosting an NBA team: Louisville, Kentucky; Las Vegas, Nevada; and Norfolk, Virginia.[5]

NATIONAL FOOTBALL LEAGUE

As indicated in Table 2.2 of Chapter 2, a dozen of the NFL teams had relocated from one area to another before the 1950 season. That group of 12 involves three current clubs: the Spartans' move from Portsmouth to Detroit—and renaming the Detroit Lions—in 1934; the Redskins' relocation from Boston to the nation's capital to play as the Washington Redskins in 1937; and the Rams' move from Cleveland to Los Angeles in 1946 and then 48 years later to eastern Missouri to perform as the St. Louis Rams. The remaining nine teams that are listed in Table 2.2 canceled operations and their franchises folded. As a result, after the 1949 regular season, 29 of 32 clubs originally entered the league as expansion franchises or had transferred into the NFL from rival professional football groups.[6]

To begin the 1950 season, the NFL's American Football Conference (AFC) consisted of six teams. One year earlier, the New York Giants, Philadelphia Eagles, Washington Redskins, and Pittsburgh Steelers had played in the Eastern Division (ED) and the Chicago Cardinals in the Western Division (WD), and the Cleveland Browns had transferred into the AFC from the All American Football Conference (AAFC). Furthermore, the NFL's seven-team National Football Conference (NFC) included the Chicago Bears, Detroit Lions, Green Bay Packers, and Los Angles Rams from the WD, and the New York Yankees, Baltimore Colts, and San Francisco 49ers from the AAFC.

For why, when, and where some of these teams had moved from sites in cities to other metropolitan areas after the 1950 season, and for how the NFL had changed its internal structure in 1970, the first and second parts of Table 4.3 were developed. These parts denote the corresponding years, teams' former and relocation cities—or leagues—and the clubs' premove and postmove performances Consequently, the next two sections of this chapter discuss the two groups of teams in the table since they had changed their home-site locations or had moved into the NFL.

Table 4.3
NFL Team Relocations, Transfers, and Performances, Selected Seasons

Year	Team	From	To	Performance Premove	Performance Postmove
Relocations					
1952	Yankees	New York	Dallas	.100	.083
1960	Cardinals	Chicago	St. Louis	.199	.451
1982	Raiders	Oakland	Los Angeles	.563	.775
1984	Colts	Baltimore	Indianapolis	.206	.250
1988	Cardinals	St. Louis	Phoenix	.353	.354
1994	Rams	Los Angeles	St. Louis	.312	.375
1994	Raiders	Los Angeles	Oakland	.542	.396
1996	Browns	Cleveland	Baltimore	.479	.343
1997	Oilers	Houston	Memphis	.354	.500
1998	Oilers	Memphis	Nashville	.500	.813
Transfers					
1950	Baltimore Colts	AAFC	NFL	.083	.083
1950	Cleveland Browns	AAFC	NFL	.941	.805
1950	New York Yankees	AAFC	NFL	.548	.341
1950	San Francisco 49ers	AAFC	NFL	.758	.489
1970	Boston Patriots	AFL	NFL	.267	.262
1970	Buffalo Bills	AFL	NFL	.216	.207
1970	Cincinnati Bengals	AFL	NFL	.261	.428
1970	Denver Broncos	AFL	NFL	.318	.350
1970	Houston Oilers	AFL	NFL	.564	.203
1970	Kansas City Chiefs	AFL	NFL	.762	.641
1970	Miami Dolphins	AFL	NFL	.300	.827
1970	New York Jets	AFL	NFL	.705	.405
1970	Oakland Raiders	AFL	NFL	.903	.694
1970	San Diego Chargers	AFL	NFL	.609	.401

Note: The columns Year, Team, From, and To, and of the Premove and Postmove Performance are defined in Table 4.1. The AAFC is the former All American Football Conference and AFL is the former American Football League.

Source: *Official 2001 National Football League Record & Fact Book* (New York: National Football League, 2001), 290–99, and National Football League," at http://www.nfl.com, accessed 8 August 2005.

Relocations

Because of such factors as inferior performances in their respective divisions and/or conferences, below-average attendances at home games, being located in low-rated television and radio markets, and sale and purchase of a franchise between various groups and construction of a new stadium at another site in a different area, it was between the early 1950s and late 1990s that 10 NFL teams had moved to other cities. After relocating to new sites, these clubs' average winning percentage during seasons increased from .360 to .434. Even so, the performances of the Texans in Dallas, Raiders in Oakland, and Ravens in Baltimore had each declined relative to how these teams succeeded in games while playing at their respective premove sites. In short, the NFL teams that are represented in Table 4.3 tended to win more games in their stadiums and elsewhere during the seasons following the years from when they had moved. However, as stated previously, some of them did not prosper at their relocated sites in the short, long, or very long run.

The Yankees, for example, experienced serious financial problems after moving from New York to Texas and being renamed the Dallas Texans. As such, the club was forced to fold and thus not operate after the 1952 season. Furthermore, the Cardinals failed to thrive after more than 40 years in Chicago and then 28 in St. Louis, and also the NFL Raiders played for 12 years each in Oakland and Los Angeles. Finally, the Oilers left Houston, Texas after the 1996 season to play in Memphis and then two years later as the Tennessee Titans to compete in Nashville where a new stadium was constructed for the team. Given these facts, the following paragraphs contain some observations about the history of specific teams mentioned in this group.

Because the NFL New York Yankees won approximately 33 percent of its regular season games in 1950–1951, the franchise had financial losses of more than $1 million. As a result, in 1952 multimillionaire Giles Miller purchased the team from the NFL for $300,000 and moved it from New York City to Dallas, Texas, to play at home in the 75,000-seat Cotton Bowl. While operating as the Dallas Texans in the 1952 season, the club finished with a win-loss record of 1–11, and its opponents scored 427 points. This performance and an estimated loss of $250,000, in part, led to the franchise's demise.

After playing at home in 52,000-seat Comiskey Park and winning a total of seven games in the 1957–1959 regular seasons, the Cardinals were financially weakened. Thus in 1960, owners Violet Wolfner and Joseph Griesedieck moved the team from Chicago to eastern Missouri to compete in the league's EC with the nickname St. Louis Cardinals. During the next 28 NFL seasons, the club did not win a division or conference title, and its home attendances lagged while playing in St. Louis' 60,000-seat Busch Memorial Stadium. Frustrated with the club's outlook, Violet Wolfner's son—who was also the franchise's owner—Bill Bidwill decided the team would improve its performances and become a profitable business at another site in a different city. So in 1988 he moved the team from St. Louis to Arizona to play in Tempe's 73,521-seat Sun Devil Stadium. After being renamed the Arizona Cardinals in 1994, the team lost a wild card game to the Dallas Cowboys in 1999. Seven years later, the team has agreed to open its 2006 season in a yet-to-be-named, $355 million 70,000-seat stadium in Glendale, Arizona. When available, this facility should boost the team's home attendances, revenues, and profits, and inspire the Cardinals' coaches and players to win more games in the NFC's ED.

Subsequent to winning two Super Bowls and then an antitrust case that was filed against the NFL, the Raiders' owner Al Davis decided to relocate his club from the City of Oakland to southern California in 1982. During the majority of 13 seasons, the Raiders had above-average attendances and performances while playing at home in Los Angeles' 92,000-seat Memorial Coliseum. According to Davis, however, the Raiders sacrificed millions of dollars in revenues and profits because it had to share the Los Angeles area's sports market with the NFL Rams and several other major and minor league professional sports teams. This predicament, in part, compelled Davis to return his team in 1994 to Oakland, where the team won the AFC WD in 2000–2002 and finished runner-up to the Tampa Bay Buccaneers by a score of 48–21 in Super Bowl XXXVII.

While the franchise was located in Baltimore, Maryland, the Colts won a Super Bowl in 1971 but had to compete each season with the Washington Redskins to attract the support of football fans and households within the clubs' metropolitan area. When Baltimore government officials refused to subsidize the construction of a modern stadium to replace the city's 60,000-seat Memorial Stadium for the Colts during the early 1980s, owner Robert Irsay became disillusioned about the team's future and moved it from Baltimore to central Indiana in 1984 to play at home in Indianapolis' new 60,272-seat RCA Dome. From the late 1980s to mid 1990s, the Colts had struggled to win games against its rivals in the AFC's Eastern and then South Division. However, since drafting quarterback Peyton Manning in 1998 and acquiring running back Edgerrin James and wide receiver Marvin Harrison, the Colts team has become a threat each season to win a division and an AFC championship. Manning's ability to accurately pass a football, combined with the receiving skills of Harrison, has established

NFL records in yards gained and touchdowns scored, and James has run for at least 1,000 yards during more than one season. If these three players avoid serious injuries and are not traded to another NFL team, then the Colts should win one or more division and conference titles, and eventually a Super Bowl.

To increase the club's attendances and revenues in a much larger metropolitan area, Art Modell moved the Browns from its home site in Cleveland's 74,400-seat Municipal Stadium to the Maryland, where it became the Baltimore Ravens in 1996. One year later, the Oilers relocated from Houston to Memphis and then—renamed the Tennessee Titans—to perform at home in Nashville. Each of these teams' owners was motivated to move their operations, in part, because of the construction of a new taxpayer-subsidized facility at the postmove sites. That is, the Ravens play in Baltimore's 69,100-seat M&T Bank Stadium and the Titans in Nashville's 67,000-seat Coliseum. Indeed, these AFC teams' average attendances at home games have increased since they relocated, climaxing in 2001, when the Ravens won a Super Bowl. However, because of communication breakdowns between the teams' coaches and players and the gradual improvements of divisional rivals, since 2002 the Ravens and Titans have not performed as well as the media expected them. Whether these two franchises can consistently succeed in their respective divisions will likely depend on how effectively they play defense and on the clubs' special teams and place kickers—not necessarily on the skills of each team's quarterbacks, running backs, and wide receivers.

Transfers

After the NFL and AAFC merged in 1949 and the NFL and AFL in 1969, Table 4.3 indicates that 4 clubs had transferred into the NFL from the AAFC in 1950; 20 years later, 10 franchises from the AFL transferred to the NFL as well. In total, the average winning percentage of this 14-team group declined from .516 to .438 in a number of seasons after they had shifted into the NFL—which has become an increasingly prosperous, popular, and entertaining professional sports league. In fact, the only former AAFC or AFL teams that significantly improved in performances during the three seasons following their transfer into the NFL were the AFC Cincinnati Bengals and Miami Dolphins: The Bengals won CD titles in the 1970 and 1973 seasons, and the Dolphins concluded its 1970–1975 seasons in the ED with a total of 67 wins, 12 losses, and one tie. Remarkably, in 1973 the Dolphins finished at 14–0–0 and defeated the Washington Redskins 14–7 to win Super Bowl VII, and one year later ended its season at 12–2–0 and beat the Minnesota Vikings 24–7 in Super Bowl VIII. In contrast, because key players were traded or had retired and due to tough competition from their AFC divisional rivals, the various teams of the Chargers, 49ers, Jets, Oilers, and Raiders played much worse on average for a few seasons after they had shifted from the AFL to their respective postmove sites.

In each decade of NFL seasons since the 1960s, the most successful clubs that had transferred from the AFL were the Dolphins in the 1970s, the 49ers in the 1980s, the Broncos in the 1990s, and the Patriots in the early 2000s. Because they participated in one or more of the Dolphins' three appearances in Super Bowls between 1970 and 1979, the teams' best players included Most Valuable Players Jake Scott and Larry Csonka, and quarterback Bob Griese. During the 1980s, it was quarterback Joe Montana and wide receiver Jerry Rice that excelled for the 49ers and led the team to three Super Bowl championships. Likewise, the Broncos won league titles in 1998–1999 because of the accurate passing efforts of quarterback John Elway and the speed of running back Terrell Davis. Finally, the NFL championships won by the Patriots in 2002, 2003, and 2005 primarily resulted from the leadership of quarterback Tom Brady and the strategies to win games as developed by coach Bill Belichick and his offensive and defensive coordinators.

Since moving from their premove to postmove sites in years between the early 1950s to late 1990s, the Los Angeles Raiders and St. Louis Rams rank as the most successful NFL relocated clubs, whereas the Dallas Texans and Chicago/St. Louis/Arizona Cardinals have been the least impressive teams. From the group of 14 franchises that had transferred in total from the AAFC and AFL, the best performing teams have been the Denver Broncos and Miami Dolphins, and the least successful clubs include the former New York Yankees and Houston Oilers.

Since the league has lucrative contracts with a number of cable, satellite, and television networks, and a generous internal revenue sharing policy, the New Orleans Saints is the most likely NFL team to relocate from its current site before 2007 or 2008. This move is anticipated because the Superdome was seriously damaged during and after Hurricane Katrina had smashed the Louisiana coast and caused the City of New Orleans to flood in August–September 2005. If the Saints relocate, the new site would be in the Las Vegas, Los Angeles, or San Antonio area. Meanwhile, in the small sports market of the Indianapolis area, local taxpayers have agreed to fund a new downtown stadium for the Colts, and in 2006 or 2007 the Arizona Cardinals plan to move into a new 63,000-seat stadium in the City of Glendale. However, if the Saints continues to play its home games in New Orleans after the 2005 season, then an NFL expansion team will be placed in Los Angeles by 2008 or 2009. Before 2010, the NFL owners will also approve an existing and/or new franchise to locate in Las Vegas or the San Antonio area.

NATIONAL HOCKEY LEAGUE

As reflected in Chapter 2's Table 2.3, in 1920 owner Percy Thompson moved the NHL Bulldogs—which began to play ice hockey games in 1917—from the City of Quebec to Hamilton, Ontario, and renamed the club the Hamilton Tigers. Then in 1925, owner Bill Dwyer shifted the Tigers from Hamilton to New York City to perform as the New York Americans. After a name change to Brooklyn Americans in 1941 and 17 relatively unsuccessful seasons in New York, the franchise was canceled in 1942 when the NHL discontinued subsidizing the Americans' operations, including its regular season games played in 15,000-seat Madison Square Garden.[7]

Besides the relocations of the Quebec Bulldogs and Hamilton Tigers, the other two movements of NHL teams that had occurred before the 1950 season were the Pirates from Pittsburgh to Philadelphia to play as the Philadelphia Quakers in 1930, and four years later the Senators from Ottawa to St. Louis to compete as the St. Louis Eagles. Accordingly, the Quakers suspended operations when it finished fifth in the American Division with a win-loss-tie record of 4–36–4, and then folded after experiencing financial losses of $100,000 in the 1930 season. The St. Louis Eagles, meanwhile, went broke in 1935 when the club placed fifth in the Canadian Division's final standings at 11–31–6. When the Eagles' owner declined to invest more operating capital into the franchise, the NHL purchased the club from that owner and then redistributed its players among the existing eight NHL teams.

Between the 1950 and 1975 regular seasons, the league decided to expand in size from a total of 6 clubs to 16. Then, after the 1975 season, the NHL added 8 new franchises, and 4 had transferred into the league from the defunct World Hockey Association (WHA). The years that the various teams moved or transferred, and the names and locations of these clubs appear in Table 4.4, and so do each of their performances at the premove and postmove sites for an equivalent number of seasons. Consequently, the next section of this chapter discusses the professional ice hockey teams that relocated from one area to another after 1950. Then the contents identify and examine the four clubs that transferred from the WHA into the NHL in 1979.

Table 4.4
NHL Team Relocations, Transfers, and Performances, Selected Seasons

Year	Team	From	To	Performance Premove	Postmove
Relocations					
1976	Seals	Oakland	Cleveland	116	120
1976	Scouts	Kansas City	Denver	77	113
1980	Flames	Atlanta	Calgary	260	245
1981	Rockies	Denver	New Jersey	157	143
1994	North Stars	Minneapolis	Dallas	220	205
1995	Nordiques	Quebec	Denver	245	306
1996	Jets	Winnipeg	Phoenix	174	255
1997	Whalers	Hartford	Raleigh	195	244
Transfers					
1979	Edmonton Oilers	WHA	NHL	249	254
1979	Hartford Whalers	WHA	NHL	252	193
1979	Quebec Nordiques	WHA	NHL	267	221
1979	Winnipeg Jets	WHA	NHL	280	163

Note: The columns Year, Team, From, and To are defined in Table 4.1. The teams that merged within the NHL, such as the Cleveland Barons and Minnesota North Stars in 1978, are excluded from Table 4.4 because team mergers within a single league are not relocations or transfers. The two columns below Performance are, respectively, the total number of points scored by the teams during one-, two-, or three-seasons at their premove and postmove sites—that is, the seasons prior to and following relocation. WHA is the World Hockey Association and NHL is the National Hockey League.

Source: "National Hockey League," at http://www.nhl.com, accessed 8 August 2005.

Relocations

The Oakland Seals—which was renamed the California Golden Seals in 1970—had defaulted on its debts that year, and between 1967 and 1975 the franchise was operated by four different groups of owners. Because the club's attendances at home averaged less than 6,000 per game in the 13,100-seat Oakland/Alameda County Coliseum, and since the team finished at the bottom of its division during the 1972–1975 NHL seasons, it was apparent that the Golden Seals must vacate the Oakland area to play at a site in another city. Thus in 1976, owner Mel Swig moved his team from Oakland to northwest Ohio and renamed it the Cleveland Barons. After becoming broke again in 1977 and then being resold to multimillionaire George Gund for $5.3 million, the Barons played the 1977 season and lost approximately $3 million while operating in Cleveland's 20,000-seat

Richfield Coliseum. As a result, in 1978 the team merged its assets with the Minnesota North Stars. Because of numerous owners and coaches, and the club's inferior performances in the East and Adams Division, the Oakland/California Golden Seals was one of the least successful NHL expansions and relocated franchises of all time.

In the NHL's 1974–1975 regular seasons, the Scouts' attendances while playing at home in Kansas City's 16,300-seat Kemper Arena averaged 7,300 per game, and during these seasons the team finished in fifth place of the Smythe Division, scoring a total of 77 points. So in 1976, owner E.G. Thompson sold the franchise to a syndicate headed by Jack Vickers, who two years later moved the team from Kansas City to Denver and changed its name to the Colorado Rockies. While playing in Denver's 16,100-seat McNichols Sports Arena, the Rockies averaged about 8,400 fans per game for six seasons but struggled to score enough points in the Smythe Division to make the league's playoffs. After the 1981 season, Peter Gilbert purchased and then resold the team to businessmen John McMullen and John C. Whitehead. Rather than incur more losses while competing in Denver, McMullen and Whitehead immediately moved the club to New Jersey, where it was renamed New Jersey Devils. In the 1994, 1999, and 2002 NHL seasons, the Devils played outstanding ice hockey and won three Stanley Cups. Furthermore, while playing at home in the 19,100-seat Continental Airlines Arena in East Rutherford, New Jersey, the Devils usually have performed in each season before 15,000–17,000 fans per game.

As an expansion franchise that was established in 1972, the Flames' attendances in Atlanta's 15,278-seat Omni Coliseum had exceeded 11,000 per game. During most of the NHL seasons, however, the team placed either third or fourth in the Patrick Division. After owner Tom Cousins—who had bought the franchise in 1977—reported that the club finished with an operating loss of $2 million in the 1979 NHL season, he sold it for an undisclosed price in 1980 to a syndicate that moved the team from Atlanta to Calgary and changed the club's name to the Calgary Flames. While performing in Calgary's 17,100-seat Pengrowth Saddledome Arena, the Flames finished first in the Smythe Division with 117 points and won a Stanley Cup in 1989 by defeating the Montreal Canadiens. With respect to the 2005 season, the Flames' four competitors in the WC's Northwest Division were the Vancouver Canucks, Minnesota North Stars, Edmonton Oilers, and Colorado Avalanche.

During the 1990s, four NHL clubs relocated to sites in other cities. Except for when the team finished runner-up to the champion New York Islanders in 1981 and Pittsburgh Penguins in 1991, the Minnesota North Stars on average had finished in third or fourth place of the Adams or

Norris Divisions. Despite attendances each season that frequently exceeded 13,000 per game in Minneapolis's 15,100-seat Metro Sports Center, the team was sold in 1994 to businessman Thomas Hicks, who then moved the club from Minnesota to northern Texas to play as the Dallas Stars in the city's 18,000-seat Reunion Arena. Since moving to Dallas, the team has attracted 16,000–18,000 fans per game in the Reunion Arena and later in the 18,000-seat American Airlines Center, and won titles in the EC's CD in the 1996–1997 seasons. The Stars' best results, however, occurred in the 1998 season, when the club finished first in the WC's Pacific Division (PD) with 51 wins and 114 points, and then won a Stanley Cup by defeating the Buffalo Sabres. Evidently, the Stars must appeal to ice hockey fans in the Dallas area because of the team's performances at games and the excitement generated by such players as Jason Arnott, Jere Lehtinen, and Mike Modano.

Since 1979, the NHL Nordiques had struggled each season to earn a profit while playing at home in the 15,700-seat Colisee de Quebec Arena, which was located in the small sports market of Quebec, Canada. After a successful 1994 season—when the club won the EC's Northeast Division with 30 wins and 65 points but was later defeated in the playoffs—the Nordiques' owner decided to move the team from Quebec to Denver in 1995 to exist as the Colorado Avalanche. Similar to how the Stars performed on its rink in Dallas, for several seasons the Avalanche have played before capacity crowds in Denver's 18,100-seat Pepsi Center. This large attendance occurred, in part, because the club won PD titles in the 1996–1997 seasons and the Northwest Division in the 1998–2002 seasons, and a Stanley Cup in 2001 after defeating the New Jersey Devils. Indeed, the Avalanche is a very popular and entertaining sports team in the Denver area, and from a financial perspective, it is a successful business enterprise that operates to generate abundant revenues and an economic profit.

The Winnipeg Jets joined the NHL in 1979 after the franchise's owners Bob Graham and Barry Shenkarow jointly paid an expansion fee of $6 million to enter the league. While playing at home in the small city of Winnipeg, the club's attendances averaged about 13,000 spectators per game in the city's 15,400-seat Winnipeg Arena. However, the Jets never performed well enough to excel and win the Central, Norris, or Smythe Division titles. As a result, in 1996 the franchise's owners moved the team from Winnipeg to the state of Arizona and renamed it the Phoenix Coyotes. The Coyotes' attendances in Phoenix's 16,210-seat American West Arena averaged about 15,500 per game during the 1996–1999 seasons. But since the early 2000s, attendances have declined to approximately 13,500 for each game when the team plays at home in the 17,500-seat Glendale Arena. After existing for two years in the WC's CD, the Coyotes team was switched to the PD, in which it competes against such rivals as the San Jose Sharks and Anaheim Mighty Ducks. To win a division title and successfully advance in the NHL playoffs, such Coyotes' players as Ladislav Nagy, Paul Mara, and Mike Comrien must lead the team during games while applying their skills to score points and achieve exceptional performances.

Between 1979 and 1997, the New England Whalers—which was renamed the Hartford Whalers in 1979—played its home games in the city's 15,633-seat Civic Center Coliseum. In contrast to the Dallas Stars and Colorado Avalanche, the Whalers failed to win more than one title while performing for various seasons in the Adams, Northeast, Norris, or Patrick Division. Because of declining attendances at its home games in the Coliseum and a new arena that was scheduled to be built for the team after it relocated, the Whalers moved from Hartford to Raleigh, North Carolina, after the 1996 season and became the Carolina Hurricanes. As such the club won an EC Southeast Division (SD) title in 1999, and three years later the Hurricanes played for a Stanley Cup but was defeated by the Detroit Red Wings. Since the 2001 season, the Hurricanes' attendances in Raleigh's 18,763-seat RBC Center have averaged more than 15,000 per game because the team is exciting, competitive, and well coached. To entertain ice hockey fans in the RBC Center—which is also the home court of the North Carolina State University basketball team—the Hurricane's top scorers in points during the 2005 season included Cory Stillman, Eric Staal, Justin Williams, and Rod Brind'Amour.

Transfers

The World Hockey Association (WHA) existed as a league from 1972 to 1979. In the 1972 season there were 12 teams in the league, and during the next seven years some of its teams bankrupted and dissolved, such as the Baltimore Blades, Calvary Cowboys, and Ottawa Civics. Meanwhile, a few expansion clubs had entered the WHA, including the Cincinnati Stingers, Indianapolis Racers, and San Diego Mariners. While operating as a private business, the league incurred losses of about $12 million per year. Consequently, in 1979 the WHA disbanded and according to an agreement that was concluded with the NHL, four of its veteran clubs transferred into the senior league. It cost each of these four teams a $6 million fee to join the NHL and another $1.5 million to compensate the WHA franchises that had not transferred into the NHL.[8]

After the four clubs switched leagues, from 1979 to 1984 the home-game attendances increased for the Oilers in Edmonton, Whalers in Hartford,

Nordiques in Quebec, and Jets in Winnipeg. That is, the number of spectators in attendance at their arenas rose for the Oilers from an estimated 450,000 in 1979 to 680,400 in 1984, and for the Whalers from 394,300 to 548,100, for the Nordiques from 429,700 to 603,200, and for the Jets from 531,800 to 574,400. Furthermore, the teams' performances had changed in the seasons following their transfer into the NHL. With respect to league championships, for example, the Oilers won a Stanley Cup in 1984–1985 and 1987–1988, and in 1990. In contrast to the Oilers, the other three clubs failed to emerge from any of the playoffs they had participated in, and thus did not compete in a championship series. As such, the Whalers, Nordiques, and Jets each relocated to other sites during the mid to late 1990s as indicated in Table 4.4. In other words, the Oilers have been the only former WHA team to play at its original site from 1979 to 2003 and in the NHL's 2005 season. If the team can maintain its attendances at home in Edmonton's 17,100-seat Rexall Place to at least 16,000 per game, then the Oilers will be financially capable of retaining its headquarters and home rink in that southwestern Canadian city.

If the two groups of NHL franchises in Table 4.4 are consolidated into one listing, six, or 50 percent, of them scored more total points during seasons at their postmove sites than they did for the same number of seasons at the premove sites. The most improved clubs of the combined groups include the Denver Rockies, Colorado Avalanche, and Phoenix Coyotes. In contrast, the teams that had scored significantly fewer points and fell in performances were three of the former WHA members: the Hartford Whalers, Quebec Nordiques, and Winnipeg Jets. In short, the table indicates that about one-half of the 12 clubs each scored about the same number of points and achieved similar results in performances at their premove sites as they accomplished in later seasons at the postmove sites.

MAJOR LEAGUE SOCCER

In early 2006, MLS officials announced the first relocation of an existing team. That move occurred because the Earthquakes attracted a total of only 13,037 fans to its home games in San Jose's Spartan Stadium during the 2005 season. To continue as a franchise in MLS, a decision was made to move the club from northern California to Texas and be nicknamed Houston 1836, which was the year that the City of Houston was founded. The league chose Houston as a site because of the area's large population, and especially since the city is the home of approximately 1.7 million Hispanic people, who traditionally prefer soccer to other sports.

To establish a diversified fan base in southeastern Texas and likewise exploit the local market, Houston 1836 is scheduled to play its first three MLS seasons in 32,000-seat Robertson Stadium, and also to compete in a series of "friendly" matches against clubs from Mexico. Furthermore, English- and Spanish-speaking television stations in Houston will broadcast the team's games. Regarding Houston 1836's future prospects in forthcoming seasons, MLS commissioner Don Garber said, "We have always believed that a combination of the diversity and the passion of the city's sports fans and the size of the market would lead to success for an MLS team. We've also had great success with the international markets, maybe as much as we've had in any city."[9]

SUMMARY

Chapter 4 identifies and discusses the post-1950 movements and transfers of sports teams within and between selected professional leagues. These reorganizations of teams influenced the structure, conduct, and operation of divisions and conferences in the AL and NL of MLB, and also those in the NBA, NFL and NHL. In total, there were 48 relocations and 22 transfers of clubs affecting these leagues including, respectively, 11 and 0 in MLB, 19 and 4 in the NBA, 10 and 14 in the NFL, and eight and four in the NHL. Tables 4.1–4.4 document and examine these types of reorganizations, listing in columns the years when relocations and transfers had occurred, the names of the teams and their former and new sites by city, and each of the club's premove and postmove performances.

With respect to the sports leagues, in MLB the AL's Athletics and Senators and the NL's Braves have each moved twice since 1950; the other baseball teams that relocated once have continued to exist at their respective sites. Despite the previous failures of two Senators' teams to remain in the nation's capital as a home site, the Washington Nationals—which was the former Montreal Expos—had a somewhat successful 2005 season while playing in the Washington, DC, area.

Regarding the NBA, 9 clubs had moved between 1950 and 1970 and another 10 after 1970; in 1976 there were four franchises that transferred from the ABA into the NBA. Interestingly, the teams that moved performed differently in winning percentages after relocating to another site. Meanwhile, most of the former ABA teams won fewer games during seasons after they had transferred into their rival's league. Because of structural damages to the Louisiana Superdome, after the 2006 season the NBA Hornets may leave New Orleans to a site in another city.

Except for the Memphis Oilers and New York Yankees, as of 2006 the existing NFL teams that previously had moved and those that transferred from other professional football leagues are reasonably secure at their current locations. Even so, between 2008 and 2010 the league will place one expansion or relocating team in Los Angeles and perhaps another one in the Las Vegas or San Antonio area. Unless a new stadium is constructed for each of them in the next few years, the New Orleans Saints and Minnesota Vikings are the most likely NFL clubs to leave their respective cities.

Due to high operating costs and relatively low revenue streams, the movements of one or more NHL clubs to other sites have an above-average probability of occurring before the 2007 or 2008 season. However, the league may decide to buy out and then merge some of the teams that exist in a region of the United States, or simply terminate the weakest of these franchises.

5

Expansions and Mergers of Alternative Leagues since 1876

Chapters 1–4 focus on the types of reorganizations that had occurred within—and the transfers of teams between—several of the primary and other professional sports leagues. Besides the different changes affecting the structures of these specific organizations, during the late 1800s and from the 1900s to early 2000s, a number of alternative U.S. professional sports leagues and their member teams were formed and scheduled regular seasons and perhaps conducted postseasons and championship series. Indeed, some of the inferior leagues that were mentioned but not highlighted in the previous chapters had only existed in the short run and as competitive businesses and options for fans because the sports markets preferred one or more of the teams playing in a dominant league such as the National Basketball Association (NBA) and National Football League(NFL).

A few of the secondary professional leagues or associations contained in Chapters 1–4 for each sport include baseball's Players League, American Football Leagues I–III, National Basketball League, and hockey's National Hockey Association and World Hockey Association. Nevertheless, because of commercial, demographic, economic, legal, and sport-specific reasons, many local and regional sports markets in metropolitan areas of North America were not fully developed and thus unable to support and sustain the operations of the Players League and other such organizations. As a result, they eventually failed.

To extend the scope and analysis of topics discussed in earlier parts of this book, Chapter 5 identifies and examines the various expansions, mergers, and cancellations that occurred within some of the more prominent alternative leagues—and between these and the primary leagues—in each of the sports during and after the late 1800s. The leagues and teams highlighted and selected for discussion in this chapter were recognized and admired by million of American sports fans, and therefore these entities played an important role in the development and growth of the industry's business activities in cities of the United States.

To review two of the former chapters' contents, the various teams listed in the tables and examined in Chapter 1 were members of baseball's Early National League and the National Football League and National Hockey League; the Basketball Association of America, National Basketball League, and National Basketball Association; and the American Soccer League. With respect to the topics in Chapter 3, the numerous teams played in the American League or National League of Major League Baseball, and in the National Football League, National Basketball Association, National Hockey League and Major League Soccer.

In contrast, the alternative sports leagues and associations selected for and portrayed in Chapter 5 had approved the entry of one or more expansion teams that were not listed in the tables contained in Chapters 1 or 3. Furthermore, these former and current sports organizations and their respective teams were competitors such that, in part, they challenged the power and authority of some elite leagues mentioned in the previous paragraph, including Major League Baseball and the National Football League, National Hockey League and National Basketball Association.

Therefore in this chapter, there are three tables of information. In turn, each table has columns listing the respective years and names of expansion teams that played within each of the alternative leagues, and other columns that denote the performances of the different clubs in various seasons and postseasons, and columns providing some characteristics about the teams' home sites and their areas.

To be specific, Chapter 5 is divided into four sections. The first section that follows next involves the expansions of secondary sports leagues and associations in professional baseball, football and basketball for the years 1891 to 1976, while the second section explores the expansions of teams in one each professional soccer league and ice hockey association that occurred between 1967 and 1984. Then the third section examines new franchises that entered professional football, women's basketball and men's soccer organizations during 1984 to 2005, and the fourth section discusses the expansion teams in women and men's basketball leagues with respect to the early 2000s.[1]

ALTERNATIVE LEAGUES I

Prior to the establishment of baseball's minor Columbian League—renamed the Federal League (FL) during 1913—the other alternative leagues in professional baseball that had existed for at least one season included the National Association of Professional Baseball Players (NAPBP) in 1871–1875, Union Association (UA) in 1884, and Players League (PL) in 1890. As discussed in Chapter 1, a total of 14 teams had joined the NAPBP between 1871 and 1875. Nonetheless, because of the league's reputation of being disorganized and experiencing excessive turnover of its franchises each season, and the financial instability of the teams' operations, and their lethargic performances in games, the NAPBP's expansion clubs are excluded from and not analyzed in this chapter. Furthermore, due to financial problems and competition from baseball's Early National League (ENL) and American Association (AA), the UA and PL had each folded after one year. Thus, the UA in 1884 and PL in 1890 did not have an opportunity to add new teams prior to and following these seasons. Therefore in baseball, this portion of Chapter 5 highlights the histories and performances of expansion clubs in the AA and FL.

According to the information in Table 5.1, on average the AA's 14 expansion teams existed approximately two seasons and won at least 41 percent of their games. With respect to how long some of the teams had played in the AA, the large-market Brooklyn Bridegrooms competed for seven seasons and New York Metropolitans five, and the small-market Columbus Solons lasted for three campaigns. Meanwhile, eight, or 57 percent, of the clubs did not establish local, regional, or national fans bases and had to terminate their operations after one season. These franchises included, for example, the Rochester Broncos in 1890 and Philadelphia Athletics in 1891.

Furthermore, although each team had played near or above .500, it was inevitable that the Columbus Buckeyes and Toledo Maumees would fail to exist for many seasons since they played their home games at sites located in relatively small to midsized cities of Ohio. Despite each team finishing first in a regular season and winning an AA pennant, in postseason tournaments the Metropolitans was defeated by the National League (NL) Providence Grays in 1884 and the Bridegrooms by the NL New York Giants in 1889. In short, the Bridegrooms and Metropolitans were the two most successful expansion teams in the AA. The Washington Nationals and Indianapolis Hoosiers, meanwhile, had the lowest winning percentages and each of them played for only one year and finished, respectively, in 13th and 12th place in the league's 1984 regular season.

The AA and NL merged when four AA teams accepted buyouts and stopped performing and another four ceased operating and joined the NL after the 1891 baseball season. This meant that the former league was terminated before the start of the 1892 regular season. Twenty-two years after the AA-NL had successfully consolidated, the six-team Columbian

Table 5.1
Expansions of Alternative Leagues I, by Team, Selected Seasons

Year	Team	Performance		Population	
		W-L%	Champion	Total	Rank
AA (1882–1891)					
1883	Columbus Buckeyes	.484	0	.1	33rd
1883	New York Metropolitans	.479	1	1.2	1st
1884	Brooklyn Bridegrooms	.487	1	.6	3rd
1884	Indianapolis Hoosiers	.271	0	.1	24th
1884	Washington Nationals	.190	0	.2	14th
1887	Cleveland Blues	.338	0	.3	10th
1888	Kansas City Cowboys	.363	0	.2	24th
1889	Columbus Solons	.490	0	.1	30th
1890	Rochester Broncos	.500	0	.2	22nd
1890	Syracuse Stars	.433	0	.1	31st
1890	Toledo Maumees	.515	0	.1	34th
1891	Cincinnati Kelley's Killers	.430	0	.3	9th
1891	Philadelphia Athletics	.525	0	1.1	3rd
1891	Washington Senators	.326	0	.3	14th
FL (1913–1915)					
1914	Baltimore Terrapins	.425	0	.6	7th
1914	Brooklyn Tip Tops	.480	0	4.7	1st
1914	Buffalo Blues	.508	0	.4	10th
AFL (1960–1969)					
1966	Miami Dolphins	.285	0	1.0	26th
1968	Cincinnati Bengals	.267	0	1.2	21st
ABA (1967–1976)					
1972	San Diego Conquistadors	.360	0	1.2	23rd

Note: The columns Year and Team are self-explanatory. Performance includes W-L%, which is the average winning percentage of each expansion team during its regular seasons at the site, and Champion, which is the total number of league championships that were won by each team. Population includes Total and Rank, which are respectively, the total population in millions and rank of each U.S. urban area or Standard Metropolitan Statistical Area (SMSA) based on the year entered in column one. The American Association is designated as AA, Federal League as FL, American Football League as AFL, and American Basketball Association as ABA.

Source: *Official Major League Baseball Fact Book 2005 Edition* (St. Louis, MO: Sporting News, 2005), 186–87; *Official 2001 National Football League Record & Fact Book* (New York: National Football League, 2001), 297–99; "American Basketball Association," at http://www.remember-theaba.com, accessed 8 August 2005; *The World Almanac and Book of Facts* (New York: World Almanac Books, 1950–2004); "Sports History," at http://www.hickoksports.com, accessed 13 September 2005.

League was formed as a U.S.- based minor league. Then before the 1913 season began, its name was changed to Federal League, and some of its member teams played their home games in relatively low-populated cities such as Covington, Kentucky, and Indianapolis, Indiana, while other clubs competed at home in more populated markets like Chicago and St. Louis, Missouri. During the 1913 season, the franchise based in Covington was moved from Kentucky to eastern Missouri to perform as the Kansas City Packers, and one year later, the FL added three new teams. In fact, each of the expansion clubs played in small-sized ballparks that had less than 20,000 seats. That is, the teams and their stadiums were the Terrapins in Baltimore's Terrapin Park, Tip Tops in Brooklyn's Washington Park, and Blues in Buffalo's Federal League Park. Also, in 1914 Baltimore and Buffalo hosted no MLB clubs.

After winning at least 50 percent of their games in 1914, during the next season, each of the three teams finished below fifth place in the FL's final year. In the end, it was the league's losses of $2 million, bankruptcies of some teams, and the untimely death of Tip Tops owner Robert Ward that, in part, pressured the FL to conclude an agreement with organized baseball and withdraw its antitrust suit against the AL and NL but then fold in 1915. That is, with MLB franchises playing baseball games at home in 11 prominent U.S. sports markets in 1915—with two each clubs in Boston, Chicago, Philadelphia, and St. Louis, and three in the New York City area—it was inevitable that the FL could not continue to operate and would eventually expire. Consequently, the FL had opened its first season as a minor league with six teams in 1913, and two years later finished as a major league with eight clubs being active in the final standings and challenging MLB in Brooklyn, Chicago, Pittsburgh, and St. Louis.

During the late 1950s, National Football League (NFL) officials rejected applications that had been submitted from several wealthy and prominent football enthusiasts who wanted to own and operate expansion teams in the league. As a result of being denied entry into the NFL, in 1960 businessman Lamar Hunt received the support of and commitment from at least six ownership groups that wanted to be included in the formation of a new professional football league. Thus Hunt and his colleagues met and established the American Football League (AFL). Besides becoming an organization, the AFL also filed an antitrust suit against the NFL for illegally amending its bylaws and maneuvering contractual agreements to allow new expansion teams to be placed in Dallas in 1960 and Minnesota in 1961, and permitting the NFL Cardinals to move from Chicago to St. Louis before the 1960 season.

In its initial season, the AFL consisted of four teams each in the Eastern Football Conference (EFC) and Western Football Conference (WFC). However, for the AFL to market and differentiate itself from the NFL, in 1961 the two conferences were changed, respectively, by being renamed the Eastern Division (ED) and Western Division (WD). Because of a strong demand for professional football in several of the nation's local markets, the AFL—after competing for six seasons—decided to increase the total number of teams and accept bids from entrepreneurs who would locate new clubs at sites in midsized cities where football was a popular sport and a strong fan base could be established, and that lacked an NFL club.

Thus in 1966, a syndicate headed by general partners Joe Robbie and Danny Thomas Enterprises paid the AFL team owners a total of $7.5 million in fees to permit their franchise to join the league, be nicknamed Miami Dolphins, and play at home in the city's 74,200-seat Orange Bowl. While it competed in the league's ED, the Dolphins' best season was in 1968, when the team finished in third place with five wins and eight losses. Since becoming an NFL team in 1970, the Dolphins has won division and conference titles, triumphed in two Super Bowls, and finished runner-up to the league's champions in 1972, 1983 and 1985.

Two years after the Dolphins became a professional football franchise based in Miami, an investment group led by principal owner Paul Brown spent $7.5 million as a fee to enter a team—the Cincinnati Bengals—to perform in the AFL and at home in the city's 45,000-seat Nippert Stadium. While playing in the league during the 1968 and 1969 seasons, the Bengals finished in fifth place each season in the WD. As a member of the NFL's American Football Conference (AFC) since 1970, the club has appeared in but narrowly lost two of the league's championship games: to the San Francisco 49ers by scores of 26–21 in Super Bowl XVI and 20–16 in Super Bowl XXIII. Nevertheless, despite many years of inferior performances the Bengals' quarterback Carson Palmer and wide receiver Chad Johnson have combined on offense to inspire the team and propelled it to win the AFC's North Division in the 2005 NFL season. The skills and achievements of these two players and their teammates denote that this franchise should improve its performances in future seasons and especially while playing in Cincinnati's 65,600-seat Paul Brown Stadium.

Although several of the teams in the American Basketball Association (ABA) had moved to sites in other cities during the league's nine seasons, there was only one expansion since NBA teams existed in the most prolific U.S. sports markets. Even so, in 1972 owner Leonard Bloom paid ABA officials $1 million to allow his team—the San Diego Conquistadors—to join and play in the league. While performing at home in San Diego's 3,200-seat Peterson Gymnasium and in arenas at other teams' sites, the club had won about 36 percent of its total games. Despite being sold by Bloom in 1975 for $2 million to Frank Goldberg and being renamed San Diego Sails, the team continued to flounder while playing before small audiences in San Diego's Golden Hall Arena. Finally, after winning only 3 of 11\games at the beginning of the 1975 ABA season, the franchise was folded by Goldberg in November of that year.[2]

ALTERNATIVE LEAGUES II

The next two groups of expansion teams to be highlighted and evaluated in this chapter had existed as members of the North America Soccer League (NASL) and World Hockey Association (WHA). The expansion years and the names and performances of these clubs are reported in columns one through four of Table 5.2. Also, column five of the table lists the total population of the teams' areas as of the expansion year and in column six is the population rank of each area—except for the cities of Montreal, Toronto, and Vancouver, British Columbia, in Canada.

To maximize the quality and presence of the sport in North America by establishing a larger fan base, in 1968 the United Soccer Association (USA)—which had imported a number of foreign clubs in its initial season—and the National Professional Soccer League (NPSL)—which formerly included 10 teams consisting of U.S. and international talent—decided to merge and form the NASL. As a result of combining the most prestigious amateur and professional soccer leagues existing in America and Canada, the NASL teams were able to lure and hire several outstanding players, who then attracted thousands of soccer fans to attend their teams' home and away games. However, because the league included a number of marginal franchises whose owners had limited financial capital and scarce resources, the NASL dwindled in size from 17 teams in 1968 to 5 in 1969. As the league regained its respectability and exposure in the media after 1969, it gradually admitted the entry of new teams and flourished during many of the regular seasons that were scheduled in the mid to late 1970s to the very early 1980s.

Before highlighting and discussing some of the unique expansion teams that are listed in Table 5.2, a few facts about the NASL's 17-year history are interesting to recall. First, the number of games played by teams in the league ranged from a total of 14 per team in 1972 to 32 during each season of 1980–1982; second, the number of clubs varied

Table 5.2
Expansions of Alternative Leagues II, by Team, Selected Seasons

		Performance		Population	
Year	Team	W-L%	Champion	Total	Rank
NASL (1967–1984)					
1970	Rochester Lancers	.462	1	.9	37th
1970	Washington Darts	.603	0	2.9	7th
1971	Montreal Olympiques	.367	0	2.7	–
1971	New York Cosmos	.640	5	11.6	1st
1971	Toronto Metros	.486	0	2.6	–
1973	Philadelphia Atoms	.474	1	4.7	4th
1974	Baltimore Comets	.479	0	2.1	14th
1974	Boston Minutemen	.468	0	3.9	6th
1974	Denver Dynamos	.329	0	1.4	24th
1974	Los Angeles Aztecs	.537	1	6.9	3rd
1974	San Jose Earthquakes	.395	0	1.2	30th
1974	Seattle Sounders	.548	0	1.4	23rd
1974	Vancouver Whitecaps	.609	1	1.0	–
1974	Washington Diplomats	.511	0	3.0	8th
1975	Chicago Sting	.531	2	6.9	3rd
1975	Hartford Bicentennials	.347	0	1.0	36th
1975	Portland Timbers	.486	0	1.0	34th
1975	San Antonio Thunder	.386	0	.9	37th
1975	Tampa Bay Rowdies	.521	1	1.3	25th
1978	Colorado Caribous	.266	0	1.5	21st
1978	Detroit Express	.571	0	4.4	5th
1978	Houston Hurricane	.501	0	2.6	11th
1978	Memphis Rogues	.323	0	.9	40th
1978	New England Tea Men	.531	0	3.9	6th
1978	Philadelphia Fury	.348	0	4.8	4th
1983	Team America	.333	0	3.5	9th
WHA (1972–1979)					
1974	Indianapolis Racers	.343	0	1.1	32nd
1974	Phoenix Roadrunners	.443	0	1.1	31st
1975	Cincinnati Stingers	.442	0	1.3	26th
1975	Denver Spurs	.341	0	1.4	22nd

Note: The columns Year, Team, Performance, and Population are described in Table 5.1. The – indicates that the population of three Canadian cities were not ranked as SMSAs and thus not reported in various editions of *The World Almanac and Book of Facts* and in the U.S. Census. The North American Soccer is indicated as NASL and World Hockey Association as WHA.

Source: "North American Soccer League," at http://www.nasl.com, accessed 13 September 2005; "World Hockey Association," at http://www.wha.com, accessed 13 September 2005; *The World Almanac and Book of Facts* (New York: World Almanac Books, 1970–1980).

from a low of 5 in 1969 to a high of 24 in 1978 to 1980; third, the teams' attendances averaged 9,100 spectators during each of the 17 seasons; the lowest average was 2,888 in 1969 and the highest 14,400 in 1980; and fourth, there were 24 NASL franchises that existed for five or more years before folding their operations, even though most of the teams' rosters were significantly reshuffled by the league after each of the seasons had been completed.

As denoted in column one of Table 5.2, the NASL had expanded by 14 teams between 1970 and 1974 inclusive and then by 12 from 1975 to 1983. These 26 clubs, on average, played at least five seasons and won about 46 percent of their games and a total of 12 championships. Based on their performances, the most successful of the NASL expansion teams was the New York Cosmos. In 14 seasons, this franchise won the most games at 221, had the highest proportion of wins at 64 percent, attracted the most attendance of any team at 30,000–40,000 per game, and earned a total of five championships while playing a portion of its games at home in four different stadiums. Indeed, the club excelled, in part, after a great Brazilian player named Pele signed a three-year, $4.5 million contract in 1975. Besides the Cosmos in New York, the Vancouver Whitecaps, Washington Darts, and Chicago Sting were also very competitive teams. As a group, these clubs won three championships and 58 percent of their games. In contrast, 9, or approximately 33 percent, of the NASL's expansion teams won less than 40 percent of their total games; the worst of these clubs included the Colorado Caribous, Memphis Rogues, and Team America.

Regarding other features about some of the expansion teams that are listed in Table 5.2, the clubs that followed the large-market Cosmos in average attendances were teams located in small to midsized cities such as the Seattle Sounders and Tampa Bay Rowdies—which each attracted 18,000 spectators per game—and then the San Jose Earthquakes and Vancouver Whitecaps, with 15,000 each per game. Interestingly, the Earthquakes were popular for 11 seasons while playing home games in San Jose's 31,000-seat Spartan Stadium despite recording a below-average winning percentage. In contrast, the teams that attracted less than 4,000 in average attendances during their existence included the Baltimore Comets, Hartford Bicentennials, Montreal Olympiques, and Washington Darts. After two NASL seasons of competition, the Comets moved from Baltimore to Las Vegas and the Darts from Washington, DC, to Miami, and the Bicentennials and Olympiques each folded as franchises after playing three seasons in the league.

Several of the 26 NASL expansion teams played their games at home in relatively large football stadiums. For example, the Atoms performed in Philadelphia's 68,000-seat Veterans Stadium for four seasons, the Express in Detroit's 80,300-seat Silverdome for three seasons, Dynamos in Denver's 75,100-seat Mile High Stadium for two seasons, and Team America in Washington, DC's 45,000-seat RFK Stadium for one season. Furthermore, three teams that did not move to another site decided to change their names after one or more seasons. For example, in 1977 Hartford was renamed Connecticut Bicentennials, in 1979 the Metros began playing as Toronto Blizzard, and in 1983 San Jose became Golden Bay Earthquakes. In short, some of the new NASL teams played their home games in oversized stadiums since soccer-only facilities did not exist at those sites, and other clubs changed their nicknames as a marketing gimmick.

During the late 1970s, price and wage inflation escalated causing market interest rates to soar in the United States. In turn, the inflation cost franchise owners more money and additional resources to operate their professional soccer teams. Therefore, as the debts accumulated for many of the league's organizations between 1978 and 1981, 17 teams collapsed and had to terminate their charters with the NASL. Meanwhile, the number of games played per team declined from 32 for 21 clubs in 1981 to 24 for 9 in 1984, and the teams' average attendances per game fell from approximately 14,100 to 10,700 during this four-season period. In summary, it was the overspending by many NASL team owners to hire and compensate high-priced U.S. and foreign players, the fact that sports fans did not support their local professional soccer clubs, and the country's inflated economic performances during the late 1970s and early 1980s that were contributing factors that forced the league to close down and dissolve in March 1985.

Organized in 1971 by businessmen Garry Davidson and Dennis Murphy as a sport venture and alternative to the NHL, the WHA launched its initial season one year later with six teams each in the ED and WD—whereby eight were based at sites in the United States and four in Canada. In general, the league's officials had planned to locate WHA clubs in midsized Canadian and small American cities that did not host NHL franchises, and to place some clubs in large U.S. markets that were the home sites of NHL teams. After a series of relocations by a few of the WHA franchises, in 1974 the league expanded by two teams. Specifically, investors John Weissart and Dick Tinkhaur paid an expansion fee totaling $2 million to the WHA franchise owners to permit their team—the Indianapolis Racers—to perform in the city's 17,000-seat Market Square Arena, which was also the home site of the NBA Indiana Pacers. Besides the Racers, in 1974 a syndicate headed by investor Bert Gaetz provided $2 million in fees for the Phoenix Roadrunners to play at home in the city's 12,800-seat Veterans Memorial Stadium.

As indicated in Table 5.2, the Racers existed for four WHA seasons in Indianapolis plus a portion of a fifth season. In total, the club won 118, or 35 percent, of its games. After filing for bankruptcy in 1975 and two years later being sold by owner Paul Deneau to Nelson Skalbania for $1 million, the Racers folded its operations midway through the 1978 season when its win-loss-tie against league opponents was 5–18–2. Meanwhile, during three regular seasons in Phoenix, the Roadrunners compiled a record of 106–114–18 in the league's final standings. However, as a result of its poor performances in Veterans Memorial Stadium and severe revenue shortages, it was necessary for Gaetz's group to cancel the franchise before the 1977 season. In retrospect, the Racers and Roadrunners failed because they experienced low attendances while playing games in their home arenas, did not receive enough exposure from the print media in the Indianapolis and Phoenix areas, and simply provided inferior ice hockey entertainment to their local and regional fans.

To grow the sport by penetrating midsized markets in the United States, the WHA added two new franchises in 1975. For an expansion fee of $2 million per franchise, businessmen Brian Heekin and Bill DeWitt were permitted to enter the Cincinnati Stingers into the league to perform at home in the city's 15,820-seat Riverfront Coliseum. In four WHA seasons, the Stingers won 142, or 44 percent, of its total games. Nevertheless, due to financial and managerial problems, the franchise canceled its operations and folded in 1979. Second, the WHA allowed entrepreneur Ivan Mullenix to locate his Spurs team in Denver and play at home in the city's 16,800-seat McNichols Sports Arena. After 14 wins, 26 defeats, and one tie, and operating losses estimated at $2 million while playing one-half of a season in Denver, Mullenix moved his franchise to Canada and changed the club's name to Ottawa Civics. Since the team continued to lose money while playing in Ottawa's 10,500-seat Civic Center, the Civics folded after completing the league's 1975 season.

For several reasons, the WHA had to disband in 1979. That is, the failure to continue operating as a business occurred, in part, because the league's large market teams could not effectively compete for sports fans against their NHL rivals and thus were forced to terminate or move to sites in cities of other areas. Furthermore, some WHA teams had no alternative but to sign a number of ice hockey players who were committed to and controlled by NHL reserve contracts. As a result, such great superstars as Bobby Hull, Gordie Howe, and Derek Sanderson were paid extremely high salaries by their teams. In fact, the average salary of WHA players exceeded $50,000 per season versus $30,000 for NHL players. Therefore, after huge financial losses and multiple but unsuccessful attempts to merge with the NHL, the WHA shut down after completing its last season and in 1979 four of its teams—the Winnipeg Jets, Quebec Nordiques, Edmonton Oilers, and Hartford Whalers—were given the right to switch into the NHL.[3]

ALTERNATIVE LEAGUES III

The three groups of expansion teams discussed in this section of Chapter 5 were members of either a former men's professional football or soccer league, or previously performed in a current women's basketball league. With respect to these sports organizations, they consist of the expansion clubs that existed and competed in the United States Football League (USFL) and Men's Premier Soccer League (MPSL), and that currently perform or had played in the Women's National Basketball Association (WNBA). Because of the teams' different histories, locations, and performances, this part of the chapter is limited to reporting the facts and circumstances of when, where, and how each of the league's expansions and any mergers had evolved.[4]

In contrast to the typical NFL season, Donald Dixon established the USFL and scheduled its teams' games before the fall and winter months. Consequently, during the spring and early summer months of 1983, the USFL played its first season with four teams each entered in an Atlantic, Central, and Pacific Division (AD, CD, and PD). Because the majority of USFL teams were located in large sports markets, these clubs' average attendances had exceeded 24,000 per game and the league earned relatively high ratings on the broadcasts of local and regional radio and television stations. To penetrate other Standard Metropolitan Statistical Areas, in 1984 the USFL's commissioner Chet Simmons and president Peter Spivak decided to add five new clubs to the league. (The names, performances, and area populations and population ranks of the five expansion franchises are reported in Table 5.3.) Furthermore, to reposition its member teams for competitive purposes, in 1984 the USFL was reorganized into the AD and Southern Division (SD) as units of the Eastern Conference, and the CD and PD as components of the Western Conference. One year later, however, the division titles were dropped, leaving each of the existing teams to compete in one of the two conferences.

As indicated in the table, the five clubs that entered the league in 1984—whose owners each paid a fee of $6 million—had an average win-loss percentage of 36 percent, won zero championships, and played at home in stadiums located in small to midsized metropolitan areas. For example, the Bulls performed in Jacksonville's 80,200-seat Gator Bowl; the Showboats in Memphis's 50,200-seat Liberty Bowl; the Outlaws in Tulsa's 40,300-seat Skelly Stadium (in 1985 they played as the Arizona Outlaws in Tempe's 70,100-seat Sun Devils Stadium); the Maulers in Pittsburgh's 60,100-seat Three Rivers Stadium; and the Gunslingers in San Antonio's 32,000-seat Alamo Stadium. Despite playing games in stadiums within mediocre markets relative to the sites of the big-city NFL teams, the USFL expansion clubs' average attendances at home varied with the Bulls at 45,000 per game and the Showboats at 28,500, Outlaws at 19,000, Maulers at 22,800 and Gunslingers at 13,000.

Regarding each of the teams' brief history in the league, the Bulls was an average performing club for two years and thus merged with the Denver Gold franchise after the 1985 season and then disbanded when the USFL folded in 1986; although the team was above average in performances, the Showboats' owner Logan Young had depleted his cash account before the 1984 season, and new owner Billy Dunavant operated the club for two years, and then in early 1986 Dunavant canceled the franchise; after playing the 1984 season based in Tulsa, the Outlaws merged with the Arizona Wranglers and played its second season in Tempe as the Arizona Outlaws before disbanding in 1986; because of winning only five of its games in the 1984 USFL season before home crowds of less than 23,000 per game, the Maulers' owner Edward DeBartolo Sr. terminated his franchise before the 1985 season had begun; and when the Gunslingers' owner Clinton Manges missed some of the salary payments that he owed to players who had performed in the 1985 season, the team folded before the end of the year.

After the league was awarded only $1 in damages by a court from a lawsuit that it filed against the NFL for antitrust violations, and because several of its teams had deficits and struggled to pay their debts, sports journalists printed a number of controversial articles declaring that the USFL was bankrupt and in financial ruin. As a result of this negative publicity and some teams' failure to renegotiate stadium leases at their home sites, the league was forced to cease operating in late 1985 and then fold before beginning another season.

To offer a different brand of entertainment and market it to a diverse audience of sports fans who lived in urban areas across the United States, the WNBA was formed and initiated its first season in spring 1997. During that season the league consisted of eight teams, which were each located at sites in large or midsized U.S. cities. After evaluating the teams' markets and total and per-game attendances, and since the league's television ratings had revealed a positive response from fans about the 1997 season, the WNBA officials decided to add a number of new franchises to play in the league. As such, the expansion teams and their respective performances, and the total population and population rank of the clubs' areas, are provided in the various columns of Table 5.3.

Regarding this group of new franchises—but excluding the Chicago Sky—four teams joined the WNBA during the late 1990s and another four in 2000. Because of potential advertising revenues from their sponsors and the availability and convenience of modern basketball arenas, the eight WNBA clubs had located and played at sites in cities of metropolitan areas that hosted an affiliated NBA team. Since their expansion years, the eight teams have won an average of approximately 44 percent of their regular season games. The Miracle, however, struggled in popularity while based in Orlando and thus had to relocate in 2003; moreover, the Miami Sol and Portland Fire folded in 2002 after each team existed for three seasons in the league. In contrast, the Detroit Shock and Seattle Storm have been the two most successful expansion clubs in the WNBA because of the number of seasons they have played and league championships won, and their average winning percentages.

To perform as an expansion team in the league's Eastern Conference, the Chicago Sky became the WNBA's 14th franchise when it began to play in the 2006 season. As a consequence of receiving operating subsidies and other business opportunities from the NBA Chicago Bulls, the Sky will compete in its home games at the 6,500-seat UIC Pavilion, which is located on the campus of the University of Illinois at Chicago. Regarding the Sky's front office personnel, former Boston Celtics center and Hall of Fame inductee Dave Cowens is coach and general manager and Michael Alter—who is one of the nation's largest private commercial real estate developers—is the club's owner and chairman. Furthermore, besides being a former coach of a women's high school basketball team and playing the sport at the University of Richmond in Virginia, the Sky's president and chief executive officer, Margaret Stender, served as president of juice drinks for PepsiCo and also of ready-to-eat cereals for the Quaker Oats Company.[5]

Depending on how effectively the Sky operates as a sports franchise and business in the Chicago area and due to other relevant factors, before 2010 the WNBA is expected to further expand its size and add one or more teams in cities that currently host NBA franchises. With respect to which

Table 5.3
Expansions of Alternative Leagues III, by Team, Selected Seasons

Year	Team	Performance		Performance	
		W-L%	Champion	Total	Rank
USFL (1983–1985)					
1984	Jacksonville Bulls	.416	0	.8	50th
1984	Memphis Showboats	.500	0	.9	41st
1984	Oklahoma Outlaws	.389	0	.9	40th
1984	Pittsburgh Maulers	.166	0	2.4	15th
1984	San Antonio Gunslingers	.333	0	1.2	33rd
WNBA (1997–present)					
1998	Detroit Shock	.473	1	5.4	8th
1998	Washington Mystics	.372	0	7.3	4th
1999	Minnesota Lynx	.444	0	2.9	16th
1999	Orlando Miracle	.468	0	1.5	30th
2000	Indiana Fever	.435	0	1.6	29th
2000	Miami Sol	.500	0	3.9	12th
2000	Portland Fire	.385	0	2.2	23rd
2000	Seattle Storm	.454	1	3.5	13th
2005	Chicago Sky	NA	NA	9.2	3rd
MPSL (2003–2004)					
2004	Albuquerque Asylum	.750	0	.7	58th
2004	Idaho Wolves	.000	0	.2	–
2004	Sacramento Knights	.533	0	1.8	25th
2004	Salinas Valley Samba	.593	0	.2	–
2004	Sonoma Valley FC Sol	.562	0	.1	–

Note: See Table 5.1 for the meanings of Year, Team, Performance, and Population, and Table 5.2 for interpreting the – in column six. NA denotes that the data for the Chicago Sky's Performance is not available. The United States Football League is denoted as USFL, Women's National Basketball Association as WNBA, and Men's Premier Soccer League as MPSL.

Source: "United States Football League," at http://www.usfl.com, accessed 13 September 2005; "Women's National Basketball Association," at http://www.wnba.com, accessed 13 September 2005; "Men's Premier Soccer League," at http://www.mpsl.com, accessed 13 September 2005; *The World Almanac and Book of Facts* (New York: World Almanac Books, 1984–2004).

U.S. cities, the most attractive new sites to place new WNBA teams in the east and south are, respectively, in Boston and Philadelphia, and Atlanta and Memphis. Relative to the southwest, west and pacific regions of the United States, the most promising cities to consider for expansions include Dallas and Denver, and San Diego and/or San Francisco. Because other cities were either the home sites of former NBA or WNBA teams or lack a fan base that will support woman's professional basketball games, the sites with least potential are located in Cleveland, Miami; Milwaukee; New Orleans; Portland, Oregon; and Orlando, Florida in the United States, and Montreal, Toronto, and Vancouver, British Columbia, in Canada.

The final expansion teams contained in Table 5.3 are those that existed in the Men's Premier Soccer League (MPSL). This Division III professional sports organization, which was officially organized in early to mid 2003, established a mission to provide skilled athletes with an opportunity to perform against each other in soccer games at a relatively high level of competition. MPSL teams are and have been located in small cities and very small metropolitan areas in Arizona, California, Idaho, Nevada, New Mexico, and Utah. After six teams had each played 15 games in the league's first regular season, the Arizona Suaharos defeated the Utah Salt Ratz and won a championship in 2003.

To play in the 2004 season, the MPSL decided to add five new clubs. As indicated in Table 5.3, the Albuquerque Asylum was the most competitive of these expansion teams. That is, in 2004 the Asylum ended in second place behind the Chico Rooks but was defeated by the Suaharos in the playoffs. Although the remaining four expansion teams did not qualify for the postseason, the Utah Salt Ratz beat the Suaharos to become the 2004 MPSL champion.

ALTERNATIVE LEAGUES IV

Thus far Chapter 5 has identified, listed in tables, and discussed the various expansion teams in nine of the alternative professional sports leagues that were or are based in the United States. To continue the discussion, this section of the chapter highlights the new franchises that were added to a duo of other secondary leagues during specific years. That is, to the National Women's Basketball League (NWBL) and American Basketball Association (ABALive). Given the title, purpose, and scope of this chapter, the expansion clubs in these two leagues are the final groups of professional sports organizations that were researched and studied as topics.[6]

When it was formed in 2001, the professional component of the NWBL consisted of teams populated by women who formerly played basketball in Division I, II, or III college and university programs, or who had competed for a few seasons while members of one or more U.S. or foreign semiprofessional or professional basketball clubs. In fact, during one regular season or another a fraction of these athletes were listed on the active rosters of WNBA and national European teams. Thus, the NWBL's franchises have each contained a wide range of talented young and middle-aged rookie and veteran players. Since 2001, some of these women included the WNBA Houston Comets' Sheryl Swoopes, Indiana Fever's Tamika Catchings, Detroit Shock's Ruth Riley and Swin Cash, New York Liberty's Becky Hammon, and such former collegiate and WNBA superstars as Rebecca Lobo, Shea Ralph, and Kara Wolters.

The NWBL's first year in operation was in 2001, when the Atlanta Justice, Birmingham Power, Mobile Majesty, and Kansas City Legacy had competed against each other in the regular season. Then in the following four seasons, several groups applied and gained admission to participate in the league as owners of expansion franchises. In turn, these groups fielded new teams that played, such as the Chicago Blaze and Springfield Spirit beginning in 2002; Grand Rapids Blizzard, Houston Stealth, and Tennessee Fury in 2003; Colorado Chill and Dallas Fury in 2004; Lubbock Hawks and San Jose Spiders in 2005; and San Diego Siege and San Francisco Legacy in 2006. The Siege, which play some games at home in the city's 2,000-seat Harry West Gymnasium—located on the campus of San Diego City College—hired Delaware native David McElwee to be the team's general manager and employed a former WNBA Utah Starzz coach, Fred Williams, as its first head coach. Moreover, the Siege is the NWBL's second club to be placed in a city near the U.S. West Coast. Thus, it will be interesting to observe whether the Siege, Legacy, and Spiders become intraleague rivals and to determine whether these clubs are able to generate enough cash flows to afford the transportation payments for games played at sites in other cities.

Because a large number of sports fans in urban areas were indifferent about buying tickets and attending NWBL games, some of the league's original and expansion teams have folded. These terminations included the Majesty after the 2001 season, Justice and Legacy after the 2002 season, Blizzard after the 2003 season, and Stealth after the 2004 season. When the 2005 season ended, the failed franchises were the Dallas Fury—which had relocated from Tennessee in 2003—and the Blaze, Hawks, and Power. Thus the Chill, Siege, Spiders, and Legacy competed in the NWBL's 2006 regular season. According to a message received from McElwee, the league's pro cup champions and runners-up were, respectively, the Stealth and Fury in 2003, Fury and Chill in 2004, and the Chill and Fury in 2005. Because of the large disparities in operating revenues and costs that have occurred among some of the franchises in recent seasons, these terminations and championships indicate that superior and inferior NWBL teams located in large, midsized, and small markets were equally likely to be unstable and forced to disband.

Unsurprisingly, this six-year-old national women's basketball league actively seeks applications, funds, and resources from prospective owners of franchises. Indeed, to apply for membership and become an owner, investors must complete a brief form that specifies a city as a future location of a team. If the respective NWBL officials approve that document, then the applicant must pay $100 in fees and complete a detailed application and submit it to the league for review. The third step in the process is for the applicant to attend at least three NWBL home games, meet the existing teams' owners and preview their operations, and also be prepared to sign a franchise agreement at an owners' meeting and make an initial payment of at least $40,000. To qualify and enter a team in the league for the 2007 season, the cost of purchasing a franchise is $75,000, and the annual expenses to operate a club are estimated at $125,000. Furthermore, the league requires that each franchise must host nine home games between the months of February and March 2007. In short, the NWBL is a risky but growth-oriented league that offers an opportunity for investors to support women's professional basketball teams that operate and are located at sites in some small, midsized, and large cities of areas across the United States.

According to its online mission statement, the Indianapolis-based ABALive was formed in 2000 to provide fast-paced and fan-friendly professional basketball to people of all ages at a reasonable price, and to extend an opportunity for coaches and players to display their talents in a competitive environment. Furthermore, in the long run this alternative men's professional basketball league expects to become a nationally recognized organization whose franchises are located in major U.S. and international markets. Based on information from its Website and other sources, the ABALive has played five seasons as of 2006 and experienced mixed results as a sports business.

During the 2000 season, the ABALive consisted of eight teams with sites located in cities that varied in population, that is, from Los Angeles and Chicago to Kansas City and Memphis. When that season concluded, four franchises had folded and one relocated, and joining the league as expansion teams in 2001 were the Phoenix Eclipse, Kentucky Pro Cats, and Southern California Surf. Then, to reorganize its structure and schedule, the ABALive decided to cancel the 2002 season. In 2003, the league opened and added new teams that were based in Fresno and Long Beach, California; Las Vegas; New Jersey; and Juarez and Tijuana of Mexico. Meanwhile, the only original team remaining active after the 2000–2001 regular seasons was the Kansas City Knights.

To begin the 2004 season, the ABALive had expanded by approximately 27 teams. However, when that season ended, some of the league's expansion teams had folded, such as the Cincinnati Monarchs, Hermosillo (Mexico) Seris, Portland Reign, New Jersey Skycats, and Utah Snowbears.

These and other teams were forced to terminate their operations because of weak attendances at home and away games, lack of exposure in the media, insufficient cash inflows from the local broadcast of games on radio and/or cable television, and the reluctance of the teams' owners to provide more money as inputs to keep their franchises in existence.

According to a report published on the league's Web site, a total of 15 different individuals and groups were interested in owning an ABALive team to participate in the 2006 season. These potential owners had headquarters or offices in such cities as Baton Rouge, Lake Charles, and New Orleans in Louisiana; Ontario and Ventura in California; Orlando, Florida, and Vancouver in British Columbia. Also, in an email message dated February 2003, the league's cofounder and chairman Joe Newman expressed an interest in locating teams to play at sites in the Dominican Republic and Puerto Rico, and in other nations of Central America and various countries of the Caribbean. In short, the ABALive plans to develop a stable and successful league initially in the United States and later globally, and to exist as an option for local basketball fans and not as a threat to the NBA.

Besides the two secondary leagues discussed before in this section of the chapter, a few facts and other types of information were collected about teams in the American Basketball League, National Women's Football Association, and Women's Professional Football League. After researching these leagues' documents, it was tedious to identify and pinpoint the appropriate years and the names and performances of their expansion teams, and to obtain accurate data each season about these organizations because many of the clubs temporarily or permanently shut down or had transferred to other sites before or while the regular seasons were played. Furthermore, to preserve their cash balances in order to operate as businesses in another year, some of the alternative leagues canceled a number of teams' games before or during specific seasons. Because of such inconsistent team records, seasons, and performances, these three leagues and their expansions, mergers, and other reorganizations are not analyzed.

SUMMARY

In contrast to similar topics discussed in Chapters 1 and 3, this chapter highlights and examines the expansions, mergers, and other reorganizations that occurred in several alternative professional sports leagues—and between them and prominent leagues—in selected years from the late 1800s to early 2000s. While they had existed or currently operate at their sites in U.S. cities, some of these rival men and women's teams established a fan base in areas and invaded the markets of the nation's major professional sports teams, including those in MLB, NFL, NBA, NHL, and MLS.

Most secondary sports leagues failed to thrive in the long run for several reasons. Some of these parent organizations were undercapitalized and had operating deficits and relatively high debts. Others, meanwhile, had inferior-performing teams in divisions and conferences, perhaps inefficient commissioners and administrators, and frequent turnover of franchise owners. Because alternative leagues receive little exposure in the media, it was very difficult for their expansion teams to be profitable and generate sufficient amounts of operating revenues from fans at games and from local and regional radio and television broadcast rights.

Based on the number of seasons played and the success of their teams, the most superior and inferior secondary leagues among the groups discussed here are the AA and FL in baseball, AFL and USFL in football, ABA and NWBL in basketball, WHA in ice hockey, and the NASL and MPSL in soccer. Regarding other leagues that were mentioned in this chapter's sections, the WNBA was and is able to survive and schedule games for regular seasons and in postseasons because of the operating subsidies that each of its teams receive from an NBA franchise and/or the commissioner's office. Furthermore, the ABALive is a high-growth league. As such, it focuses each year on expansion and, in part, relies for its income on the fees and revenues from new teams in order to continue operating as a business and competitive professional basketball league in the sports industry.

6

Team Relocations and Transfers in Alternative Leagues since 1876

Chapters 2 and 4 describe the movements of sports teams from one metropolitan area to another and the transfers of clubs between a number of professional leagues that once existed or are currently based in the United States. Specifically, Chapter 2 contains the movements and transfers of teams that occurred prior to 1950 while Chapter 4 focuses on those that took place since 1950. As reflected in these two chapters, during their existence the most prominent sports leagues in the United States have consisted of the Early National League and Major League Baseball's American and National Leagues, and the National Football League and Basketball Association of America, National Basketball League and National Basketball Association, National Hockey League, and the American Soccer League and Atlantic Coast League. Moreover, between 1996 and 2005, there were no relocations of teams within or transfers into Major League Soccer.

Besides the dominant organizations, some clubs—as members of less prominent or secondary leagues—moved their headquarters and operations to sites in other cities or had shifted into a rival league in the same sport. Chapter 6 identifies and analyzes these particular relocations and transfers. It contains—for a selection of alternative U.S. sports leagues—the specific year and the names of teams and their performances at the respectivepre- and postmove sites with respect to various regular seasons and postseasons.

Thus in this chapter, there are three tables that provide some relevant statistics and other information about the teams. The first table includes a total of four alternative leagues and a number of relocated teams that performed in professional baseball and basketball; the second table consists of one each soccer and ice hockey league and their respective teams' movements; and the third table lists the relocated clubs of two former secondary football leagues. Although several other less popular professional sports and sports organizations have emerged in the United States and folded since the late 1800s—or have continued to operate for various seasons with clubs at sites in rural and urban areas—their histories and team movements and transfers have not been accurately recorded or completely documented in the literature. Therefore, the activities, events, and business operations of these leagues and their teams are not cited and discussed in this or the other chapters.

ALTERNATIVE LEAGUES I

This portion of Chapter 6 concentrates on the relocations of teams in baseball's Union Association (UA) and Federal League (FL), and in basketball's American Basketball Association (ABA) and Women's National Basketball Association (WNBA). Organized in September 1883 as a national professional league to attract the nation's baseball fans and compete for market share against the American Association (AA) and Early National League (ENL), the UA held its only season in 1884 in which it consisted of 10 teams located at sites in cities that ranged in population from Boston and Chicago to Cincinnati and Kansas City. After a series of regular season games, some of the UA's clubs experienced attendance problems in their home ballparks because they either did not win enough games, played in markets that hosted and supported other local professional sports teams, and/or were performing at sites in small and very small metropolitan areas. As denoted in Table 6.1, a few of the league's teams had to exit from their original locations.[1]

After the Unions played 25 games, some officials of the Pennsylvania Railroad—which was the club's owner—decided to move the team from its tiny market in Altoona to the state of Kansas where it would perform as the Kansas City Cowboys and at home in Athletic Park. When the league's 1884 season concluded, the Unions and Cowboys clubs combined had won a total of 22, or 21 percent, of their contests and finished 61 games behind the St. Louis Maroons, who won the UA pennant that season.

Besides the Unions' relocation, during August 1884 the Browns franchise left South Side Park in Chicago and moved its headquarters temporarily to Pittsburgh, Pennsylvania, and then permanently to the state of Minnesota, where it played as St. Paul Whitecaps. Even so, in 1884 the Chicago-Pittsburgh-St. Paul teams won less than 45 percent of their games and finished in eighth place of the league's final standings.

Table 6.1
Team Relocations in Alternative Leagues I, Selected Seasons

	Team		Performance	
Year	From	To	Premove	Postmove
UA (1884–1884)				
1884	Altoona Unions	Kansas City Cowboys	.240	.203
1884	Chicago Browns	St. Paul Whitecaps	.451	.250
1884	Philadelphia Keystones	Wilmington Quicksteps	.313	.111
1884	Wilmington Quicksteps	Milwaukee Grays	.111	.667
FL (1914–1915)				
1914	Indianapolis Hoosiers	Newark Peppers	.575	.526
ABA (1967–1976)				
1968	Anaheim Amigos	Los Angeles Stars	.321	.423
1968	Minnesota Muskies	Miami Floridians	.641	.551
1968	New Jersey Americans	New York Nets	.462	.218
1968	Pittsburgh Pipers	Minnesota Pipers	.692	.462
1969	Houston Mavericks	Carolina Cougars	.295	.500
1969	Minnesota Pipers	Pittsburgh Pipers	.462	.345
1969	Oakland Oaks	Washington Capitols	.769	.524
1970	Los Angeles Stars	Utah Stars	.423	.679
1970	New Orleans Buccaneers	Memphis Pros	.500	.488
1970	Washington Capitols	Virginia Squires	.524	.655
1973	Dallas Chaparrals	San Antonio Spurs	.333	.536
1974	Carolina Cougars	Spirits of St. Louis	.560	.381
WNBA (1997–present)				
2003	Utah Starzz	San Antonio Silverstars	.625	.353
2003	Orlando Miracle	Connecticut Sun	.500	.529

Note: Year is when the clubs moved from their Premove to Postmove sites. Based on the number of years the teams existed at each of the sites, Performance is the average winning percentages of the baseball and basketball clubs for one, two, or three seasons while at the Premove and Postmove sites, or before and after a relocation or transfer had occurred. The Union Association is designated as the UA, Federal League as FL, American Basketball Association as ABA, and Women's National Basketball Association as WNBA.

Source: *Official Major League Baseball Fact Book 2005 Edition* (St. Louis, MO: Sporting News, 2005), 186–87; "American Basketball Association," at http://www.remembertheaba.com, accessed 8 August 2005; "Women's National Basketball Association," at http://www.wnba.com, accessed 13 September 2005.

The final two relocations of UA teams were the Keystones, which moved from Philadelphia to Wilmington, Delaware, during the 1984 season, and after two wins that season the Quicksteps then relocated from Wilmington to Milwaukee and made a nickname change to become the Milwaukee Grays. While performing from its base in that southeastern city of Wisconsin, the club won two-thirds of its games but disbanded when the UA folded in January 1885 because only five member teams attended the league's winter meetings. Interestingly, in 1884 there were no AA or ENL baseball clubs that had sites in Altoona, Kansas City, St. Paul, Wilmington, and Milwaukee, although one AA and ENL team existed in Philadelphia and one ENL club played in Chicago. In short, the UA Browns and Keystones had to relocate from their sites because of the intense competition for fan support from other professional baseball league's clubs.

Before becoming recognized as a major league, the FL had existed as a minor league in 1913. In that year, owners C. E. Clark and J. Spinney moved the Blue Sox from very small-market Covington, Kentucky, to Missouri and renamed the team Kansas City Packers, which then proceeded to win a total of 148, or approximately 49 percent, of its games during the 1914–1915 FL regular seasons. Meanwhile, after winning the regular season and a FL pennant in 1914 the Hoosiers were sold by owners James A. Ross and J. E. Krause to Harry Sinclair and P. J. White, who then moved the team from small-market Indianapolis, Indiana to the state of New Jersey, where it became known as Newark Peppers. In 1915, the Peppers finished in fifth place and six games behind the FL champion Chicago Whales. Indeed, that was the final season of the Packers, Peppers, and the league's other six clubs because the FL disbanded following an agreement negotiated with officials from organized baseball—that is, the AL and NL. Thus, during its brief history, the FL had exciting pennant races each season, although the majority of its teams incurred significant financial losses. This outcome is in contrast to the clubs in MLB, which reportedly broke even or earned small amounts of operating profit.

As indicated in Table 6.1, four ABA teams moved in 1968, three each in 1969 and 1970, one in 1973, and another in 1974. After struggling to establish a fan base while playing at home in the 7,800-seat Anaheim Convention Center during the late 1960s and then being sold for $450,000, the Amigos' owner Jim Kirst moved his team from Anaheim to Los Angeles so that it could perform as the Los Angeles Stars in the city's 15,350-seat Sports Arena. Unable to coexist in southern California and share the area's sports market with the NBA Los Angeles Lakers, in 1970 the Stars was resold for $850,000 to Bill Daniels, who then relocated it from Los Angeles to play at home in the 12,166-seat Salt Palace in Salt Lake City, Utah. While performing as Utah Stars, the team beat the Kentucky Colonels in seven games to win an ABA title in 1971 and three years later finished runner-up to the champion New York Nets. However, the Stars had financial problems and went out of business while playing its games in the 1975 season. Even so, because of all-star center Zelmo Beaty and guard Jimmy Jones, and due to coach Joe Mullaney, the Stars won nearly 70 percent of regular season games while located in Salt Lake City. In the end, the Stars' move from large-market Los Angeles to Utah was an unavoidable and risky strategy and not in the long-term interests of the franchise.

After playing the 1967 ABA season, in part, at the 15,500-seat Metropolitan Sports Center in Minnesota, the Muskies moved from the Minneapolis area to southern Florida and performed in at least four home-site arenas as Miami Floridians. Since the team had no superstar players for local basketball fans to cheer at the club's home games that were held in the cities of Jacksonville, Miami, St. Petersburg, and West Palm Beach, the Floridians disbanded in 1972. In other words, the sport of professional basketball played by ABA teams was not supported locally in Minneapolis or throughout Florida during the late 1960s and early 1970s.

Besides the movements of the Amigos, Stars, and Muskies from their respective sites, in 1967 the New Jersey Americans also became an ABA franchise when businessman Arthur Brown paid the league an entry fee of $30,000. However, because of below-average performances in games played at home in the 5,500-seat Teaneck Armory in Teaneck, New Jersey, Brown was compelled to relocate the team from that city to Long Island and change its name to the New York Nets. After being renamed New Jersey Nets and appearing in eight playoffs, winning a league championship in 1974, and averaging almost 8,000 per game in attendances at the Commack Arena, Island Garden, and Nassau Coliseum, the Nets had the necessary experiences and assets to join the NBA when the ABA disbanded in 1976. This transfer into a rival league cost the Nets' owner Roy Boe—who had purchased the club in 1969 from Brown—a sum of $8.8 million. This amount included payments of $3.2 million to the NBA, $4 million to the New York Knicks for invading that club's territory, and $1.6 million to compensate the ABA teams that did not shift into the NBA.

After Gabe Rubin's Pittsburgh Pipers defeated the New Orleans Buccaneers in seven games to win an ABA championship in 1967, he moved the team from Pittsburgh to Minneapolis. But due to lack of enthusiasm of the club's performances at its home-site games, in 1969 the Pipers left Minneapolis and returned to Pittsburgh to play at home in the 15,500-seat Metropolitan Sports Center. Unfortunately, this ABA club did not appeal to basketball fans in western Pennsylvania's sports market, which evidently preferred to support the NFL Pittsburgh Steelers and NL Pittsburgh Pirates. So in 1970, Rubin sold the franchise to Metro Sports, and the team became known as Pittsburgh Condors. Nevertheless, because of low attendances and increasing financial losses and debts while operating in the Pittsburgh area, the team canceled its operations and folded after the 1971 season.

The Houston Mavericks joined the ABA in 1967, and during two seasons the club played poorly in its arena before home crowds that averaged 1,300 per game. In 1969 a syndicate headed by William Witmore sold the franchise to James Gardiner. Then Gardiner moved the club from Houston to North Carolina to perform as the Carolina Cougars in arenas in Charlotte, Greensboro, Raleigh, and Winston-Salem. Because the Cougars were an average team without a substantial fan base, in 1973–1974 a group led by Harry Weltman purchased the team for $2.2 million and then relocated it from Charlotte to the state of Missouri, where it existed as Spirits of St. Louis and played at home in the city's 18,000-seat St. Louis Arena. After two mediocre seasons in St. Louis and announcing a move to Salt Lake City, the Spirits became unpopular in its market area and folded before the 1976 ABA season was expected to begin.

Two years after joining the league as an original franchise, the Oakland Oaks won a championship in 1969 primarily because of scoring leader Rick Barry, Rookie of the Year Warren Armstrong, all-ABA player Doug Moe, and coach Alex Hannum. Even so, the regular season attendances of less than 2,500 per game motivated entertainer Pat Boone and his partners to sell the franchise in 1969 for $2 million to Earl Foreman, who then moved the team from Oakland to Washington, DC, and renamed it the Washington Capitols. After playing one season at home in the 7,000-seat Washington Coliseum, Foreman moved the club from Washington city to the state of Virginia to play basketball games in various arenas located in Hampton, Norfolk, Richmond, and Roanoke. Although players such as the great Julius Erving and 7-foot center Swen Nater attracted local fans in these cities to the team's home games, the Virginia Squires was not successful as a business venture and thus failed after finishing the 1975 season in last place of the ABA's Eastern Division.

While located in New Orleans and playing home games in gymnasiums on the campuses of Loyola University and Tulane University and in the city's Municipal Auditorium, the Buccaneers averaged about 2,600 spectators per game for three seasons. Despite playing for a league championship in 1968 and a division title in 1969, the franchise was sold to P. L. Blake purchased in 1970 and renamed the Memphis Pros after Blake moved it to Tennessee to play its home games in the 10,860-seat

Mid-South Coliseum. After a change in names from Memphis Pros to Memphis Tams and then to Memphis Sounds, and being resold in 1972 and again in 1974, the club had accumulated a large amount of liabilities and debts, which forced it to declare bankruptcy in 1975. The ABA tried to revive the franchise by announcing a relocation from Memphis to Maryland and renaming the team Baltimore Claws. Nevertheless, before the end of the 1975 ABA season, the Sounds disbanded operations and shut down.

Between 1967 and 1973, the Dallas—renamed Texas and then Dallas—Chaparrals played competitively as a team in its home games for four seasons in Fort Worth's 18,500-seat Tarrant County Convention Center and Lubbock's 10,400-seat Municipal Coliseum, and then for two seasons in Dallas's 9,300-seat Moody Coliseum. Following the club's sale by owner Gary Davidson and his investment group to a syndicate, in 1973 the team was moved from its site in Dallas to play as the Spurs at home in San Antonio's 10,200-seat HemisFair Arena. After the conclusion of three regular seasons, the club had appeared in three ABA playoffs and averaged 7,400 per game in attendances. Consequently, in 1976 the San Antonio Spurs became an NBA team when its owners paid a fee of $3.2 million to the league plus a payment of $1.6 million to the ABA teams that did not participate in the league's merger with the NBA.

Collectively the average winning percentage of the 12 ABA clubs listed in column two of Table 6.1 declined from .498 at their premove sites to .480 at the postmove locations. Whereas five of the teams became more competitive after relocating, seven others experienced a decrease in winning percentages at their postmove sites. For example, the Stars in Los Angeles outperformed the Amigos, which had played at home in Anaheim, and the Capitols in Washington won fewer games per season than did the Oaks in Oakland. In short, when the 1975 ABA season ended, the New Jersey Nets, San Antonio Spurs, Indiana Pacers, and Denver Nuggets each continued to operate as sports enterprises after transferring into the NBA.

Due to disappointing attendances at home and experiencing financial problems, after the 2002 season two WNBA teams were compelled to move to other sites. During six seasons while playing a portion of its games at home in Salt Lake City's 19,900-seat Delta Center, the Utah Starzz won about 63 percent of its total games and qualified for the league's playoffs in 2001 and 2002. Nevertheless, when the NBA San Antonio Spurs received the minimum 6,000 season ticket deposits that were necessary to obtain a WNBA franchise, the Starzz—renamed San Antonio Silverstars—relocated from Utah to Texas to perform at home in San Antonio's 18,500-seat SBC Center. Since moving to San Antonio, the club has won less than 40 percent of its regular season games and struggles each year to qualify for the league's playoffs.

With respect to another relocation of a WNBA team, in 2003 the Miracle moved from playing at home in the 17,300-seat TD Waterhouse Centre in Orlando to performing at home in the 10,000-seat Mohegan Sun Arena in Uncasville, Connecticut. After being renamed the Connecticut Sun by its owner—who is from the Mohegan Native American tribe— the club competed in three consecutive WNBA playoffs. In short, since 2003 the average winning percentage declined from .562 for the Starzz and Miracle to .441 for the Silverstars and Sun. Furthermore, the Sun has been a more successful business and well-coached team in the league than has the Silverstars.

ALTERNATIVE LEAGUES II

In this section, the discussion involves one group of teams that played as members of an alternative professional soccer league and another group that performed as clubs in a secondary ice hockey league. Regarding the first group, in 1968 the National Professional Soccer League and United Soccer Association consolidated its operations and merged to form a single entity, the North American Soccer League (NASL). In its first season, the league consisted of four divisions and a total of 17 teams. Then during the 1969–1971 seasons, 15 of its clubs folded; the Montreal Olympiques, New York Cosmos, Rochester Lancers, Toronto Metros, and Washington Darts each joined the NASL as expansion teams.[2]

As depicted in Table 6.2, between 1972 and 1984 there were 17 teams in the NASL that had moved from their respective sites to athletic stadiums in other cities. In total, the group's performances per season improved after relocating. That is, the total points scored by the 17 teams increased on average from 102 at their premove sites to 120 at the postmove locations. In fact, 11, or 64 percent, of these clubs had more total points at their postmove than premove sites. Yet, some of the most competitive teams such as the New England Tea Men and Fort Lauderdale Strikers scored fewer points while playing at their postmove sites in, respectively, Jacksonville, Florida, and Minnesota. In contrast, some of the premove inferior teams like the Connecticut Bicentennials, Colorado Caribous, and Philadelphia Fury each recorded significantly more points after relocating and while performing when named as, respectively, the Oakland Stompers, Atlanta Chiefs, and Montreal Manic.

For demographic and economic reasons, a few of the NASL franchises had multiple relocations. To illustrate, the Darts played two seasons in the Washington, DC, area before relocating to southern Florida in 1972 and being renamed Miami Gatos. Then the Gatos—renamed Toros—moved from Miami to Fort Lauderdale to play as the Strikers during the 1977

Table 6.2
Teams Relocations in Alternative Leagues II, Selected Seasons

Year	Team From	To	Performance Premove	Postmove
NASL (1968–1984)				
1972	Washington Darts	Miami Gatos	111	44
1976	Denver Dynamos	Minnesota Kicks	85	138
1976	Baltimore Comets	San Diego Jaws	87	82
1977	Miami Toros	Fort Lauderdale Strikers	63	161
1977	San Antonio Thunder	Team Hawaii	107	106
1977	San Diego Jaws	Las Vegas Quicksilver	82	103
1978	Connecticut Bicentennials	Oakland Stompers	72	103
1978	Las Vegas Quicksilver	San Diego Sockers	103	164
1978	St. Louis Stars	California Surf	104	115
1978	Team Hawaii	Tulsa Roughnecks	106	132
1979	Oakland Stompers	Edmonton Drillers	103	88
1979	Colorado Caribous	Atlanta Chiefs	81	121
1980	New England Tea Men	Jacksonville Tea Men	154	141
1980	Memphis Rogues	Calgary Boomers	126	151
1981	Detroit Express	Washington Diplomats	129	135
1981	Philadelphia Fury	Montreal Manic	98	141
1984	Fort Lauderdale Strikers	Minnesota Strikers	136	115
WHA (1972–1979)				
1973	New York Golden Blades	New Jersey Knights	68	68
1973	Ottawa Nationals	Toronto Toros	74	86
1973	Philadelphia Blazers	Vancouver Blazers	76	55
1974	New Jersey Knights	San Diego Mariners	68	90
1974	Los Angeles Sharks	Michigan Stags	50	46
1974	Michigan Stags	Baltimore Blades	46	–
1975	Denver Spurs	Ottawa Civics	29	–
1975	Vancouver Blazers	Calgary Cowboys	76	86
1976	Toronto Toros	Birmingham Bulls	53	66

Note: Table 6.1 defines Year and the two columns for Team. The Premove and Postmove Performance are each the total number of points scored for one, two, or three seasons by a team. For example, the Darts scored 111 points in the 1971 season and the Gatos 44 in the 1972 season. The – indicates that the Baltimore Blades and Ottawa Civics did not play one season. The North American Soccer League is designated as NASL and World Hockey Association as WHA.

Source: "North American Soccer League," at http://www.nasl.com, accessed 13 September 2005 and "World Hockey Association," at http://www.wha.com, accessed 13 September 2005.

season. Finally, in 1984 the Strikers relocated from Fort Lauderdale to a site in Minnesota for one season. Interestingly, the Strikers was a more successful team in Fort Lauderdale than in Minnesota, and more competitive than in previous seasons when named the Washington Darts, Miami Gatos, and Miami Toros. Other franchises that changed sites and their names at least twice were team combinations consisting of the Baltimore Comets-San Diego Jaws-Las Vegas Quicksilver, San Antonio Thunder-Team Hawaii-Tulsa Roughnecks, and Connecticut Bicentennials-Oakland Stompers-Edmonton Drillers. Indeed, because of relatively low relocation costs, these types of team movements were more common within the NASL than within the other sports leagues that were researched and included in this and the other chapters.

To elaborate, the following are seven special aspects about the NASL's history and some teams as members of the group. First, despite positive or negative changes in performances per season, a number of the NASL clubs decided to cancel operations after spending one or more years at their postmove sites and prior to 1985, when the league had folded: the Atlanta Chiefs, Calgary Boomers, California Surf, Minnesota Kicks, and Washington Diplomats in 1981; the Edmonton Drillers in 1982; and the Montreal Manic in 1983. This relatively large count of team cancellations suggests that the league began to increasingly decline as an organization and unravel as a business during the late 1970s to early 1980s.

Second, the Jacksonville Tea Men withdrew from the NASL and joined the American Soccer League II (ASL II) in 1982, and two years later the San Diego Sockers and Minnesota Strikers became teams that transferred into the Major Indoor Soccer League (MISL). The Tea Men, Sockers, and Strikers were each very competitive clubs while playing in the NASL during several of the league's regular seasons. Nonetheless, these clubs' owners were uncertain about the NASL's future and thus chose to shift their teams into other professional soccer leagues.

Third, the only team in the group to win an NASL championship was the Tulsa Roughnecks, which played soccer games aggressively and defeated the Toronto Blizzard 2–0 in 1983. The runners-up to the league's champions included the Washington Darts in 1970, Miami Toros in 1974, and Ft. Lauderdale Strikers in 1980. Invariably, the two teams that won multiple titles during the league's 17 seasons in existence were the New York Cosmos with five and Chicago Sting with two. Other than the Cosmos and Sting—which had joined the league, respectively, in 1971 and 1975—there were 10 championship teams that are not listed in columns two and three of Table 6.2. For example, such NASL teams as the Los Angeles Aztecs, Rochester Lancers and Philadelphia Atoms each excelled during at least one season.

Fourth, the two clubs that scored the most points at their premove sites were the New England Tea Men and Fort Lauderdale Strikers: The Tea Men scored 154 points during the 1978 through 1980 seasons and the Strikers accumulated 136 points from 1977 to 1983. Even so, these two clubs never won a league title because the Cosmos and Sting earned a total of five NASL championships during the 1977 through 1983 seasons. After relocating and changing their nicknames, the San Diego Sockers and Fort Lauderdale Strikers had the two highest point totals. During seven seasons each, the Sockers won at least one Western Division title as a member of the Pacific Conference (PC), and the Strikers finished first in the Eastern Division of the Atlantic Conference (AC).

Fifth, the most inferior performers at their premove and postmove sites were, respectively, the Miami Toros and Connecticut Bicentennials, and the Miami Gatos and San Diego Jaws. As such, the Toros and Gatos failed to be consistent each season when they played home games in Miami's Orange Bowl Stadium, and the Jaws recorded only 82 points in the 1976 season and placed fifth in the Southern Division of the PC. The Bicentennials changed its first name from Hartford to Connecticut in 1977 and then ended in fourth and fifth place during two consecutive seasons in the Northern Division of the AC while competing at home in Dillon Stadium and the Yale Bowl. Thus, due to a number of erratic and disappointing performances in games played at home that resulted in attendance and financial problems, each of these teams ultimately moved to sites in cities of other metropolitan areas.

Sixth, in evaluating the NASL franchises that relocated to one or more sites and had changed their nicknames at least once, the highest average winning percentages per season were achieved by the trio of Darts-Gatos-Strikers at .549 and Jaws-Quicksilver-Sockers at .509. In contrast, the two groups of teams with the lowest average winning percentages were the Stompers-Drillers at .384 and Stars-Surf at .417. Thus the other clubs that moved had won between 42 percent and 50 percent of their total games. Consequently, after measuring the performances of all teams during their seasons of play, the New York Cosmos and Vancouver Whitecaps were the two most successful clubs in the league's history; they each won more than 60 percent of games and scored in excess of 365 points. In contrast, the majority of relocating teams had average to below-average performances while they existed in the NASL.

Seventh, some sports experts contend that besides the high cost and risk of operating as a major soccer league based in the United States, the NASL folded because of overexpansion, an excessive number of franchise ownership turnovers and team movements, and the scheduling of games in oversized football stadiums. Evidently, the lease payments were exorbitant for the California Surf to play at home in Spartan Stadium and for the Edmonton Drillers to compete in the Commonwealth and Clarke Stadiums, and for the Atlanta Chiefs in Atlanta Fulton County and Bobby Dodd Stadiums, Calgary Boomers in McMahon Stadium, Minnesota Kicks in Metropolitan Stadium, Washington Diplomats in RFK Stadium, and Montreal Manic in Olympic Stadium. Therefore each of these teams had folded, in part, because the sum of their revenues from gate receipts, sponsors and sales of merchandise, and cash inflows from other sources failed to cover the total fixed expenses of operating in large and underutilized facilities at their home sites.

The second group of clubs listed in Table 6.2 had played for various seasons in the World Hockey League (WHA) between 1972 and 1979. According to the table, there were nine relocations that involved a total of 14 teams. The circumstances of each movement reveal some interesting facts about these franchises and their teams' performances.

After paying the league an entry fee of $25,000 in 1972, the New York Raiders' owners Neil Shayne and Norman Dachs sold the franchise to the WHA, which then resold it for $1.5 million to a private syndicate. When that club—which was renamed the New York Golden Blades—went broke in 1973, the WHA repurchased the franchise from the syndicate and then sold it for $800,000 to a partnership. These owners then moved the team from New York to New Jersey's 4,000-seat Cherry Hill Arena to perform as New Jersey Knights. However, because of more financial difficulties, in 1974 the new owners relocated the club from New Jersey to southern California and renamed it San Diego Mariners. After playing its home games without passion and before small crowds in San Diego's 12,800-seat Sports Arena, the Mariners franchise was canceled in 1977. Thus, it was money, marketing problems, and management deficiencies that caused this franchise to be terminated by its last owner—billionaire Ray Kroc, the founder of McDonalds Corporation.

During the 1972 WHA season, the Ottawa Nationals played most home games before small audiences in the city's 10,700-seat Civic Center Arena. Then businessman John Bassett bought the franchise from its owners for $1.8 million and moved the team from Ottawa to a rink, the 4,800-seat Varsity Arena in Toronto, Canada. Three years after being nicknamed Toronto Toros, Bassett became discouraged because of the local community's inadequate support of his team. As a result, in 1976 he decided to move the club from Toronto to exist—as the Birmingham Bulls—at home in the 16,800-seat Birmingham-Jefferson Civic Center, Alabama. Nevertheless, because of the Bulls' inability to score points and establish a strong fan base in the Birmingham area, the franchise was canceled in 1979. In the end, the sports fans in the cities of Ottawa, Toronto, and Birmingham were not enthusiastic about WHA teams that did not play entertaining and competitive ice hockey games and win championships.

Before the 1972 WHA season began, the Miami Screaming Eagles' owner Herb Martin sold his franchise for $210,000 to James Cooper, who then transferred the team from Miami to Pennsylvania to perform at home games as the Blazers in Philadelphia's 8,000-seat Civic Center. Unable to generate profits while playing in the Civic Center, the team was sold again in 1973 and then moved from Philadelphia to the 16,100-seat Pacific Coliseum in Vancouver, Canada. In that year, the newly named Vancouver Blazers scored 55 points and finished fifth in the WHA's West Division (WD). After two more dismal seasons in Vancouver, the team's new owner—Neonex International Ltd.—moved the club from Vancouver to play as the Cowboys in Calgary's 7,400-seat arena, which was named the Calgary Corral. After experiencing revenue shortages from low gate receipts and little money from local sponsors, in 1977 the Calgary Cowboys' franchise went bankrupt and decided to discontinue operations and disband.

In its first season as an original team in the WHA's WD, the Los Angeles Sharks ended in sixth place with a win-loss-tie record of 25–53–0 and incurred a significant financial loss. When a syndicate of investors purchased the Sharks franchise from owner Leonard Bloom in 1974 for $2.5 million, the group moved the team—later renamed Michigan Stags—from Los Angeles to play in Detroit's 12,100-seat Cobo Arena. After the Stags went broke during the 1974 season, the WHA relocated the club to eastern Maryland so that it could perform as the Blades in Baltimore's 11,200-seat Arena. When unable to attract a new owner and investors, the Blades went out of business to avoid more financial problems before the start of the 1975 WHA season.

For a fee of $2 million, the WHA authorized owner Ivan Mullenix to enter the Denver Spurs into the league in 1975 as an expansion team. Despite playing its home games in Denver's 16,000-seat McNichols Sports Arena, the Spurs struggled to win games against its rivals and attract local sports fans. Thus during the league's 1975 season, Mullenix moved his club from the state of Colorado to Canada so that it could perform as Ottawa Civics and play at home in the city's 9,800-seat Civic Center. However, because of $2 million in operating losses, the Civics franchise was canceled in 1976.

Interestingly, the various WHA teams that are listed in columns two and three of Table 6.2 did not play in a league championship series. Moreover, each of the clubs failed to survive either before or after the WHA-NHL merger in 1979. In short, it was the league's best teams—the Edmonton Oilers, New England Whalers, Quebec Nordiques, and Winnipeg Jets— that were most qualified and prepared to transfer into the NHL.

ALTERNATIVE LEAGUES III

In 1973, Orange County California attorney Gary Davidson—who had a major role in forming the ABA and WHA—persuaded a total of 12 investors or syndicates of owners to each pay $100,000 and purchase a franchise in the World Football League (WFL). This new organization's mission, in part, was to place teams in at least five large U.S. markets and challenge the NFL clubs that existed in those locations, although six, or 50 percent, of the WFL teams played in cities with SMSA populations of fewer than one million residents. The new league also negotiated a lucrative television contract, but it expired in one year. To implement its first season in July 1974, the WFL was composed of four teams each in the Eastern, Central, and Western Division (ED, CD, and WD). Since some of the initial owners were not qualified or experienced enough to operate a franchise in an alternative professional football league, a number of the WFL teams had to change sites before playing a game, as denoted in the first portion of Table 6.3.[3]

An original WFL franchise was the Boston Bulldogs. During early summer 1974, Bulldogs owner Howard Baldwin reevaluated his investment in the franchise and sold the club for personal reasons to Bob Schmertz, who then moved it from Boston to New York and changed its name to New York Stars. Shortly thereafter, a syndicate purchased the Stars from Schmertz and relocated the team from New York to North Carolina to perform as the Charlotte Hornets and at its home site in the city's 24,000-seat American Legion Memorial Stadium. In two consecutive seasons, the team won a total of 16 games and finished in second place and then third in the league's ED. When the WFL folded during late 1975, the Hornets franchise had no alternative but to disband.

The Houston Texans was a WFL franchise that was originally planned to be located in Memphis, Tennessee. After averaging 18,700 fans per game midway into the 1974 season, the Texans' owner Steve Arnold moved his club from Houston to Louisiana and renamed it the Shreveport Steamer to play in the city's 30,000-seat State Fair Coliseum. During the 1974–1975 seasons, the Steamer won a total of 12, or approximately 38 percent, of its games, ended in fourth place and then one year later third in the WD, and averaged 17,000 per season at home games. Subsequent to being resold by Arnold to John Atkins in 1975, the franchise was canceled when the WFL folded.

Table 6.3
Team Relocations in Alternative Leagues III, Selected Seasons

Year	Team		Performance	
	From	To	Premove	Postmove
WFL (1974–1975)				
1974	Boston Bulldogs	New York Stars	NA	NA
1974	New York Stars	Charlotte Hornets	NA	.516
1974	Houston Texans	Shreveport Steamer	NA	.375
1974	Washington Ambassadors	Virginia Ambassadors	NA	NA
1974	Virginia Ambassadors	Florida Blazers	NA	.700
1975	Florida Blazers	San Antonio Wings	.700	.538
USFL (1983–1985)				
1984	Boston Breakers	New Orleans Breakers	.611	.444
1984	Philadelphia Stars	Baltimore Stars	.889	.583
1984	Washington Federals	Orlando Renegades	.167	.278
1985	New Orleans Breakers	Portland Breakers	.444	.333

Note: Table 6.1 defines Year, Team and the columns titled From and To, and Performance and the columns labeled Premove and Postmove. The NA means that the team relocated before playing regular season games at the premove and/or postmove sites. The World Football League is designated as WFL and United States Football League as USFL.

Source: "World Football League," at http://www.wfl.com, accessed 13 September 2005 and "History: United States Football League," at http://www.oursportscentral.com, accessed 23 December 2005.

Even with three name changes—from the Washington Capitals to Washington Ambassadors and then to the Washington-Baltimore Ambassadors—owner E. Joseph Wheeler was unable to finalize a stadium contract for his club with some officials from the city of Washington. Thus before the 1974 season opened, Wheeler moved the Ambassadors a relatively short distance or from Washington, DC, to Norfolk, Virginia. Almost immediately after that event, Wheeler sold his team to a syndicate that relocated the club from Norfolk to Orlando in central Florida. Renamed the Florida Blazers, the team played at home in Orlando's 30,000-seat Tangerine Bowl and won an ED title in its initial season. Then in December 1974, the team was defeated by a score of 22–21 in the league's championship World Bowl game by the Birmingham Americans. However, due to financial problems and home attendances of less than 16,000 per game, the WFL took control of the Blazers. As an investment, in 1975 businessman Norm Bevan purchased the club, renamed it the Wings, and then moved it to San Antonio, a growing city in southeastern Texas. After winning seven and losing six regular season games—and some of those games to rivals at home in San Antonio's 30,000-seat Alamo Stadium—the Wings disbanded in 1975 because the WFL ceased to exist as a league.

In summary, it was because of incompetent franchise owners, underfinanced investors, team coaches who lacked experience and name recognition, inferior football players, and the negative publicity as a result of the media reporting the discounting of tickets by teams to inflate their attendances at games that, in total, caused the WFL to go out of business. In fact, the league disbanded before the 1975 season had concluded.

To offer its games in the spring of each year rather than in the fall, the United States Football League (USFL) was organized by Donald Dixon in 1982, and initially the league consisted of 12 franchises. Accordingly, one team each played at home in the seven largest U.S. metropolitan areas, the eighth in 10th-ranked Washington, DC, and the other four in midsized cities. With respect to movements of teams in the USFL, a few franchises decided to relocate before and some after the league's opening season in 1983. To illustrate, the Boston Breakers was an original USFL team. Although the club was successful on the field against its opponents, the Breakers had the league's lowest attendance at 12,800 per game while playing at home in Boston's 20,500-seat Nickerson Field. Before the 1984 season started, entrepreneur Joe Canizaro purchased the franchise from owner Randy Vataha and moved the club from Boston to southern Louisiana. Then Canizaro changed the club's name to New Orleans Breakers. Despite an increase in average attendance in 1984 to 30,600 while playing at home in the 30,500-seat Superdome, a disappointing winning percentage of .444 forced the team to relocate from New Orleans to Oregon, where it became known as Portland Breakers and scheduled home games in the city's 32,500-seat Civic Stadium. However, as a result of a decrease in average attendance to about 20,000 and a season of dismal performances in its games before hometown fans, the Breakers folded in 1985 because the league ceased to exist.

In the 1983 and 1984 seasons, respectively, the Philadelphia Stars placed runner-up to the Michigan Panthers 24–22 for the league's title and then defeated the Arizona Wranglers 23–3 to win a USFL championship. Yet the Stars' average attendance was below 20,000 while playing at home in Philadelphia's 72,200-seat Veterans Stadium. So in 1984, owner Myles Tannenbaum moved his club from Philadelphia to Maryland, where it performed at home in Baltimore's 45,000-seat Byrd Stadium. In 1985, businessman Steve Ross purchased the Stars from Tannenbaum for $3 million. One year later, the team disbanded when the USFL folded.

Berl Bernard owned the Washington Federals, which was an original USFL franchise. After the team played two dismal seasons in the nation's capital at 54,800-seat RFK Stadium, Bernard sold his club to Sherwood Weiser, who in turn resold it to Donald Dizney. Before the 1985 season began, Dizney moved the team from Washington, DC, to play in Orlando's 50,000-seat Citrus Bowl. Before competing there, he renamed the club Orlando Renegades. Even so, in 1986 the Renegades franchise had to terminate its operations when the USFL folded.

For a few key facts about the seven USFL teams listed in Table 6.3, each season the attendances of the Boston and Portland Breakers, and the Philadelphia Stars and Washington Federals averaged fewer than 20,000 per game when they played at home in their stadiums. Furthermore, the two teams with the highest average attendances per game in one season were the New Orleans Breakers' 30,550 and Baltimore Stars' 28,350 in 1984. Regarding some of the teams' performances, the Philadelphia Stars and Boston Breakers had the highest average winning percentages and the Stars appeared in two league championship games. Finally, the Baltimore Stars became the 1985 USFL champion by defeating the rival Oakland Invaders by a score of 28–24.

During the USFL's three-year history, franchises were sold and purchased at a rapid pace. This high turnover rate created significant problems for the teams' coaches, players, fans, and communities. Furthermore, the league was inferior to the NFL because of its disparities with respect to television income and clubs' per-game attendances, and the failures of USFL franchises in such large markets as Boston, Chicago, Detroit, Philadelphia, and Washington, DC. In the end, the USFL disbanded after the 1985 season when a court awarded it $1 in damages as a result of a lawsuit filed against the NFL for antitrust violations. Since there was no merger between these rival football leagues, all of the USFL's 14 teams had to dissolve.

SUMMARY

This chapter discusses the movements of teams within eight alternative professional leagues and the transfers of clubs between leagues in the same sport during years from the late 1800s to early 2000s. In fact, there were two groups of clubs each in baseball, basketball, and football, and one each in ice hockey and soccer. The total number of team relocations and transfers during this period of years—relative to the eight leagues—was 55. This number includes 5 in baseball, 14 in basketball, 10 in football, 9 in ice hockey, and 17 in soccer. To highlight these activities, Chapter 6 contains three tables that indicate respectively the years, teams' nicknames before and after relocating and/or transferring, and the clubs' performances for various seasons at their premove and postmove sites.

Due to demographic, economic, and financial factors and various sport-specific reasons, one team relocated within the "major" Federal League and 17 moved within the North American Soccer League. This vast difference in the number of team movements across the eight organizations suggests that a portion of franchise owners were not totally committed to their league's mission and thus became easily demoralized after being defeated by their rivals and losing a majority of games in regular seasons. Meanwhile, other owners were impatient in marketing and promoting their teams and unable to attract local fans to hometown games. Finally, some owners were simply sensitive about and less tolerant in sustaining financial losses while operating in their home arenas, ballparks, and stadiums. Consequently, the turnover rates and movements of teams in the alternative leagues were relatively higher per season than the rates and average number of relocations among teams in the dominant or primary leagues that are featured in Chapters 2 and 4

7

Conclusion

Since the late 1800s a number of primary and secondary professional sports leagues have established their headquarters and existed in the United States. Some of these organizations failed after a year, whereas others struggled but succeeded to operate for numerous seasons. Whether they have remained active and survived or not, the leagues were compelled to change their composition and thus reorganize. That is, for various demographic, economic, financial, and sport-specific reasons, the team's management decided to realign their structures and form conferences and perhaps divisions within these conferences. Furthermore, at one time or another most of the sports leagues added more teams and/or downsized by eliminating a number of their franchises. Therefore, the purpose of Chapters 1–6 is to document and discuss when, why, and how selected leagues had reformed and either continued to operate or fold as groups in the competitive sports industry.

Beginning in the late 1800s and throughout the 1900s and early 2000s, two of the common ways that leagues adjusted to market conditions were expansion and merger. In other words, to maximize profits, each year some of the teams in these leagues attempted to extend their longevity by moving from a site in a city to another metropolitan area and then playing games at home in a new or renovated arena, ballpark, or stadium. Although this strategy was implemented according to plans, a few of the leagues still could not sustain their operations and inevitably failed. As a result, a hundred or more professional sports teams disbanded. Yet, some clubs continued to exist and perform because they had transferred into a rival league.

This chapter highlights and discusses the different types of reorganizations by league and sport, and gives an overview of history for the benefit of educators, commentators, researchers, and sports fans. As such, in two sections it summarizes the results of various leagues' transformations during the pre- and post-1950 eras. Then some implications are discussed about the future prospects of specific leagues.

LEAGUE EXPANSIONS/MERGERS

Pre-1950

According to column two of Table 7.1, between 1876 and 1950 a total of 85 new sports teams had joined six different professional leagues. Based on

Table 7.1
League and Team Reorganizations, by Sport, Selected Seasons

League (Seasons)	League Expansions		Team Relocations/Transfers	
	Pre-1950	Post-1950	Pre-1950	Post-1950
Baseball				
AA (1882–1891)	14	NA	0/8	NA
AL (1901–2005)	0	7	2/0	6/0
ENL (1876–1900)	14	NA	3/0	NA
FL (1914–1915)	3	NA	1/0	NA
NAPBP (1871–1875)	0	NA	0/6	NA
NL (1901–2005)	0	7	0/0	5/0
UA (1884)	0	NA	4/1	NA
Football				
AAFC (1946–1949)	0	NA	0/4	NA
AFL (1960–1969)	NA	2	NA	0/10
NFL (1922–2005)	25	9	12/0	10/0
USFL (1983–1985)	NA	5	NA	4/0
WFL (1974–1975)	NA	0	NA	6/0
Basketball				
ABA (1967–1975)	NA	1	NA	12/4
BAA (1946–1948)	0	NA	0/11	NA
NBA (1949–2005)	0	18	0/0	19/0
NBL (1937–1948)	0	NA	0/6	NA
WNBA (1996–2005)	NA	9	NA	2/0

Table 7.1 (continue)

League (Seasons)	League Expansions		Team Relocations/Transfers	
	Pre-1950	**Post-1950**	**Pre-1950**	**Post-1950**
Ice Hockey				
NHL (1917–2005)	6	21	4/0	8/0
WHA (1972–1979)	NA	4	NA	9/4
Soccer				
ASL I (1921–1933)	23	NA	0/6	NA
EPSL II (1928–1929)	0	NA	0/5	NA
MLS (1996–present)	NA	4	NA	0/0
MPSL (2003–2004)	NA	5	NA	0/0
NASL (1967–1984)	NA	26	NA	17/0

Note: NA is Not Applicable, which means that the league did not exist in the sport's seasons during pre- or post-1950. Transfers are the number of teams that had shifted between leagues primarily because of mergers.

Source: See sources in the tables of Chapters 1–6.

the experiences of two such groups that existed in the United States before those in the other sports had formed, prior to 1950, baseball's AA and ENL added 28, or approximately 33 percent of the total, expansion clubs. Even so, these teams won an average of only 41 percent of their regular season games. Due to poor performances, low attendances at home-site games, sales of teams to new owners, and financial problems, several of the AA franchises disbanded after one season, and so did some ENL expansion teams.

After the AA and ENL each grew in size and then dissolved, from 1922 to 1949 it was the NFL and ASL I that, in total, expanded by admitting 48 new clubs to perform in their conferences and/or divisions for various seasons. With respect to the teams' circumstances, 15, or 66 percent, of the NFL expansions folded within six seasons. Consequently, only 8, or 32 percent, of football's pre-1950 expansion clubs played six or more NFL seasons at their original sites. Regarding the ASL I, 23 soccer teams joined the league between 1921 and 1933. After one season of competition, nine, or approximately 39 percent, of these expansion franchises disbanded. Apparently, the clubs had inferior coaches and players, attracted few sports fans to their home games, and desperately lacked enough revenues to operate.

Besides the number of pre-1950 expansion clubs in the AA, ENL, NFL, and ASL I, the FL added three teams in 1914 and the NHL six in 1924–1926. Because four, or 66 percent, of the expansion ice hockey teams have continued to perform in the league's regular seasons through the early 2000s, the NHL's pre-1950 reorganizations have been relatively more successful in the long run than those that had occurred in the other leagues. Finally, nine, or 60 percent, of the leagues that had existed prior to 1950 did not add new teams.

To avoid teams from competing for players in the same sport and for other economic reasons, some of the dominant and/or secondary leagues compromised and then consolidated their organizations. With respect to which leagues were affected, such combinations included the AA-ENL-PL in 1891, AL-NL in 1903 and ASL I-EPSL II in 1929, and 20 years later the AAFC-NFL and ABA-NBA. Consequently, each of these five mergers resulted in fewer professional sports leagues and fewer teams in metropolitan areas, diminished the rate of increase in player's salaries, and granted more market power to the surviving leagues and their respective franchises.

Post-1950

Table 7.1's column three indicates that 13 of the professional leagues added a total of 118 new teams between 1950 and 2005. In contrast, the WFL was the only group that did not expand the number of clubs during the post-1950 era. To penetrate sports markets in 65 areas, the most ambitious organization was the NASL and then the NHL and NBA. As denoted in Chapter 5's Table 5.2, the NASL's 26 expansion clubs won about 46 percent of their games while they existed between 1970 and 1984.

Between 1967 and 2000, the NHL welcomed 21 clubs as new members. That is, 6 joined the league in the 1960s and 1970s; there were 7 more in the 1990s; and 2 in 2000. Several of the expansion teams that were located in small and midsized cities struggled to fill their arenas for home games and compete for division and/or conference titles. Indeed, if any of the 30 current NHL franchises continue to founder, before 2010 one or more of them could fold or be encouraged to relocate to sites in cities of metropolitan areas within the United States.

As indicated in Chapter 3's Table 3.3, there were 18 expansion teams that entered the NBA between 1961 and 2004. Because of inferior performances, small fan bases, financial issues, and/or ownership problems, 6, or 33 percent, of these franchises have ceased to exist at their original locations. Nevertheless, as of the 2005 season, this group of 18 teams has succeeded to win eight NBA titles and finish runners-up to league champions in seven postseasons. Interestingly, the Charlotte Bobcats became an NBA expansion team in 2004, which was two years after the Charlotte Hornets relocated from the state of North Carolina to Louisiana and adopted the nickname New Orleans Hornets. Although the Bobcats fail to consistently win as a member of the Eastern Conference's Southeast Division, the team plays with enthusiasm and effort at home in a new yet-to-be-named arena before 13,000–16,000 fans per game.

After receiving antitrust exemptions and thus permission from U.S. federal courts, the AFL-NFL merged in 1970 and so did the ABA-NBA in 1976. As a result, since the mid to late 1970s, four major team sports based in the United States have been operating as economic cartels that control the entries and locations of their respective teams. In turn, the annual profits and market values of these franchises have tended to appreciate. Consequently, consumers pay high ticket prices to attend teams' home and away games, players demand and receive lucrative salaries and perquisites, owners generate increasing amounts of wealth from their investments in professional sports enterprises, and municipalities issue bonds and use local taxpayer money to finance the construction of new sports facilities and/or the renovation of existing arenas, ballparks, and stadiums.

To summarize this section of the conclusion, since their original seasons the NFL has expanded by 34 teams and NHL 27. Meanwhile, the former NASL added 26 new clubs in 18 years and the ASL I enlarged by 23 in 13. In contrast, between the late 1800s and early 2000s there were no expansion teams in baseball's NAPBP and UA, football's AAFC and WFL, basketball's BAA and NBL, and soccer's EPSL II. Because of business, financial, and economic risks, these latter sports organizations were conservative and thus not prepared or motivated to use expansion as a strategy to penetrate new markets in U.S. metropolitan areas and provinces in Canada.

TEAM RELOCATIONS/TRANSFERS

Pre-1950

During this era of regular seasons, playoffs, and championship series for 15 of the professional sports leagues, column four of Table 7.1 denotes that a total of 26 teams moved from their home cities to sites in other areas and 47 clubs transferred into another league. If the expansions listed in column two are excluded, before 1950 the sports leagues that restructured the most to least were those in baseball and then basketball, football, soccer, and ice hockey. Consequently, in the following paragraphs of this section the first topic discussed is the relocations within leagues prior to 1950, and second is the transfers between leagues during this period of years.

Regarding the total 10 movements that occurred within four baseball leagues, five, or 50 percent, of the clubs improved in winning percentages after relocating to their postmove sites. Furthermore, only the two AL clubs that relocated had survived after the 1901 baseball season.

As denoted in Chapter 2's Table 2.2, between 1924 and 1949, there were 12 NFL clubs that moved their operations to sites in cities of other areas. Seven, or approximately 59 percent, of these clubs had higher winning percentages after they relocated. In short, prior to 1950, the majority of NFL clubs had moved from playing at home in obsolete stadiums that were located in small to midsized cities into new or renovated facilities in more populated areas within larger sports markets.

The third group of teams that moved—from 1900 to 1950—played in the NHL. While performing in regular seasons at their postmove sites, these four clubs did not win a division title and eventually each of them folded. Due to competition among the six established NHL franchises from the 1940s to early 1970s, the league's next relocation phases occurred for teams in the mid to late 1970s and then in the early 1980s and mid 1990s.

As a result of reorganization, before 1950 a number of teams had shifted between leagues in the same sport. These specific clubs are discussed in Chapter 2 for the primary leagues and in Chapter 6 for the alternative leagues. During this period, a sum of 47 teams had transferred from eight into four existing or new leagues. Some teams decided to become affiliates of another league when their respective parent organizations dissolved due to merger, whereas other clubs became attached to another sports group because their league simply went of business.

Post-1950

Column five of Table 7.1 lists the number of team relocations that occurred within selected leagues from 1950 to 2005 and the number of clubs that had transferred between leagues in the same sport. According to the table, a total of 98 teams in 11 sports leagues moved to sites in other cities and 18 shifted from and into 3 rival leagues. Specifically, there were 11 movements of teams in baseball, 20 in football, 33 in basketball, and 17 each in ice hockey and soccer. After 1950, the first, second, third, and fourth largest number of movements by teams per league were 19, 17, 12, and10, which are reported in, respectively, Table 4.2 for the NBA, Table 6.2 for the NASL, Table 6.1 for the ABA, and Table 4.3 for the NFL. Relative to the number of transfers by sport, 10 teams had shifted from the AFL into the NFL, and 4 each had transferred from the ABA into the NBA and WHA into the NHL.

Besides clubs in the NBA, NASL, ABA, and NFL, a total of 40 teams relocated within a group of seven sports leagues. As reflected in column five of Table 7.1, there were several clubs that had transferred from one league to another between 1950 and 2005. That is, 10 teams shifted from the AFL to NFL in 1970, and 4 each had transferred from the ABA to the NBA in 1976 and from the WHA to the NHL in 1979.

In conclusion, since the late 1800s, there have been 124 sports teams that changed their locations within professional leagues and 65 clubs that transferred between leagues. Therefore, across each sport, the 189 relocations and transfers per league were composed of 25 teams in ice hockey, 28 in soccer, 36 in baseball, 46 in football, and 54 in basketball. If these numbers are added to the expansions in each of the sports leagues, the reorganizations totaled 392, including 56 in ice hockey, 81 in baseball, 82 in basketball, 86 in soccer, and 87 in football. Consequently, these sums indicate that professional ice hockey leagues restructured the least while football leagues initiated the most reorganizations.

FUTURE IMPLICATIONS

The frequency and type of reorganizations within and between the various professional sports leagues, and those involving the respective franchises, certainly affected their decisions about how to implement reforms, and whether as business and entertainment enterprises they could continue to exist, successfully perform, and profitably operate into the future. Consequently, there are a number of potential opportunities and controversial issues that one or more of the leagues are likely to experience in the future relative to what had influenced them since becoming established organizations in the twentieth and twenty-first centuries. Some important matters that may challenge the leagues and member franchises throughout the early 2000s include (1) their revenue sharing policies, (2) disparities in the metropolitan areas' population and wealth among large, midsized, and small market teams, (3) global expansion, (4) clubs' local, regional, and national fan bases, and (5) other specific events and trends that are related to each of the sports. As a result, the following are nine observations that indicate why and how the history of reorganizations, as discussed in Chapters 1–6, have changed and will likely affect the future plans, operations, and growth of the U.S.-based professional leagues.

First, the inequalities in teams' annual payrolls and thus their regular season and postseason performances have occurred, in part, because each of them play games against their opponents at home in facilities that are located within demographically different market areas. Across the sports leagues, this fact suggests that clubs with home sites in such cities as Milwaukee, Orlando, and Portland are at a competitive disadvantage in earning power and winning titles relative to those that are based in Chicago, Los Angeles, and New York. The contrasts in generating revenues and winning championships are especially apparent between teams in divisions of MLB but less so among clubs in conferences of the NFL, NBA, and MLS. Meanwhile, in 2005 the NHL signed a new collective bargaining agreement with its players union whereby a larger share of the league's total revenues is to be redistributed from large- to small-market teams. Because it has become increasingly difficult for sports officials such as commissioners and groups like executive committees to justify and convince some franchise owners to transfer their incomes to other teams, the professional leagues will be less likely to approve any expansions and/or movements to sites in areas with relatively small populations and low-rated television and radio markets. In short, it is midsized cities that are and will be the most attractive places in the United States for new and existing professional sports clubs to locate and play their games at home.

Second, the knowledge of—and international demand for—American professional sports brands and events has significantly increased since the 1970s–1980s. This phenomenon implies the emergence of potential fan bases, which makes a number of foreign cities viable sites for teams of leagues that decide to evaluate and implement reorganization strategies. In other words, after the hype and exposure that will evolve from the 2008 Summer Olympics in Beijing, there will be economic incentives and business opportunities for MLB and the other four leagues to eventually sponsor a division of four to six teams that will operate somewhere in midsized to large cities within nations of Asia, Europe, and perhaps Central and/or South America. A baseball group affiliated with MLB, for example, could be established with teams playing in such countries as the Dominican Republic, Mexico, Panama, Puerto Rico, and Venezuela. Furthermore, the NFL Europe exists as a professional league to exploit sports markets within Western European cities, and basketball and the NBA are very popular in many regions of Asia and Eastern Europe. However, because of the owner's lockout that terminated the 2004 regular season, the NHL needs to reclaim and then grow its fan base in North America. Thus, this league is unlikely in the short run to open new sites and expand or relocate existing teams overseas. Similarly, it will be 5–10 years before MLS is organizationally and financially capable of placing teams beyond the U.S. borders.

Third, to promote and further extend their marketing programs with respect to the number and location of franchises, each of the sports leagues require increasing amounts of revenues from national broadcasting rights and thus cable and satellite networks. Since these revenues are equally shared among the member clubs of a league and are especially critical to the survival of small and some midsized market teams, the gradual decline in television ratings for regular season games offered by MLB, the NBA, and the NHL is an ominous trend that these leagues must reverse. Therefore, the amounts of income from national, regional, and local television and radio contracts are ultra-important factors that the sports leagues must consider when contemplating future expansions, mergers, and other kinds of reorganizations. Moreover, these monies affect the level of competitive balance between teams in the divisions and conferences of leagues and in turn, the clubs' media coverage and exposure, and the penetration of their markets.

Fourth, based on its 10-year history, MLS has a specific set of organizational issues to confront. The league's teams, which have marginally expanded their local and regional fan bases since the late 1990s, require the support of investors, sponsors, and taxpayers who are committed and willing to provide financial capital and pay for the construction of modern soccer stadiums so that these clubs can attract more spectators and generate additional revenues at their home games. Also, as the markets for professional soccer emerge and develop across cities in the United States, MLS will be motivated to authorize and move one or more of its weakest existing teams to sites in these areas. In fact, the first MLS relocation occurred during early 2006 when the Earthquakes relocated from San Jose, California, to southeastern Texas and changed the club's name to Houston Dynamo. Furthermore, if the league's newest expansion teams—Chivas USA and Real Salt Lake—are able to remain popular and draw impressive attendances to their home games, then MLS will place teams into cities with large Hispanic populations. Even though a U.S. women's professional soccer league folded during the early 2000s, the sport and MLS have a reasonable opportunity to penetrate some of the popular sports markets in the U.S. southeast, southwest, and west, and thrive at these locations.

Fifth, the WNBA is a unique and relatively new professional basketball league. To supply a schedule of games each season, the league's franchises are highly dependent on receiving operating subsidies provided by their respective NBA teams. Therefore, the WNBA is regulated to expand and/or relocate existing clubs into cities that are home sites of NBA clubs. Indeed, in 2006 the WNBA agreed to place an expansion club named the Chicago Sky in the northeast Illinois area. Assuming the league survives, this action suggests that other U.S. populated areas are prime sites as future locations for new and current WNBA teams.

Sixth, the ABALive and NWBL are secondary, fragile, and probably temporary leagues. That is, they are not in direct competition for players or markets with, respectively, the NBA or WNBA. Rather, the two former leagues exist in the short run to provide sports entertainment to men's and women's basketball fans who live in very small, small, and midsized communities. To exist from one season to the next, the ABALive has encouraged investors to fund and operate expansion franchises, and the league's existing teams occasionally withdraw from and shift to alternative sites. The NWBL, meanwhile, remains limited in size and attempts to establish a presence in local markets by giving fans an opportunity to attend low-key games played by women who formerly were WNBA and/ or Division I college players. Because the ABALive and NWBL are not perceived to be serious threats or rivals to superior basketball leagues, an eventual merger of the ABALive and NBA, and of the NWBL and WNBA are remote events.

Seventh, the majority of league reorganizations affect the relationships of coaches, players, and their families. To illustrate, some players are identified, drafted, and reassigned to perform for an expansion team that plays at home in a different city. Also, when a sports club moves to another area, the franchise's personnel must decide whether to relocate their households and residences to the postmove location. As a result, these two reorganizations could create financial and other personal hardships for teams' coaches and athletes, which in part influences their performances in games. Historical evidence suggests that expansion clubs must exist for five or more years to become competitive in a given division or conference. Alternatively, relocated teams play only about average in seasons after moving despite a significant increase in attendances at home games held in their postmove arenas, ballparks, or stadiums.

Eighth, when evaluating local markets for expansion and relocating professional teams, the attractiveness of small, midsized, and big cities and areas may vary by sport. In other words, a city or area may contain a proportionately large fan base that enthusiastically attends games played in professional baseball and basketball but not in football, ice hockey, or soccer. These intersport deviations in support are based, in part, on such factors as the clubs' competitiveness, entertainment value and tradition, teams' relations with the local media and community, and fans' perceptions of the franchises' owners, coaches, and players. Furthermore, two or more teams located within a market may have different levels of support. Sports fans in the New York area, for example, preferred the Dodgers and Yankees to the Giants but rooted for these three baseball teams as opposed to the NBA Knicks, NHL Rangers, and NASL Cosmos. Even so, because of population size and amount of aggregate wealth—and despite movements of some large-market clubs as the Raiders and Rams—cities like Los Angeles, New York, Boston, and Chicago are desirable home sites for new and existing professional sports franchises.

Ninth, in the future, MLB, the NFL, the NBA, and the NHL will be increasingly reluctant to expand and approve the entry of new clubs. Indeed, the owners of franchise within these leagues especially resist sharing any revenues earned from their venues and television broadcasts with other division and conference teams. Also, the cost of operating professional sports clubs has risen, and that suggests being a millionaire is not necessarily sufficient wealth to be an owner of a team. Hence, a growing number of business entrepreneurs may invest money in new and current clubs of such secondary sports leagues as the ABALive and NWBL. In contrast, because of franchises' financial problems, leagues will likely permit member teams to relocate from their present sites to other areas. Since the 1960s, these relocations occurred when sponsors and local taxpayers refused to provide teams with subsidies to finance the construction of new—or renovation of existing—arenas, ballparks, and/or stadiums. Consequently, before 2015, some of the leagues' sports teams will be playing games at home in obsolete facilities and thus seek public funds to upgrade their facilities with more seats and amenities.

In the end, these nine implications will determine which of the current leagues will succeed or fail in the future. It is crucial, therefore, that decision makers be aware of and respect the relevant business history of—and facts about—expansions, mergers, and other reorganizations that had occurred within and between professional sports leagues in the United States.

Notes

INTRODUCTION

1. See Stephen H. Hardy, "Entrepreneurs, Organizations, and the Sports Marketplace," *Journal of Sport History 13* (1986), 14–33.

2. For studies of the expansion and relocation of teams in professional sports leagues, see Frank P. Jozsa, Jr., "An Economic Analysis of Franchise Relocation and League Expansion in Professional Team Sports, 1950–1975," (doctoral dissertation, Georgia State University, 1977), and Frank P. Jozsa, Jr., and John J. Guthrie, Jr., *Relocating Teams and Expanding Leagues in Professional Sports: How the Major Leagues Respond to Market Conditions* (Westport, CT: Quorum Books, 1999).

3. Baseball club franchise moves from 1946 to 1972 are discussed in James Quirk, "An Economic Analysis of Team Movements in Professional Sports," *Law and Contemporary Problems 38* (Winter/Spring 1973), 42–66. Other conclusions about relocation are, in part, derived analytically and empirically by James Quirk and Mohamed El Hodiri in "The Economic Theory of a Professional Sports League," in Roger G. Noll, ed., *Government and the Sports Business* (Washington, DC: The Brookings Institution, 1974), 33–80.

4. These and other topics, such as the special privileges received by professional sports clubs from the U.S. federal government, are highlighted and discussed in some articles of *Government and the Sports Business.*

5. For why government should not distort the marketplace to encourage the relocation of sports teams, see James Gattuso, "Congress and Rule-Making," *Society* (May/June 1986), 6–10.

6. A compelling argument has been made to reduce the entry barriers of leagues, thereby allowing more teams to exist and giving fans a better opportunity to attend

professional sports games. See Arthur T. Johnson, "Balancing Interests," *Society* (May/June 1986), 11–16.

7. Some of the controversies and effects of revenue sharing in professional football are presented in David Meggyesy, "The National Football League Monopoly," *Society* (May/June 1986), 16–21.

8. To analyze the sports business from a multidisciplinary perspective, see Paul D. Staudohar and James A. Mangan, eds., *The Business of Professional Sports* (Champaign: University of Illinois Press, 1991).

9. Charles C. Euchner, *Playing the Field: Why Sports Teams Move and Cities Fight to Keep Them* (Baltimore, MD: John Hopkins University Press, 1993),1–5.

10. Because professional sports franchises have an impact on their communities, many local politicians seek public funds to finance the construction of new sports facilities. This topic is discussed in Kenneth L. Shropshire, *The Sports Franchise Game: Cities in Pursuit of Sports Franchises, Events, Stadiums, and Arenas* (Philadelphia: University of Pennsylvania Press, 1995), 1–10.

11. See Robert Draper, "Spoils Sports: Houston Professional Sports Teams Threaten to Relocate," *Texas Monthly* (January 1996), 110–16.

12. These observations are expressed in an article by Stephen F. Ross titled "Break Up the Sports League Monopolies," in Paul D. Staudohar and James A. Mangan, eds., *The Business of Professional Sports* (1991), 152–73.

13. For some aspects of the sports business during the 1990s, see Paul Attner, "How Professional Sports Governs Expansion Will Mean Success or Failure for the 21st Century," *The Sporting News* (18 March 1991), 13–19, and Jerry Crasnik, "How to Build a Baseball Franchise," *The Sporting News* (30 June 1997), 27.

14. See Gary Stix, "Blackballing the Inner City," *Scientific American 269* (September 1993), 152.

15. Professional sports franchises' contributions to generate jobs and increase payrolls in communities, and to provide financial returns to local taxpayers are analyzed in two publications: Mark S. Rosentraub, *Major League Losers: The Real Costs of Sports and Who's Paying for It* (New York: Basic Books, 1997), 1–15, and John J. McCormick, "Playing Stadium Games: The Urge to be a Big-League Town Has Turned Civic Pride Into a Costly—and Vain—Obsession," *Newsweek* (30 June 1997), 55.

16. To read how six cities improved their infrastructures to prepare for the arrival of new professional sports teams, see Melissa Minker, "Expansion," *SportsTravel* (January 1997), 30–34.

17. The mission, organization, and interest of FANS, including the resolutions regarding the relocation of sports clubs, was available during the late 1990s on the group's Web site at http://www.consumers.com, accessed 10 February 1997.

18. For whether the Triad area in North Carolina had a realistic opportunity to host a baseball team in the late 1990s and the results of the referendum, see Justin Catanoso, "Loading the Bases in North Carolina?" *Business Week* (7 April 1997), 98–99, and "Voters Reject Triad Referendum For Baseball Stadium," at http://www.cnnsi.com, accessed 6 May 1998.

19. See Bob Hille, "TSN's Best Sports Cities," *The Sporting News* (30 June 1997), 14–23. As an aside, in 2005 some U.S. cities that ranked as good locations to expand included Las Vegas, Nevada; Louisville, Kentucky; Nashville, Tennessee; Pittsburgh, Pennsylvania; and Tampa Bay, Florida, for an NBA team; and Portland, Oregon; San Antonio, Texas; Las Vegas, Nevada; Orlando, Florida; and Sacramento, California, for an MLB club. Furthermore, in a survey conducted by American City Business Journals, the best sites for sports teams in 2004 were Los Angeles; Philadelphia; Orlando, Florida; Houston, Texas; and Portland, Oregon. See, respectively, "Topping the Expansion List," at http://www.cnnsi.com, accessed 12 August 2005, and G. Scott Thomas, "Los Angeles Scores as Best Place for Sports Teams," at http://www.msnbc.msn.com, accessed 12 August 2005.

CHAPTER ONE

1. For the NAPBP's history and this league's teams, see Dan Nichols, "Major League Franchise Information," at http://www.baseball1.com, accessed 16 September 2005, and "Complete Team Index," at http://www.baseball-reference.com, accessed 15 September 2005.

2. The expansions in the ENL were determined from "The First Major League (1875–1889)," at http://www.hickoksports.com, accessed 27 August 2005; *Official Major League Baseball Fact Book 2005 Edition* (St. Louis, MO: Sporting News, 2005), 171–204; and "Schedule Overview 1901–1998," at http://www.baseball1.com, accessed 16 September 2005. The ownership histories, attendance records, and radio and television incomes of teams in several professional sports leagues are available in James Quirk and Rodney D. Fort, *Pay Dirt: The Business of Professional Team Sports* (Princeton, NJ: Princeton University Press, 1992), 378–511.

3. To read about the NFL's expansion clubs and their performances, see the *Official 2001 National Football League Record & Fact Book* (New York: National Football League, 2001), 290–301; "NFL Franchise Chronology," at http://www.hickoksports.com, accessed 27 August 2005; and "National Football League (NFL) History," at http://www.rauzulusstreet.com, accessed 12 August 2005.

4. The chronology and evolution of these pre-NHL amateur ice hockey leagues and associations are in "Amateur Hockey Association," at http://www.en.wikipedia.org, accessed 24 September 2005, and "List of Ice Hockey Leagues," at http://www.en.wikipedia.org, accessed 16 September 2005.

5. See the "National Hockey League," at http://www.en.wikipedia.org, accessed 27 August 2005; "National Hockey League (NHL) Expansion History," at http://www.rauzulusstreet.com, accessed 12 August 2005; and "NHL Franchise Origins," at http://www.infoplease.com, accessed 12 August 2005.

6. For example, statistics about the various Boston Bruins clubs, players and championships are available on the Web site "Boston Bruins," at http://www.en.wikipedia.org, accessed 27 August 2005, and for the team's performances each season see "Stanley Cup Record Year-by-Year," at http://www.bostonbruins.com, accessed 27 August 2005. The annual awards won by NHL players are reported in *The World Almanac and Book of Facts* (New York: World Almanac Books, 2004), 940–44.

7. The NBL's history is reported in "Encyclopedia: National Basketball League," at http://www.nationmaster.com, accessed 27 August 2005, and "National Basketball League," at http://www.hickoksports.com, accessed 27 August 2005.

8. For the ABL's original and expansion teams and their locations, see "American Basketball League 1925–55," at http://www.en.wikipedia.org, accessed 29 September 2005.

9. The various dates and events about the BAA and/or NBA franchises are reported in "NBA Growth Timetable," at http://www.basketball.com, accessed 20 September 2005; "NBA Franchise History," at http://www.hickoksports.com, accessed 27 August 2005; "National Basketball Association," at http://www.rauzulusstreet.com, accessed 12 August 2005; and "Basketball History," at http://www.history-of-basketball.com, accessed 20 September 2005.

10. See Dave Litterer, "American Soccer League I (1921–1933)," at http://www.sover.net, accessed 20 September 2005, and David Goldblatt, *Soccer Yearbook 2004/5* (New York: DK Publishing, 2004), 504–5.

11. One of the readings about this unique soccer league and its teams is Dave Litterer, "American Soccer League II (New England Division)," at http://www.sover.net, accessed 21 September 2005.

CHAPTER TWO

1. For the early history of U.S.-based professional sports leagues and teams, see Frank G. Menke, *The Encyclopedia of Sports,* 5th edition (New York: A. S. Barnes and Company, Inc., 1975); Roger G. Noll, ed., *Government and the Sports Business* (Washington, DC: The Brookings Institution, 1974); Mark Pollak, *Sports Leagues and Teams: An Encyclopedia, 1871 Through 1996* (Jefferson, NC: McFarland & Company, 1997); "Major Professional Sports Leagues," at http://www.en.wikipedia.org, accessed 23 October 2005.

2. The home sites, standings, and events of the professional baseball leagues and teams are, in part, contained in the *Official Major League Baseball Fact*

Book 2005 Edition (St. Louis, MO: Sporting News, 2005); James Quirk and Rodney D. Fort, *Pay Dirt: The Business of Professional Team Sports* (Princeton, NJ: Princeton University Press, 1992); "Major League Baseball," at http://www.mlb.com, accessed 8 August 2005; "The First Major League (1875–1889)," at http://www.hickoksports.com, accessed 27 August 2005; "MLB Franchise History," at http://www.mlb.com, accessed 9 November 2004; "19th Century National League Teams," at http://www.en.wikipedia.org, accessed 19 September 2005. For a study of team relocations in MLB, see James Quirk, "An Economic Analysis of Team Movements in Professional Sports," *Law and Contemporary Problems* (Winter/Spring 1973), 42–66.

3. Some sources consulted for the early history of professional football leagues, teams, players, and events include the *Official 2001 National Football League Record & Fact Book* (New York: National Football League, 2001); *The First Fifty Years* (New York: Ridge Press/Benjamin Company, 1969); Bob Carroll, *Total Football II: The Official Encyclopedia of the National Football League* (New York: HarperCollins World, 1999); "National Football League (NFL) History," at http://www.rauzulusstreet.com, accessed 12 August 2005.

4. For books and other literature on professional ice hockey leagues and teams, see James Duplacey, *Total Hockey: The Official Encyclopedia of the National Hockey League* (New York: Total Sports, 1998): Zander Hollander and Hal Brock, *The Complete Encyclopedia of Ice Hockey* (Englewood Cliffs, NJ: Prentice-Hall, Inc., 1974); "National Hockey League," at http://www.en.wikipedia.org, accessed 27 August 2005; "History," at http://www.nhl.com, accessed 24 August 2005; James Quirk and Rodney D. Fort, *Pay Dirt,* 463–78.

5. Specific facts about the movements of such ice hockey teams as the Quebec Bulldogs, Hamilton Tigers, Pittsburgh Pirates, and Ottawa Senators are available in "NHL Relocation History," at http://www.geocities.com, accessed 15 September 2005, and at http://www.en.wikipedia.com.

6. The relocations, transfers, and performances of professional basketball teams—prior to the 1950 NBA season—are discussed in Leonard Koppett, *Total Basketball: The Ultimate Basketball Encyclopedia* (Wilmington, DE: SportClassic Books, 2004); Kenneth A. Shouler, *Total Basketball: The Ultimate Basketball Encyclopedia* (Wilmington, DE: SportClassic Books, 2003); "National Basketball Association (NBA) History," at http://www.rauzulusstreet.com, accessed 12 August 2005; "Basketball History," at http://www.history-of-basketball.com, accessed 20 September 2005; "NBA Franchise History," at http://www.hickoksports.com, accessed 27 August 2005.

7. Facts about the pre-1950 amateur and professional soccer leagues, teams, and seasons in the United States were obtained, in part, from David Goldblatt, *Soccer Yearbook 2004/5* (New York: DK Publishing, 2004); "Major League Soccer," at http://www.en.wikipedia.org, accessed 16 September 2005; "History: Major

League Soccer," at http://www.hickoksport.com, accessed 3 December 2005; Dave Litterer, "American Soccer History Archives," http://www.sover.net, accessed 23 October 2005; Idem., "Eastern Professional Soccer League II," at http://www.rsssf. com, accessed 22 October 2005.

CHAPTER THREE

1. See Michael N. Danielson, *Home Team: Professional Sports and the American Metropolis* (Princeton, NJ: Princeton University Press, 1997), 168. In addition, another book that explicitly discusses the expansion of U.S.-based professional sports leagues is Frank P. Jozsa, Jr., and John J. Guthrie, Jr., *Relocating Teams and Expanding League in Professional Sports: How the Major Leagues Respond to Market Conditions* (Westport, CT: Quorum Books, 1999).

2. The publications that were consulted about MLB expansion teams and their performances include the *Official Major League Baseball Fact Book 2005 Edition* (St. Louis, MO: Sporting News, 2005); Frank P. Jozsa, Jr., *Baseball, Inc.: The National Pastime as Big Business* (Jefferson, NC: McFarland & Company, Inc., 2006); James Quirk and Rodney D. Fort, *Pay Dirt: The Business of Professional Team Sports* (Princeton, NJ: Princeton University Press, 1992); "MLB Franchise History," at http://www.mlb.com, accessed 9 November 2004; Dan Nichols, "Major League Franchise Information," at http://www.baseball1.com, accessed 16 September 2005; *The World Almanac and Book of Facts* (New York: World Almanac Books, 1950–2004).

3. For the facts about expansion teams in the NFL, see the *Official 2001 National Football League Record & Fact Book* (New York: National Football League, 2001); Bob Carroll, *Total Football II: The Official Encyclopedia of the National Football League* (New York: HarperCollins World, 1999); James Quirk and Rodney D. Fort, *Pay Dirt,* 409–34; "NFL Franchise Chronology," at http://www.hickoksports.com, accessed 27 August 2005.

4. The histories of the American Basketball Association, Basketball Association of America, the National Basketball League, and the NBA expansion teams and their performances are, in part, discussed in Frank P. Jozsa, Jr., *American Sports Empire: How the Leagues Breed Success* (Westport, CT: Praeger Publishers, 2003); Kenneth A. Shouler, *Total Basketball: The Ultimate Basketball Encyclopedia* (Wilmington, DE: SportClassic Books, 2003); "NBA Franchise History," at http://www.hickoks-ports.com, accessed 27 August 2005; James Quirk and Rodney D. Fort, *Pay Dirt,* 446–63.

5. For detailed information about the Charlotte Bobcats and the club's new arena, see Peter St. Onge, "New Gem Shines, but for How Long?" *The Charlotte Observer* (6 November 2005), 1A, 9A, and "Charlotte Bobcats," at http://www.nba. com, accessed 1 November 2005.

6. See "NHL Expansion History," at http://www.geocities.com, accessed 15 September 2005; "NHL Expansion & Relocation Since 1967," at http://www. andrewsstarspage.com, accessed 20 September 2005; "NHL Expansion/Relocation/ Contraction," at http://www.misterpoll.com, accessed 12 August 2005; James Quirk and Rodney D. Fort, *Pay Dirt,* 463–78.

7. For facts about the various soccer leagues and teams, see Dave Litterer, "American Soccer History Archives," at http://www.sover.net, accessed 23 October 2005; "Major League Soccer," at http://www.en.wikipedia.org, accessed 16 September 2005; "Major League Soccer: History," at http://www.hickoksports. com, accessed 27 August 2005.

8. Future new sites for Major League Soccer teams are discussed in Jason Halpin, "MLS Closing in on Toronto Expansion," at http://www.mlsnet.com, accessed 15 November 2005; idem, "Expansion, Relocation Top League Agenda," at http://www.mlsnet.com, accessed 14 November 2005; Jack Bell, "Second New York-Area Team?" *New York Times* (3 May 2005), 6; Anita Chabria, "Analysis: MLS Expansion," *PR Week* (28 March 2005), 9; Charles F. Gardner, "MLS Message to Milwaukee: Build It and We Will Come," at http://www.jsonline.com, accessed 12 August 2005; Stanley Holmes, "Soccer: Time to Kick it Up a Notch," *Business Week* (22 November 2004), 74–75.

CHAPTER FOUR

1. For MLB, NFL, and NHL teams, performances and seasons, see the *Official Major League Baseball Fact Book 2005 Edition* (St. Louis, MO: Sporting News, 2005); *Official 2001 National Football League Record & Fact Book* (New York: National Football League, 2001); and James Duplacey, *Total Hockey: The Official Encyclopedia of the National Hockey League* (New York: Total Sports, 1998). Other facts and information about the professional sports teams, players and seasons are contained in *The World Almanac and Book of Facts* (New York: World Almanac Books, 1950–2004).

2. The ownership histories of teams in the professional sports leagues are summarized in James Quirk and Rodney D. Fort, *Pay Dirt: The Business of Professional Team Sports* (Princeton, NJ: Princeton University Press, 1992). For a study about the relocation of MLB, NFL, and NBA teams since 1950, see Frank P. Jozsa, Jr., and John J. Guthrie, Jr., *Relocating Teams and Expanding Leagues in Professional Sports: How the Major Leagues Respond to Market Conditions* (Westport, CT: Quorum Books, 1999).

3. Regarding the relocation of the Expos and Selig's statement, see Barry M. Bloom, "MLB Selects D.C. For Expos," at http://www.mlb.com, accessed 9 November 2004, and Mike Bauman, "At Last, Nationals Have a Future," at http:// www.mlb.com, accessed 22 February 2005.

4. The New Orleans Hornets had to select another site to play home games in the 2005 season. The discussions about that decision are reported in Jenni Carlson, "How the Hornets Ended Up in Oklahoma City," at http://www.sportsbusinessnews. com, accessed 4 November 2005. With respect to how the Charlotte Hornets and Vancouver Grizzlies had applied to move to other sites, see "Each Team Files Application for Relocation," at http://www.espn.go.com, accessed 12 August 2005.

5. Articles that discuss and, in part, evaluate cities as sites for current and relocating NBA teams are G. Scott Thomas, "Study Names Best, Worst Cities For Sports Franchises," at http://www.birmingham.bizjournals.com, accessed 15 September 2005; Daniel Rascher and Heather Rascher, "NBA Expansion and Relocation: A Viability Study of Various Cities," *Journal of Sport Management* (July 2004), 274–95. In his annual state of the league address during All-Star weekend in February 2006, NBA Commissioner David Stern stated: "The team most likely to change cities is the Supersonics" and that "Oklahoma City is 'at the top of the list' should a franchise relocate." See "Sonics the Most Likely to Move," *The Charlotte Observer* (19 February 2006), 14C, and Jim Cour, "Sonics Looking at Arena Alternatives," at http://www.netscape.com, accessed 1 February 2006.

6. Besides *Pay Dirt* and *Relocating Teams and Expanding Leagues in Professional Sports,* other sources for information and facts about team relocations and transfers in the NFL include "NFL Franchise Chronology," at http://www.hickoksports. com, accessed 27 August 2005, and Bob Carroll, *Total Football II: The Official Encyclopedia of the National Football League* (New York: HarperCollins World, 1999).

7. See Zander Hollander and Hal Brock, *The Complete Encyclopedia of Ice Hockey* (Englewood Cliffs, NJ: Prentice-Hall, Inc., 1974), and "NHL Expansion & Relocation Since 1967," at http://www.andrewsstarspage.com, accessed 20 September 2005.

8. Various aspects of this eight-year ice hockey league and its teams and seasons are included in "WHA Teams (1972–79)," at http://www.infoplease.com, accessed 12 August 2005; "World Hockey Association," at http://www.wha.com, accessed 13 September 2005; and "List of Ice Hockey Leagues," at http://www.en.wikipedia. org, accessed 16 September 2005.

9. Chris Duncan, "MLS' Newly Named Houston 1836 Seeks Local Support," at http://www.usatoday.com, accessed 26 January 2006.

CHAPTER FIVE

1. For information about mergers, reorganizations, and expansion teams in the alternative leagues, see James Quirk and Rodney D. Fort, *Pay Dirt: The Business*

of Professional Team Sports (Princeton, NJ: Princeton University Press, 1992), and "Expansion/Merger Timetable," at http://www.infoplease.com, accessed 12 August 2005.

2. Besides the readings listed in Table 5.1, other sources for baseball, football, and basketball include "Complete Team Index," at http://www.baseball-reference. com, accessed 15 September 2005; "List of Leagues of American Football," at http://www.en.wikipedia.org, accessed 16 September 2005; "Basketball History," at http://www.history-of-basketball.com, accessed 20 September 2005.

3. More data and facts about the seasons and teams in the NASL and WHA are contained in Dave Litterer, "North American Soccer League (NASL) 1967–1984," at http://www.sover.net, accessed 12 August 2005; "Major Professional Sports Leagues," at http://www.en.wikipedia.org, accessed 23 October 2005; "WHA Teams (1972–79)," at http://www.infoplease.com, accessed 12 August 2005; Mark Pollak, *Sports Leagues and Teams: An Encyclopedia, 1871 Through 1996* (Jefferson, NC: McFarland & Company, 1997).

4. See "History: United States Football League," at http://www.oursportscentral. com, accessed 23 December 2005; "Complete Team List," at http://www. databasebasketball.com, accessed 20 September 2005; Dave Litterer, "Men's Premier Soccer League," at http://www.sover.net, accessed 17 August 2005; "Soccer Development of America Announces MPSL League Expansion After Annual General Managers Meeting," *Business Wire* (9 October 2003), 1.

5. The WNBA's new expansion team Chicago Sky and its front office are discussed in Jena Janovy, "Fan's Franchise, *The Charlotte Observer* (7 July 2005), 2C, and "Chicago Sky is Ready to Soar," at http://www.wnba.com, accessed 24 December 2005.

6. In part, the histories of these leagues are discussed in "NWBL Pro League 2006—Franchise Opportunities," at http://www.nwbl.com, accessed 28 November 2005; Judy Van Handle, "NWBL Alive and Growing," at http://www. sportsbusinessnews.com, accessed 3 February 2004; "Home of the American Basketball Association: Teams 2005–2006 Season," at http://www.abalive.com, accessed 12 August 2005; "2004–2005 Expansion Teams," at http://www.abalive. com, accessed 13 April 2004.

CHAPTER SIX

1. Generally, the sources used to document and analyze the movements and transfers of teams in Alternative Leagues I are cited in Table 6.1 and Chapter 5's Tables 5.1 and 5.3. The secondary baseball and basketball leagues are also topics in, respectively, Bill James, *The New Bill James Historical Baseball Abstract* (New York: Free Press, 2003), and Kenneth A. Shouler, *Total Basketball: The Ultimate Basketball Encyclopedia* (Wilmington, DE: SportClassic Books, 2003).

2. For more information about the relocation and performances of clubs in the NASL and WHA, see the sources in Table 6.2 and Table 5.2. The history of the NASL is also discussed in Jose Colin, *The North American Soccer League Encyclopedia* (Haworth, NJ: St. Johann's Press, 2003). Furthermore, the teams and seasons of alternative ice hockey leagues are contained in Zander Hollander and Hal Brock, *The Complete Encyclopedia of Ice Hockey* (Englewood Cliffs, NJ: Prentice-Hall, Inc., 1974).

3. Some references include the "World Football League," at http://www.wfl.com, accessed 13 September 2005; "United States Football League," at http://www.usfl.com, accessed 13 September 2005; "List of Leagues of American Football," at http://www.en.wikipedia.org, accessed 16 September 2005; "Sports History," at http://www.hickoksports.com, accessed 13 September 2005.

Selected Bibliography

ARTICLES

Ascenzi, Joseph. "Ontario, Calif., Arena Effort Aided by Basketball League's Expansion Plans." *Business Press* (28 June 2004): 1.

Attner, Paul. "How Professional Sports Governs Expansion Will Mean Success or Failure for 21st Century." *The Sporting News* (18 March 1991): 13–19.

Bell, Jack. "Second New York-Area Team?" *New York Times* (3 May 2005): 6.

Carlson, Jenni. "How the Hornets Ended Up in Oklahoma City." *The Daily Oklahoman* (4 November 2005): 1.

Cassidy, Hilary. "Out with the Old … in with the New." *Brandweek* (10 May 2004): 48–52.

Catanoso, Justin. "Baseball Should Go Where the Money Is." *Business Week* (29 June 1998): 131.

———. "Loading the Bases in North Carolina." *Business Week* (7 April 1997): 98–99.

Chabria, Anita. "Analysis: MLS Expansion." *PR Week* (28 March 2005): 9.

Crasnick, Jerry. "How to Build a Baseball Franchise." *The Sporting News* (30 June 1997): 27.

Crothers, Tim. "Ice Follies." *Sports Illustrated* (25 November 1996): 62–66.

Draper, Robert. "Spoils Sports: Houston Professional Sports Teams Threaten to Relocate." *Texas Monthly* (January 1996): 110–16.

Eskenazi, Gerald. "Pro Leagues in America Eye the Globe." *New York Times* (9 April 1989): 19.

Ewing, Jack, and Laura Cohn. "Can Soccer Be Saved?" *Business Week* (19 July 2004): 46–48.

Fluke, Cecily, et al. "Bully Ball." *Forbes* (27 December 2004): 127–34.

Gattuso, James. "Congress and Rule-Making." *Society* (May/June 1986): 6–10.

Gergen, Joe. "Is Global Expansion the Wave of the Future?" *The Sporting News* (28 August 1989): 9.

Gonzalez, Simon. "Expansion Can't Explain All Big Numbers." *The Charlotte Observer* (14 July 1998): 4B.

Guier, Cindy Stooksbury. "When the Home Team Leaves." *Amusement Business* (16 June 1997): 10–12.

Hardy, Stephen H. "Entrepreneurs, Organizations, and the Sports Marketplace." *Journal of Sport History 13* (1986): 14–33.

Hille, Bob. "TSN's Best Sports Cities." *The Sporting News* (30 June 1997): 14–23.

Holmes, Stanley. "Soccer: Time to Kick It Up a Notch." *Business Week* (22 November 2004): 74–75.

Janovy, Jena. "Fan's Franchise." *The Charlotte Observer* (7 July 2005): 2C.

Johnson, Arthur T. "Balancing Interests." *Society* (May/June 1986): 11–16.

——. "Municipal Administration and the Sports Franchise Relocation Issue." *Public Administration Review* (November/December 1983): 519–28.

McAdam, Sean. "Baseball OKs Contraction." *The Charlotte Observer* (7 November 2001): 1C, 5C.

McCormick, John J. "Playing Stadium Games: The Urge to Be a Big-League Town Has Turned Civic Pride into a Costly—and Vain—Obsession." *Newsweek* (30 June 1997): 55.

Meggyesy, David. "The National Football League Monopoly." *Society* (May/June 1986): 16–21.

Mehrtens, Cliff. "League Picks Four Expansion Franchises." *The Charlotte Observer* (8 June 1999): 3B.

Minker, Melissa. "Expansion." *SportsTravel* (January 1997): 30–34.

Muret, Don. "With Total Attendance at High Mark, 11-Team CISL Considering Expansion." *Amusement Business* (13 October 1997): 20.

Onge, Peter St. "New Gem Shines, but for How Long?" *The Charlotte Observer* (6 November 2005): 1A, 9A.

Powell, Tom. "Expansion Teams Credited for Rise in Attendance for Major Pro Leagues." *Amusement Business* (16 December 1996): 57–58.

Quirk, James. "An Economic Analysis of Team Movements in Professional Sports." *Law and Contemporary Problems* (Winter/Spring 1973): 42–66.

Quirk, James, and Mohamed El Hodiri. "The Economic Theory of a Professional Sports League." In *Government and the Sports Business,* Roger G. Noll, ed. Washington, DC: The Brookings Institution, 1974, 33–80.

Rascher, Daniel, and Heather Rascher. "NBA Expansion and Relocation: A Viability Study of Various Cities." *Journal of Sport Management* (July 2004): 274–95.

Ross, Stephen F. "Break Up the Sports League Monopolies." In *The Business of Professional Sports,* Paul D. Staudohar and James A. Mangan, eds. Champaign: University of Illinois Press, 1991, 152–73.

Rozin, Skip. "Growing Pains: The Evolution of Expansion." *Sport* (December 1994): 10.

Schmitz, Brian. "Cities Adding Teams Isn't What Baseball Needs, Some Say." *The Orlando Sentinel* (11 May 2000): 1–2.

"Soccer Development of America Announces MPSL League Expansion after Annual General Managers Meeting." *Business Wire* (9 October 2003): 1.

"Sonics the Most Likely to Move." *The Charlotte Observer* (19 February 2006): 14C.

Stix, Gary. "Blackballing the Inner City." *Scientific American 269* (September 1993): 152.

Young, Hoon Lee, and Rodney Fort. "Structural Change in MLB Competitive Balance: The Depression, Team Relocation, and Integration." *Economic Inquiry* (January 2005): 158–70.

BOOKS

Betts, John Rickards. *America's Sporting Heritage: 1850–1950.* Reading, MA: Addison-Wesley Publishing Company, 1974.

Carroll, Bob. *Total Football II: The Official Encyclopedia of the National Football League.* New York: HarperCollins World, 1999.

Colin, Jose. *The North American Soccer League Encyclopedia.* Haworth, NJ: St. Johann's Press, 2003.

Danielson, Michael N. *Home Team: Professional Sports and the American Metropolis.* Princeton, NJ: Princeton University Press, 1997.

Duplacey, James. *Total Hockey: The Official Encyclopedia of the National Hockey League.* New York: Total Sports, 1998.

Euchner, Charles C. *Playing the Field: Why Sports Teams Move and Cities Fight to Keep Them.* Baltimore, MD: Johns Hopkins University Press, 1993.

The First Fifty Years. New York: Ridge Press/Benjamin Company, 1969.

Goldblatt, David. *Soccer Yearbook 2004/5.* New York: DK Publishing, 2004.

Hollander, Zander, and Hal Brock. *The Complete Encyclopedia of Ice Hockey.* Englewood Cliffs, NJ: Prentice-Hall, Inc., 1974.

James, Bill. *The New Bill James Historical Baseball Abstract.* New York: Free Press, 2003.

Jozsa, Frank P., Jr. *American Sports Empire: How the Leagues Breed Success.* Westport, CT: Praeger Publishers, 2003.

——. *Baseball, Inc.: The National Pastime as Big Business.* Jefferson, NC: McFarland & Company, Inc., 2006.

——. *Sports Capitalism: The Foreign Business of American Professional Leagues.* Aldershot, England: Ashgate Publishing, 2004.

Jozsa, Frank P., Jr., and John J. Guthrie, Jr. *Relocating Teams and Expanding Leagues in Professional Sports: How the Major Leagues Respond to Market Conditions.* Westport, CT: Quorum Books, 1999.

Koppett, Leonard. *Total Basketball: The Ultimate Basketball Encyclopedia.* Wilmington, DE: SportClassic Books, 2004.

Lowe, Stephen R. *The Kid on the Sandlot: Congress and Professional Sports, 1910–1992.* Bowling Green, OH: Bowling Green State University Popular Press, 1995.

Menke, Frank G. *The Encyclopedia of Sports.* 5th ed. New York: A. S. Barnes and Company, Inc., 1975.

Noll, Roger G., ed. *Government and the Sports Business.* Washington, DC: The Brookings Institution, 1974.

Pollak, Mark. *Sports Leagues and Teams: An Encyclopedia, 1871 Through 1996.* Jefferson, NC: McFarland & Company, 1997.

Quirk, James, and Rodney D. Fort. *Pay Dirt: The Business of Professional Team Sports.* Princeton, NJ: Princeton University Press, 1992.

Rosentraub, Mark S. *Major League Losers: The Real Costs of Sports and Who's Paying for It.* New York: Basic Books, 1997.

Sandy, Robert, Peter J. Sloane, and Mark S. Rosentraub. *The Economics of Sport: An International Perspective.* New York: Palgrave Macmillan, 2004.

Shouler, Kenneth A. *Total Basketball: The Ultimate Basketball Encyclopedia.* Wilmington, DE: SportClassic Books, 2003.

Shropshire, Kenneth L. *The Sports Franchise Game: Cities in Pursuit of Sports Franchises, Events, Stadiums, and Arenas.* Philadelphia, PA: University of Pennsylvania Press, 1995.

Staudohar, Paul D., and James A. Mangan, eds. *The Business of Professional Sports.* Champaign: University of Illinois Press, 1991.

The World Almanac and Book of Facts. New York: World Almanac Books, 1950–2004.

DISSERTATIONS

DePalma, Thomas J. "Betting Market Efficiency in the National Hockey League: An Analysis of Expansion Seasons." doctoral dissertation, University of Delaware, 2004.

Dobbs, Michael E. "The Organization of Professional Sports Leagues: Mortality and Founding Rates, 1871–1997." doctoral dissertation, University of Texas at Dallas, 1999.

Harm, Rodney Harry. "Expansion and Franchise Movement of Major League Teams in the Post World War II Era: 1945–1995." doctoral dissertation, Texas Christian University, 2000.

Jozsa, Frank P., Jr. "An Economic Analysis of Franchise Relocation and League Expansion in Professional Team Sports, 1950–1975." doctoral dissertation, Georgia State University, 1977.

Seredynski, Glen Joseph. "The Economics of the National Hockey League Expansion, Relocation, and Survival." doctoral dissertation, University of Victoria, 1991.

MEDIA GUIDES

Official Major League Baseball Fact Book 2005 Edition. St. Louis, MO: Sporting News, 2005.

Official 2001 National Football League Record & Fact Book. New York: National Football League, 2001.

INTERNET SOURCES

"Amateur Hockey Association." http://www.en.wikipedia.org.

"American Basketball Association." http://www.remembertheaba.com.

"American Basketball League 1925–55." http://www.en.wikipedia.org.

Arnett, Jeff. "There Used to be a Ballpark: How 50 Years of Relocation and Expansion Have Shaped the Game's Geography." http://www.baseballhalloffame.org.

Balashov, Sergei, and Alexei Belousenko. "Revolution in Hockey? European NHL Set to Emerge." http://www.sportsbusinessnews.com.

"Barcelona President Interested in MLS." http://www.mlsnet.com.

"Basketball Association of America." http://www.nbahoopsonline.com.

"Basketball History." http://www.history-of-basketball.com.

Bauman, Mike. "At Last, Nationals Have a Future." http://www.mlb.com.

Bloom, Barry M. "MLB Selects D.C. for Expos." http://www.mlb.com.

Bonham, Dean. "Bonham on the State of Soccer." http://www.sportsbusinessnews.com.

"Boston Bruins." http://www.en.wikipedia.org.

Carlson, Jenni. "How the Hornets Ended Up in Oklahoma City." http://www.sportsbusinessnews.com.

"Charlotte Bobcats." http://www.nba.com.

"Chicago Blackhawks." http://www.en.wikipedia.org.

"Chicago Sky Is Ready to Soar." http://www.wnba.com.

Christl, Cliff. "Texans Have a Headstart over Other Expansion Teams." http://www.jsonline.com.

"Complete Team Index." http://www.baseball-reference.com.

"Complete Team List." http://www.databasebasketball.com.

Cour, Jim. "Sonics Looking at Arena Alternatives." http://www.netscape.com.

"Defunct NHL Teams." http://www.infoplease.com.

"Detroit Red Wings." http://www.en.wikipedia.org.

Duncan, Chris. "MLS' Newly Named Houston 1836 Seeks Local Support." http://www.usatoday.com.

"Each Team Files Application for Relocation." http://espn.go.com.

"Encyclopedia: National Basketball League." http://www.nationmaster.com.

"Expansion/Merger Timetable." http://www.infoplease.com.

"FANS." http://www.consumers.com.

"The First Major League (1875–1889)." http://www.hickoksports.com.

"Franchise Information: Expansion History." http://www.mlb.com.

"Frankford Yellow Jackets." http://www.hickoksports.com.

Gardner, Charles F. "MLS Message to Milwaukee: Build It and We Will Come." http://www.jsonline.com.

"Geography of Pro Sports in the U.S. and Canada." http://www.geography.about.com.

Grathoff, Pete. "MLS Looking for Investors and Interested Cities." http://www.sportsbusinessnews.com.

Halpin, Jason. "Expansion, Relocation Top League Agenda." http://www.mlsnet.com.

——. "MLS Closing in on Toronto Expansion." http://www.mlsnet.com.

Harrow, Rick. "The Business of Soccer." http://www.sportsbusinessnews.com.

"History." http://www.nhl.com.

"History: Major League Soccer." http://www.hickoksports.com.

"History of the WPFL." http://www.womensprofootball.com.

"History: United States Football League." http://www.oursportscentral.com.

"Home of the American Basketball Association: Teams 2005–2006 Season." http://www.abalive.com.

"List of Ice Hockey Leagues." http://www.en.wikipedia.org.

"List of Leagues of American Football." http://www.en.wikipedia.org.

Litterer, Dave. "American Soccer History Archives." http://www.sover.net.

——. "American Soccer League I (1921–1933)." http://www.sover.net.

——. "American Soccer League II (New England Division)." http://www.sover.net.

——. "Eastern Professional Soccer League II." http://www.rsssf.com.

——. "Men's Premier Soccer League." http://www.sover.net.

——. "North American Soccer League (NASL) 1967–1984." http://www.sover.net.

——. "An Overview of American Soccer History." http://www.sover.net.

"Major League Baseball." http://www.mlb.com.

"Major League Soccer." http://www.en.wikipedia.org.

——. http://www.mlsnet.com.

"Major League Soccer: History." http://www.hickoksports.com.

"Major Professional Sports Leagues." http://www.en.wikipedia.org.

"Marlins Give Up on Miami Ballpark." http://www.cnnsi.com.

"Men's Premier Soccer League." http://www.mpsl.com.

"MLB Franchise History." http://www.mlb.com.

"MLB Worried about D.C. Ballpark." http://www.cnnsi.com.

"MLS Attendance Analysis: Basic Numbers." http://www.kenn.com.

"MLS Attendance Analysis: Team Averages." http://www.kenn.com.

"Montreal Maroons." http://www.sportsencyclopedia.com.

Murphy, Melissa. "WNBA Locations to Be Re-Evaluated." http://dailynews.yahoo.com.

"National Basketball Association." http://www.nba.com.

——. http://www.rauzulusstreet.com.

"National Basketball Association (NBA) History." http://www.rauzulusstreet.com.

"National Basketball League." http://www.hickoksports.com.

——. http://www.nbl.com.

"National Football League." http://www.nfl.com.

"National Football League (NFL) History." http://www.rauzulusstreet.com.

"National Hockey League." http://www.en.wikipedia.com.

——. http://www.nhl.com.

"National Hockey League (NHL) Expansion History." http://www.rauzulusstreet.com.

"National League Year in Review." http://www.baseball-almanac.com.

"National Women's Basketball League." http://www.nwbl.com.

"NBA Expansion Potential." http://www.en.wikipedia.org.

"NBA Franchise History." http://www.hickoksports.com.

"NBA Growth Timetable." http://www.basketball.com.

"NBA History." http://www.basketball.com.

"New York Rangers." http://www.en.wikipedia.org.

"NFL Franchise Chronology." http://www.hickoksports.com.

"NHL Attendance Figures." http://www.hockeyresearch.com.

"NHL Expansion and Relocation since 1967." http://www.andrewsstarspage.com.

"NHL Expansion History." http://www.geocities.com.

"NHL Expansion/Relocation/Contraction." http://www.misterpoll.com.

"NHL Franchise Origins." http://www.infoplease.com.

"NHL Prospective Cities." http://www.geocities.com.

"NHL Relocation History." http://www.geocities.com.

Nichols, Dan. "Major League Franchise Information." http://www.baseball1.com.

"19th Century National League Teams." http://www.en.wikipedia.org.

"North American Soccer League." http://www.nasl.com.

"NWBL Pro League 2006—Franchise Opportunities." http://www.nwbl.com.

"Pittsburgh Pirates (NHL)." http://www.en.wikipedia.org.

Rao, Chay. "Analysis: The Business of Hockey." http://washingtontimes.com.

"San Jose Seeking Major League Team." http://www.cnnsi.com.

"Schedule Overview 1901–1998." http://www.baseball1.com.

Schmitz, Brian. "Cities Adding Teams Isn't What Baseball Needs, Some Say." http://www.orlandosentinel.com.

Schoenfield, David. "Beantown Reigns Supreme." http://sports.espn.go.com.

"Sports History." http://www.hickoksports.com.

"Sports History: National Professional Soccer League." http://www.hickoksports.com.

"Stanley Cup Record Year-by-Year." http://www.bostonbruins.com.

Stark, Jayson. "If Not South Florida, Where Next for the Marlins." http://www.sportsbusinessnews.com.

Stewart, Regan. "Sport Cities." http://www.businessfacilities.com.

"Team-by-Team Analysis." http://www.baseball-almanac.com.

Thomas, G. Scott. "Economic Clout Makes L.A. Sports Team Choice." http://www.bizjournals.com.

——. "Los Angeles Scores as Best Place for Sports Teams." http://www.msnbc.msn.com.

——. "Study Names Best, Worst Cities for Sports Franchises." http://www.birmingham.bizjournals.com.

——. "The Methodology behind ACBJ's Study." http://www.msnbc.msn.com.

"Topping the Expansion List." http://www.cnnsi.com.

"2004–2005 Expansion Teams." http://www.abalive.com.

"United States Football League." http://www.usfl.com.

Van Handle, Judy. "NWBL Alive and Growing." http://www.sportsbusinessnews.com.

"Voters Reject Triad Referendum for Baseball Stadium." http://www.cnnsi.com.

"WHA Teams (1972–79)." http://www.infoplease.com.

"Women's National Basketball Association." http://www.wnba.com.

"World Football League." http://www.wfl.com.

"World Hockey Association." http://www.wha.com.

Index

About the Author

FRANK P. JOZSA JR. is Associate Professor of Economics and Business Administration at Pfeiffer University, where he has taught courses in the graduate studies program since 1991. He has written extensively on issues of sports business and economics, including articles in *Athletic Business*, the *Carolina Journal*, and the *Wall Street Journal Review of Books*. He is co-author of *Relocating Teams and Expanding Leagues in Professional Sports* (Quorum, 1999), and author of *Sports Capitalism, Baseball, Inc.*, and *American Sports Empire* (Praeger, 2003).